Civilian Immunity in War

Civilian Immunity in War

EDITED BY

Igor Primoratz

OXFORD
UNIVERSITY PRESS

OXFORD
UNIVERSITY PRESS

Great Clarendon Street, Oxford OX2 6DP

Oxford University Press is a department of the University of Oxford.
It furthers the University's objective of excellence in research, scholarship,
and education by publishing worldwide in

Oxford New York

Auckland Cape Town Dar es Salaam Hong Kong Karachi
Kuala Lumpur Madrid Melbourne Mexico City Nairobi
New Delhi Shanghai Taipei Toronto

With offices in

Argentina Austria Brazil Chile Czech Republic France Greece
Guatemala Hungary Italy Japan Poland Portugal Singapore
South Korea Switzerland Thailand Turkey Ukraine Vietnam

Oxford is a registered trade mark of Oxford University Press
in the UK and in certain other countries

Published in the United States
by Oxford University Press Inc., New York

© the Several Contributors 2007

The moral rights of the authors have been asserted
Database right Oxford University Press (maker)

First published 2007

British Library Cataloguing in Publication Data

Data available

Library of Congress Cataloging in Publication Data

Data available

Typeset by Laserwords Private Limited, Chennai, India
Printed in Great Britain
on acid-free paper by
Biddles Ltd., King's Lynn, Norfolk

ISBN 978–0–19–929074–1

For the unknown civilian

Acknowledgements

With the exception of Chapters 4 and 9, the papers included in this book were first presented at the international conference 'Civilian Immunity in War' I organized in collaboration with Professor Georg Meggle (University of Leipzig, Germany). The conference was sponsored by the Centre for Applied Philosophy and Public Ethics (CAPPE), the University of Melbourne division, and the Centre for Interdisciplinary Research (Zentrum für interdisziplinäre Forschung), University of Bielefeld, Germany, and held at the University of Melbourne on 3–5 December 2003. Those papers were subsequently revised for publication in the light of detailed critical discussion which each received at the conference.

I would like to thank Ms Irena Blonder, Manager of CAPPE Melbourne at the time, for invaluable help with organizing the conference, and Mr Ned Dobos, Ph.D. student at CAPPE, for preparing the index.

IGOR PRIMORATZ

Contents

Notes on the Contributors   ix

Introduction   1

Part I.   19

 1. Civilian Immunity in War: Its Grounds, Scope, and Weight   21
    Igor Primoratz

 2. Civilians and Soldiers   42
    Uwe Steinhoff

 3. Civilian Immunity in War: From Augustine to Vattel   62
    Colm McKeogh

 4. Civilian Immunity in War: Legal Aspects   84
    David Kretzmer

 5. Civilian Immunity, Forcing
    the Choice, and Collective Responsibility   113
    Seumas Miller

 6. Collateral Immunity in War
    and Terrorism   136
    C. A. J. (Tony) Coady

Part II.   159

 7. Airpower and Non-combatant Immunity: The Road to
    Dresden   161
    Stephen A. Garrett

 8. Civilian Immunity in the Precision-Guidance Age   182
    Hugh White

 9. Civilian Immunity in the 'New Wars'   201
    Paul Gilbert

10. Women, War, and International Law   217
    Véronique Zanetti

11. War and the Protection of Property   239
    Janna Thompson

Select Bibliography   257

Index   261

Notes on the Contributors

C. A. J. (TONY) COADY is Professorial Fellow at the University of Melbourne division of the Centre for Applied Philosophy and Public Ethics. He was Boyce Gibson Professor of Philosophy at the University of Melbourne from 1990 to 1998. He is the author of *Testimony: A Philosophical Inquiry* (Oxford University Press, 1992) and *Morality and Political Violence* (Cambridge University Press, in press), editor of *What's Wrong with Moralism?* (Blackwell, 2006), and co-editor (with Michael O'Keefe) of *Terrorism and Justice: Moral Argument in a Threatened World* (Melbourne University Press, 2002) and *Righteous Violence: The Ethics and Politics of Humanitarian Intervention* (Melbourne University Press, 2005).

STEPHEN A. GARRETT is Professor of International Policy Studies at the Monterey Institute of International Studies in Monterey, California. He is the author of six books and more than forty articles on international affairs, and is particularly concerned with the question of the place of ethics in foreign policy. Among his books are *Conscience and Power* (St Martin's Press, 1996) and *Ethics and Airpower in World War II* (St Martin's Press, 1993). He is currently working on a manuscript on the practical and moral questions involved in 'transitional justice': how newly democratic regimes deal with the human rights abuses of a previous authoritarian government.

PAUL GILBERT is Professor of Philosophy at the University of Hull. His books include *Terrorism, Security and Nationality* (Routledge, 1994), *The Philosophy of Nationalism* (Westview Press, 1998), *Peoples, Cultures and Nations in Political Philosophy* (Edinburgh University Press, 2000), and *New Terror, New Wars* (Edinburgh University Press, 2003).

DAVID KRETZMER is Bruce W. Wayne Professor of International Law at the Hebrew University, Jerusalem. He is the author of *The Legal Status of the Arabs in Israel* (Westview Press, 1990) and *The Occupation of Justice: The Supreme Court of Israel and the Occupied Territories* (State University of New York Press, 2002), and co-editor (with Eckart Klein) of *The Concept of Human Dignity in Human Rights Discourse* (Kluwer, 2002).

COLM MCKEOGH is Senior Lecturer in Political Science at the University of Waikato, Hamilton, New Zealand. He is the author of *The Political Realism of Reinhold Niebuhr: A Pragmatic Approach to Just War* (Macmillan, 1997) and *Innocent*

Civilians: The Morality of Killing in War (Palgrave Macmillan, 2003). He is currently researching pacifist political theory.

SEUMAS MILLER is Professor of Philosophy at Charles Sturt University and the Australian National University (joint position) and Director of the Centre for Applied Philosophy and Public Ethics (an Australian Research Council-funded Special Research Centre). His books include *Social Action: A Teleological Account* (Cambridge University Press, 2001), *Corruption and Anti-corruption* (with Peter Roberts and Edward Spence) (Prentice-Hall, 2004), and *Ethical Issues in Policing* (with John Blackler) (Ashgate, 2004).

IGOR PRIMORATZ is Professor Emeritus of Philosophy at the Hebrew University of Jerusalem, and Principal Research Fellow at the Centre for Applied Philosophy and Public Ethics, University of Melbourne. He is the author of *Justifying Legal Punishment* (Humanities Press International, 1989) and *Ethics and Sex* (Routledge, 1999) and editor of *Human Sexuality* (Ashgate, 1997), *Patriotism* (Humanity Books, 2002), *Terrorism: The Philosophical Issues* (Palgrave Macmillan, 2004), *Identity, Self-determination and Secession* (with Aleksandar Pavković) (Ashgate, 2006), and *Politics and Morality* (Palgrave Macmillan, 2007).

UWE STEINHOFF is Research Associate at the Leverhulme Program on the Changing Character of War, Department of Politics and International Relations, University of Oxford, and Affiliated Researcher at the Oxford Uehiro Centre for Practical Ethics. He is the author of *Kritik der kommunikativen Rationalität* (Mentis Verlag, 2006), *Effiziente Ethik: Über Rationalität, Selbstschaffung, Politik und Postmoderne* (Mentis Verlag, 2006), and *On the Ethics of War and Terrorism* (Oxford University Press, forthcoming).

JANNA THOMPSON is Associate Professor of Philosophy at La Trobe University in Melbourne and Honorary Fellow in the Centre for Applied Philosophy and Public Ethics. She is the author of *Justice and World Order* (Routledge, 1992), *Discourse and Knowledge* (Routledge, 1997), and *Taking Responsibility for the Past: Reparation and Historical Justice* (Polity, 2002).

HUGH WHITE is Professor of Strategic Studies at the Australian National University and a Visiting Fellow at the Lowy Institute for International Policy. From 2001 to 2004 he was the first Director of the Australian Strategic Policy Institute (ASPI). Over the two decades before that he had served as an intelligence analyst with the Office of National Assessments, as a journalist with the *Sydney Morning Herald*, as a senior adviser on the staffs of Defence Minister Kim Beazley and Prime Minister Bob Hawke, and as a senior official in the Department of Defence, where from 1995 to 2000 he was Deputy Secretary for Strategy and Intelligence.

VÉRONIQUE ZANETTI is Professor of Ethics and Political Philosophy at the University of Bielefeld, Germany. She wrote her habilitation dissertation on the ethics of humanitarian intervention and has published several articles on the ethics of international relations. Other publications include a monograph on Kant's concept of natural teleology (Brussells, 1994) and (with Manfred Frank) a commentary on Kant's philosophy of nature and aesthetics (vol. iii of *Kants Gesammelten Schriften*, Bibliothek Deutscher Klassiker (Frankfurt am Main, 1996)). She co-edited (with Steffen Wesche) *Dworkin: A Debate* (Brussells, 2000).

Introduction

I

Civilization may not aim at encompassing everything we do, but it does aim at informing most of our activities. Warfare is certainly one of them—indeed, one of our activities most in need of restraint. If we do not subject our decisions to go to war and the choices we make in the course of fighting to some civilized standards, we will fight like barbarians. Looking at the history of warfare in the last hundred years or so, one might well argue that this is precisely what we have been doing and may well continue doing in the foreseeable future.

In his 1994 Amnesty Lecture, British historian Eric Hobsbawm portrayed the twentieth century as one of return to barbarism. Barbarism, he explained, was first and foremost 'the disruption and breakdown of systems of rules and moral behaviour by which *all* societies regulate the relations among their members and ... between their members and those of other societies'.[1] This breakdown was most salient and most dangerous with regard to the rules meant to contain the use of violence, and in particular to restrain the waging of war.

In the nineteenth century, it was taken for granted that the military of a civilized country fought the armed forces of the enemy, and not enemy civilians. Even some revolutionary movements subscribed to a political analogue of this principle. Thus the programme of the Narodnaya Volya, a Russian organization that had chosen political assassination as the

---

[1] E. Hobsbawm, 'Barbarism: A User's Guide', in *On History* (London: Weidenfeld & Nicolson, 1997), 253.

method of revolutionary struggle, stated that those individuals and groups who took no part in the struggle between the regime and those fighting for its overthrow would be treated as neutrals, and their life, limb, and property would not be attacked.[2] The idea of limited war in general, and of immunity of civilians (non-combatants) in war in particular, was seen as an outcome of a process of civilization and humanization of warfare that had its roots in ancient philosophical and religious thought, had evolved as a major tradition in philosophy and moral theology in the Middle Ages, and had been systematically developed by philosophers and political and legal thinkers of the modern age until it came to be recognized as one of the most important achievements of moral progress. By the eighteenth century, major European powers had accepted civilian immunity as a central tenet of their military practice. In the last decade of the nineteenth century and the first decade of the twentieth, the principle was embedded in the Hague Conventions (1899, 1907) and thus became part and parcel of international law. But this development was then reversed on the ground: wars of the twentieth century turned out to be ever more hostile to those who were *not* doing the fighting.

Hobsbawm argues that this return to barbarism, which began with World War I, is due to a number of factors. The Great War introduced the most murderous period in history. It involved deliberate destruction of human life on a scale that had been unthinkable before. Moreover, 'the limitless sacrifices which governments imposed on their own men as they drove them into the holocausts of Verdun and Ypres set a sinister precedent, if only for imposing ever more unlimited massacres on the enemy'.[3] The idea of total national mobilization for war evolved into the theory and practice of total war: war in which the aims and the means, too, are total. This meant that the central constraint on the ways of fighting, the principle of civilian immunity, was in practice ever more eroded and eventually almost entirely discarded. This was facilitated by the demonization of the enemy, encouraged by the very nature of total war and the exigencies of democratic politics:

... The First World War was the first major war, at all events in Europe, waged under conditions of democratic politics by, or with the active participation of,

---

[2] See Z. Ivianski, 'The Moral Issue: Some Aspects of Individual Terror', in D. C. Rapoport and Y. Alexander (eds.), *The Morality of Terrorism: Religious and Secular Justifications*, 2nd edn. (New York: Columbia University Press, 1989).

[3] Hobsbawm, 'Barbarism', 256.

the entire population. Unfortunately democracies can rarely be mobilized by wars when these are seen merely as incidents in the international power-game, as old-fashioned foreign offices saw them to be. Nor do they fight them like bodies of professional soldiers or boxers, for whom war is an activity that does not require hating the enemy, so long as he fights by the professional rules. Democracies, as experience shows, require demonized enemies.[4]

The first major step in this process of making civilians ever more the victim, and indeed the target, of deadly violence in war was the naval blockade that Great Britain imposed on Germany in World War I. It continued well beyond the end of fighting, brought about widespread malnutrition and disease, and snuffed out up to 800,000 civilian lives. World War I also led to civil war in Russia, in which all sides perpetrated massacres of civilians; the bolsheviks also unleashed the 'Red Terror' with its quasi-judicial executions of (real or imagined) political opponents on a scale unprecedented in previous revolutions. Leon Trotsky, one of the architects of the 'Red Terror', subsequently claimed that modern military technology had already rendered the distinction between soldiers and civilians obsolete: 'modern warfare, with its long-range artillery, aviation, poison gases ... inevitably involves the loss of hundreds of thousands and millions, the aged and the children included, who do not participate directly in the struggle'.[5]

It might be thought that World War II proved Trotsky right with regard to the use of aircraft: it turned the names of Hamburg and Dresden, Hiroshima and Nagasaki, into metonyms for terror bombing and mass killing of civilians. Yet Trotsky was referring to the inability of the modern air force to be precise in its targeting and stay clear of civilian life, limb, and property, whereas the civilians killed in the bombing of those and many other cities and towns were targeted deliberately. The 'balance of terror', said to be preserving the peace in the Cold War period, was based on the threat that the nuclear powers would use their nuclear weapons against each other's civilian population centres. Quite a few wars of national liberation from colonial rule involved terrorism—indiscriminate killing and maiming of civilians. Mary Kaldor introduced the term 'new wars'

---

[4] Ibid. 256–7.

[5] L. Trotsky, 'Moralists and Sycophants against Marxism', in L. Trotsky, J. Dewey, and G. Novack, *Their Morals and Ours: Marxist vs. Liberal Views on Morality*, 5th edn. (New York: Pathfinder Press, 1973), 57.

to distinguish the *fin de siècle* ethnic wars in the Balkans and the Caucasus from old-style military conflicts between established states. She points out that

the strategic goal of these wars is population expulsion through various means such as mass killing, forcible resettlement, as well as a range of political, psychological and economic techniques of intimidation. This is why, in all these wars, there has been a dramatic increase of refugees and displaced persons, and why most violence is directed against civilians.[6]

In two recent cases of military intervention, those in Kosova and (initially) in Afghanistan, Western powers tried to achieve their objectives by means of air power alone, and had their aircraft fly at extremely high altitudes, where they were not in danger of anti-aircraft fire. This tactic had the predictable result of inflicting much 'collateral damage' on civilian population. This development led some commentators to wonder whether the principle of civilian immunity had been replaced by that of Western *combatant* immunity.

At the outset of the twentieth century, the number of civilians killed in war was low relative to the number of soldiers killed: one civilian per every eight soldiers. By the end of the century, the ratio had been reversed: now eight *civilians* get killed for every soldier that falls in battle.[7]

On the other hand, while this onslaught on the civilian continued apace after the end of World War II, the same period witnessed major advances in legal provisions concerning civilian immunity, and some progress with regard to trying and punishing those who had offended against the laws and customs of war that protect civilians. Most crimes tried by the International Military Tribunal at Nuremberg were crimes perpetrated against civilians. The Fourth Geneva Convention of 1949 and its two Additional Protocols, adopted in 1977, provided protection to civilian life, limb, and property in wartime more comprehensive than anything that had been in place before. This protection is now extended to all civilians, on either side of the front line. The concept of civilian is understood broadly, to include all those who are not combatants—that is, take no direct part in the hostilities. Civilians must not be attacked, or even threatened with attack. All attacks not directed at specific military targets, or using a method or means of combat

---

[6] M. Kaldor, *New and Old Wars: Organized Violence in a Global Era* (Cambridge: Polity, 2001), 8.
[7] Ibid.

that cannot be so directed, are deemed indiscriminate and are prohibited. Harm to civilians incidental to attacks on legitimate military targets must not be disproportionate to the direct military advantage aimed at.

Moreover, at least some of the major war criminals from the recent wars in the Balkans have been brought to the International Tribunal in The Hague. An International Criminal Court, designed to try war criminals from future conflicts, is being set up. These developments offer some hope that the provisions of international law of war may not remain toothless, but might, at least in some cases, be enforced, and that at least some of those who offend against them may be tried and punished for their crimes.

Thus the current situation is precarious: it gives cause for serious concern, but it also holds out hope. There is the pull of practice, which works against civilians. But there are also requirements of morality and international law, reasonably clear and far-reaching, and the hope that, at least sometimes, they can be enforced and those responsible for crimes against civilians be brought to justice.

II

Philosophers doing research on the ethics of war have made important contributions to our understanding of the principle of civilian immunity. But these contributions have been almost entirely in the form of articles or book chapters, and therefore inevitably limited in scope, if not in depth.[8] Despite the importance of the subject, so far there have been only two book-length discussions of civilian immunity, one entirely historical, the other largely so. The first is Richard Shelly Hartigan's *The Forgotten Victim: A History of the Civilian*, published in 1982. It traces the evolution of the status and fate of the civilian from 'primitive' warfare to the nineteenth century. A concluding chapter makes some brief comments on civilians'

---

[8] The most important articles are G. E. M. Anscombe, 'War and Murder', in W. Stein (ed.), *Nuclear Weapons: A Catholic Response* (London: The Merlin Press, 1961), and T. Nagel, 'War and Massacre', *Philosophy and Public Affairs*, 1 (1971/2). The former is reprinted in Anscombe's *Collected Philosophical Papers* (Oxford: Blackwell, 1981), iii; the latter in Nagel's *Mortal Questions* (Cambridge: Cambridge University Press, 1979). Valuable discussions of civilian immunity will also be found in the pertinent chapters of books such as M. Walzer, *Just and Unjust Wars*, 3rd edn. (New York: Basic Books, 2000); R. Holmes, *On War and Morality* (Princeton: Princeton University Press, 1989); and R. Norman, *Ethics, Killing and War* (Cambridge: Cambridge University Press, 1995).

predicament in the twentieth century. Hartigan's book is now dated in terms of scope, and perhaps in its assessment of the status and prospects of the civilian as well. It was published in the last decade of the Cold War, when the dominant attitude could be fairly described as

grudging acceptance that there are some innocent noncombatants, combined with a near total fatalism based on the assumption that in present or future wars the civilian cannot be practically isolated or protected. What began with blitzkriegs and progressed through firebombings has culminated in a sad acceptance that all of us are ... hostages to potential annihilation by nuclear missiles, or passive spectators of cruel guerrilla warfare in which distinctions between combatant and noncombatant often cannot be made.[9]

Hartigan's monograph was superseded by Colm McKeogh's *Innocent Civilians: The Morality of Killing in War* (2002) which is up to date, and also more comprehensive and analytical. It offers a history of the idea and practice of civilian immunity from Augustine's teaching on morally justified war to recent developments in the international law of war. It concludes with a brief account of some current debates in the ethics of war. McKeogh outlines three types of killing that have been considered pertinent to war: punitive, defensive, and consensual. Each of these three notions justifies the killing of combatants in a certain range of cases. On the other hand, none can justify intentional killing of civilians. Civilians are innocent, and therefore cannot be killed punitively. They are not fighting, and therefore cannot be killed in self-defence or defence of others. They have not joined the military, and therefore cannot be deemed to have consented to being killed. McKeogh also argues that incidental killing of civilians—killing them without intent, but with foresight, as a side-effect of acts of war directed at legitimate military targets—cannot be justified. Accordingly, he understands civilian immunity as an absolute prohibition of killing civilians knowingly, with or without intent. Only accidental killing of civilians—killing that was neither foreseen nor reasonably foreseeable—may be excused.[10]

The present book is thus a pioneering study of philosophical and legal questions concerning civilian immunity in war: the first systematic analysis

---

[9] R. S. Hartigan, *The Forgotten Victim: A History of the Civilian* (Chicago: Precedent Publishing, 1982), 2.

[10] C. McKeogh, *Innocent Civilians: The Morality of Killing in War* (Basingstoke: Palgrave Macmillan, 2002).

of all the main aspects of the subject. Contributions comprising Part I discuss the fundamental problems of the grounds, scope, and stringency of this immunity; those in Part II address a range of more specific issues arising in this connection.

The first two chapters take on directly the basic question of the ground, or grounds, of the immunity of civilians in war. In Chapter 1 I first consider two proposals for discarding the idea of civilian immunity altogether. One argues that it is unfair that the killing in war should be restricted to the healthy young men on the battlefield, and that it should rather be distributed across the entire population. The other is the claim that civilians are not really innocent, since the military act as representatives of their society. Both these arguments for rejecting civilian immunity are unacceptable. I next look into the consequentialist understanding of civilian immunity as a useful rule. This, too, is implausible, because the protection accorded to civilians is much too weak and precarious, and also because this account misses what everyone but a consistent consequentialist would consider the crux of the matter: namely, the fact that most civilians have done nothing that could make them deserve, or become liable, to be killed in war.

This fact is highlighted by the defence approach to civilian immunity, dominant in contemporary just war theory. According to this view, civilians are protected from deadly violence because or, more accurately, in so far as they are not, in the words of Michael Walzer, 'currently engaged in the business of war'. There is no *defence* against civilians. This view is explained and adopted as the sole basis of civilian immunity in war and the criterion of the proper scope of this immunity. I turn next to the responsible bystander argument for stripping some civilians of such immunity. The argument is valid, but, for different reasons, has very little purchase on reality both in authoritarian and in democratic polities. Thus the defence view provides the correct account of the ground and scope of civilian immunity in war. The stringency of the principle is a separate matter. I argue against the view of civilian immunity in war as an absolute principle, and opt for adopting it as an *almost* absolute rule. It may be overridden, but only on extremely rare occasions: when doing so is the only way to prevent, or put an end to, a true moral disaster such as genocide or 'ethnic cleansing' of an entire community. This conclusion is briefly applied to the issue of terrorism.

Whereas I argue that we should ground civilian immunity in one single principle, that of defence, Uwe Steinhoff (Chapter 2) explores the same fundamental problem, but reaches a different conclusion: a proper account of the distinction between legitimate and illegitimate targets in war must combine four different, but complementary, approaches. These are the moral guilt theory, the self-defence theory, the justifying emergency theory, and the convention theory. Steinhoff argues that the moral guilt theory cannot explain the immunity of civilians, or the lack of immunity of soldiers fighting for a just cause: the latter are innocent, and the former can be morally guilty. The self-defence theory—which he construes as referring to present attacks—enjoins immunity of civilians in war, but also that of soldiers fighting for a just cause. It even implies the immunity of soldiers fighting for an unjust cause, whenever they are not involved in a present attack (for instance, when they are asleep or cleaning their weapons). On the justifying emergency theory, which refers to a present danger, rather than a present attack, the distinction between legitimate and illegitimate targets largely corresponds to the distinction between combatants and non-combatants. But this correspondence is not complete. The convention theory comes closest to a justification of the distinction, but cannot make it absolute. Each of these approaches, then, has a valid moral principle at heart. But each proves misleading when adopted as the sole criterion for distinguishing between legitimate and illegitimate targets and acts of war. Accordingly, Steinhoff proposes that all four principles be taken into account when deciding in a particular case whether civilians may be attacked or not. He also explains how the weighing of these principles can proceed. The resulting four-tier approach would call for revision of the laws of war as they now stand in at least two significant respects. Civilians may sometimes take up arms against enemy soldiers without thereby losing their immunity. On the other hand, civilians may sometimes be directly attacked.

The next two chapters offer a historical and a legal perspective on civilian immunity, respectively. Colm McKeogh (Chapter 3) looks at two important developments in the history of the principle of non-combatant immunity. The first was the abandonment by Grotius of the attempt, made in Augustine's teaching on the morality of war, to justify killing in war in terms of the supposed guilt of those killed. The view that killing in war could be justified as punishment deserved by wrongdoing dominated

Western thought for more than a thousand years. As Paul Gilbert points out (Chapter 9), it has enjoyed something of a comeback in the 'new wars'. It can also often be discerned in the current rhetoric about the 'war on terror'. Yet, as Grotius made clear more than three and a half centuries ago, the punitive justification of killing cannot apply to modern warfare. There are insufficient grounds for the ascription of guilt to soldiers fighting on the side that lacks a just cause: as long as such soldiers fight under orders and do so in accordance with the laws of war, they are not in breach of international law. They do no wrong for which they may be put on trial. Killing them in war cannot be justified as a punishment for wrong done.

The second development discussed in McKeogh's contribution is the introduction of the principle of double effect into the ethics of war. This has had an adverse effect on the lot of civilians in war, as the principle has been used to excuse, as a side-effect, the unintended but foreseen deaths of civilians in military operations. The principle of double effect requires, among other things, that the harm of killing civilians without intent, but with foresight, be proportionate to the good to be achieved by the military action. This type of deliberation calls for the trading off of human lives against a good end. Such an approach to taking human life is at odds with fundamental moral principles for the proper treatment of human beings. McKeogh therefore argues that not only must the intentional killing of civilians remain strictly prohibited, but that all non-accidental killing of them ought to be outlawed too.

Whereas McKeogh's chapter argues for revision of the law of war, David Kretzmer's contribution gives a detailed account of the current state of that law, and indicates the main problems of its interpretation and application (Chapter 4). The law of armed conflict, or international humanitarian law, provides for the protection of civilians by means of three basic requirements. Under the principle of *discrimination* (or distinction), a party to an armed conflict is bound to distinguish between combatants and civilians: the former are a legitimate target, the latter are not. Belligerent parties are also obliged to exercise *precaution* in order to avoid harming civilians and civilian objects. Moreover, under the principle of *proportionality*, an attack against a legitimate military target must be avoided if it may be expected to cause incidental loss of civilian life, injury to civilians, or damage to civilian objects, that would be excessive relative to the concrete and direct military advantage anticipated.

Application of these principles raises an array of questions. One is the definition of 'combatant': since any person who is not a combatant is regarded as a civilian, defining combatants becomes crucial. The definition given in the Fourth Geneva Convention (1949) includes only lawful or privileged combatants: combatants who are entitled to prisoner-of-war status if captured and are immune from criminal prosecution for fighting according to the laws of armed conflict. A major point of contention is whether there is also a category of 'unlawful' or 'non-privileged' combatants, who may be legitimately targeted, but do not enjoy the privileges of lawful combatants. Obviously, those civilians who participate in hostilities are no longer immune; but what constitutes 'taking a direct part in hostilities'? Do those civilians who provide logistical support or transportation to combatants qualify? What of employees of private military companies? Another problem with the principle of discrimination concerns those civilians who lose their immunity from attack because they take an active part in hostilities. Is this loss of immunity restricted to the time during which they are directly involved in hostilities, or does it extend beyond that time? Still another relates to the protection that a belligerent party owes its own civilians. The duty to protect civilians applies not only to the adversary; a party to a conflict is bound to avoid acts that endanger its own citizens, such as using them as shields to make certain places immune from military attack, or locating military installations close to hospitals or other protected sites. What effect does non-compliance with these obligations have on the duty of the adversary to avoid harming civilians? Both the requirement of precaution and that of proportionality, which concern harming civilians without intent while attacking legitimate military targets, raise the issue of appropriate standards. What type and degree of precaution must be exercised when planning and carrying out such attacks? What is the right proportion between the importance of direct military advantage sought in an attack and the unintended, but foreseen, harm inflicted on civilians?

The final two chapters in the first part of the book explore some ways in which the scope of civilian immunity in war might be restricted. Seumas Miller brings the notion of collective responsibility to bear on the issue and argues that certain groups of civilians, under certain circumstances, may be stripped of their immunity against deadly violence, while Tony Coady examines the thinking behind the term 'collateral damage', which is often deployed to provide a licence for killing civilians as a side-effect of attacking military targets.

Miller (Chapter 5) approaches the subject in the context of a human rights-based account of the moral justification for resorting to deadly violence, and in particular for waging war. He argues that there are two neglected categories of civilians who are not *innocent* civilians, and who accordingly ought not to enjoy civilian immunity in war. They may be killed with intent, if there are weighty military considerations calling for that. The first category consists of those civilians who have a share in the collective moral responsibility for certain basic human rights violations, yet are not morally responsible for the enforcement of these violations. Such persons are neither combatants nor their leaders; nor do they necessarily assist combatants as combatants, unlike, for instance, workers in arms and ammunition factories. They may be persons holding positions of authority in the chain of command responsible for the rights violations at issue. Or they may be persons outside the chain of command who are nevertheless responsible for the basic human rights violations by virtue of having planned them, or seen to it that others shall commit them. (This raises the vexed question of the moral responsibility of intellectuals who devise and instigate policies that violate basic human rights of entire ethnic or cultural groups, which Miller does not discuss.[11]) The second category consists of the members of civilian groups who are collectively morally responsible for culpably failing to assist those who have a moral right to assistance from them. Again, such persons are neither combatants nor their leaders; nor do they necessarily assist combatants as combatants. They may be political leaders or government employees entrusted with upholding basic human rights of their citizens. These two categories overlap: there are members of civilian groups who are guilty of certain violations of basic human rights by virtue of culpably refraining from assisting the rights-bearers in question. According to Miller, civilians belonging to either of these two groups may be targeted, should there be a good military reason for doing so.

With the partial exception of McKeogh (Chapter 3), all the contributors mentioned so far discuss the principle of civilian immunity as protecting

---

[11] One recent case is that of the Serbian intellectual elite that proposed the project of Greater Serbia, instigated 'ethnic cleansing' of large parts of Former Yugoslavia, and produced propaganda whitewashing the crimes committed in its course. See I. Primoratz, 'Boycott of Serbian Intellectuals', *Public Affairs Quarterly*, 10 (1996).

civilians from harm deliberately inflicted on them. That, indeed, is of central importance in all attempts to provide moral and legal protection to civilians caught up in war. But civilians are killed and injured, and their property is destroyed, in other ways too: by violence that is not aimed at them, but nevertheless harms them as a side-effect of attacks on military targets. The moral enormity of deliberately targeting civilians tends to obscure the moral issues to do with harming them without targeting them. The term 'collateral damage', used with ever greater frequency and in an ever more cavalier manner by politicians and military spokespersons, has come to signify the casual way in which death and injury of civilians is often treated when it is not the direct and avowed purpose of military action. The contribution of Tony Coady (Chapter 6) focuses on the moral issues surrounding the infliction of such damage. Coady argues that although there is an important moral difference between harming with and without intent, this does not mean that the latter type of harming is of no moral consequence. Such indispensable moral and legal notions as 'recklessness' and 'negligence' point to the need for closer attention to the moral complexities of harm inflicted without intention.

Coady looks into the different forms of foreknowledge or lack of it that can accompany the infliction of such harm. One distinction important in this connection is that between accidental and incidental harm: harm that was not, and could not have been, foreseen by the agent, and harm that was, or could have been, foreseen. Neither type of harm is intended, but while accidental harm is beyond the agent's control, incidental harm is not. Now modern warfare, except when the fighting takes place at sea or in a desert, seems to be bound to inflict unintended, but foreseen harm on civilians. Just war theory seeks to deal with this problem by deploying the doctrine of double effect, which permits the infliction of incidental harm on civilians, provided certain conditions are met. Coady offers a brief discussion of the doctrine. Whereas McKeogh (Chapter 3) calls for discarding the doctrine of double effect, Coady insists that the doctrine, or something like it, is a necessary component of any plausible ethics of war that can proffer moral guidance in our time. But he reminds us that, although the doctrine was developed in order to *allow* for waging war in conditions that make it virtually impossible to avoid harming civilians, its spirit is *restrictive*, rather than permissive.

III

Contributions that make up the second part of the book investigate a string of more specific issues to which the principle of civilian immunity in war gives rise.

Whereas Coady draws on the doctrine of double effect as a way of maintaining the *absolute* nature of the prohibition of intentionally killing civilians, Stephen Garrett (Chapter 7) looks into a case where this absolute was first undermined and then completely set aside—that of the use of air power by Great Britain against Germany in World War II. He explores how notions of civilian immunity in wartime came to be eroded as a consequence of unrestrained air attacks on large urban areas, known as 'area bombing'. The chapter first describes the historical background to area bombing as it evolved during World War I, and the debate that took place in the interwar period among air power theorists, jurists, and political leaders about the legal and moral aspects of strategic bombing doctrine, including area attacks. Garrett goes on to examine the restrained character of British bombing tactics in the first months of World War II, and to offer an account of how and why Britain moved from a policy of limited attacks on purely military targets to one of open assault on German cities and towns. The 'area offensive' is described as unfolding in two stages over a period from early 1942 to the very end of the War. The attacks on Hamburg and Berlin are described in some detail, in order to show just what area bombing amounted to. The chapter concludes with some reflections on the relationship between the conduct of warfare and the commitment to certain fundamental values. Britain was fighting to defend freedom and democracy, yet it resorted to a method of warfare that is at odds with the values basic to a free society and a democratic polity.

For obvious reasons, the bombing of cities and towns in World War II still provides the most often cited test case for our thinking about civilian immunity. But our thinking about the moral questions faced by military commanders and political leaders needs to take account of major changes in technology that have occurred since, which impose choices different from those faced by Winston Churchill and Arthur ('Bomber') Harris. Precision-guided munitions, in particular, are changing the ways in which wars are fought, and thereby also the kinds of wars that are fought. These developments and the ways in which they affect the choices concerning civilian immunity are the subject of Hugh White's contribution (Chapter 8).

Partly because of the development and proliferation of precision guidance weapons, the tests for circumstances justifying or excusing the deliberate targeting, or incidental and accidental hitting, of civilians have become much stricter since World War II, and especially since the Vietnam War. White contends that the standards currently applied by Western militaries are in some ways tougher than those envisaged in mainstream just war theory, at least with regard to air campaigns. On the other hand, since the new technology makes it possible to attain a range of military objectives at a much lower risk and cost than ever before, the states that have such technology at their disposal are more willing to go to war. None of the major campaigns in the last two decades—Kuwait in 1991, Kosova in 1999, Afghanistan in 2001, Iraq in 2003—would have been mounted if these developments in technology had not promised a much lower level of risks and cost than, for instance, those involved in the Vietnam War. Against this background, White discusses five issues to do with civilian immunity that have arisen in these campaigns: the use of civilians as human shields, placing civilians at risk in order to reduce risks to one's own soldiers, standards of evidence concerning the nature of the target and the risks to civilians involved in attacking it, just who counts as a 'civilian', and the hardships falling short of death or injury that may legitimately be imposed on civilians.

New, 'smart' military technology may indeed, as White submits, hold out a promise of ever more discriminate use of lethal violence in war. But such technology is in the hands of states, whereas the 'new wars' that loom so large at the end of the twentieth century and beginning of the twenty-first are characterized, among other things, by the blurring of the difference between states and sub-state agents, and by the ever greater prominence of the latter in armed conflicts. Moreover, the war aims in such wars are no longer relatively limited political or economic objectives typical of traditional wars; they are, rather, territorial expansion *and* 'ethnic cleansing' of the conquered lands. These objectives cannot be achieved by waging war in accordance with the principle of discrimination; on the contrary, they enjoin advised, systematic targeting of civilian population. Paul Gilbert's contribution (Chapter 9) looks into the challenge to civilian immunity posed by the 'new wars'. These wars differ from old wars between states in being wars between peoples, defined in terms of their ethnicity, culture, or religion. They result from *discord* between such peoples, rather than from simple *disagreement* between states, and it is for this reason, Gilbert argues, that they commonly involve atrocities against enemy civilians, in breach of the principle of civilian immunity.

More specifically, 'new wars' are fought in ways that either directly target members of identity groups as members rather than as combatants, or show utter indifference to their fate by exposing them to disproportionate harm in the course of hostilities. The latter practice, even if carried out by the regular forces of states, is as much a reflection of discord as are the terrorist methods involved in the former. Terrorist tactics themselves, however, are a direct extension of the violence against members of other groups that arises from discord, and the irregular forces fighting in 'new wars' are often merely groups of people perpetrating such violence, undisciplined and contemptuous of the rules of military conduct. The two types of war differ with regard to their cause too. Whereas old wars are justified as self-defence, which leaves room for, and indeed enjoins, civilian immunity, 'new wars' seem to resurrect older ideas of just war as punishment for wrongdoing. 'Identity politics' motivating these wars is hospitable to, and more often than not combined with, crude notions of collective responsibility and guilt; this, too, helps explain the unprecedented proportion of civilian casualties. Those committed to the politics of identity lack the resources required for an adequate grounding and application of the principle of civilian immunity. If we propose to uphold it, Gilbert argues, we must do so on the basis of a different type of politics.

One of the methods of 'ethnic cleansing' used in some 'new wars' has been mass rape of women. This was especially pronounced in the war in Bosnia-Herzegovina; as Mary Kaldor writes, 'its systematic character, in detention centres and in particular places and at particular times, suggests that it may have been part of a deliberate strategy' on the part of the Serbs.[12] But then, rape has always been part and parcel of war, albeit usually committed by soldiers acting on their own and, at least in modern times, in breach, rather than fulfilment, of their military duties. Veronique Zanetti focuses on the phenomenon of rape in war and examines the ways in which

---

[12] Kaldor, *New and Old Wars*, 52.

international law has dealt with it, arguing that the special vulnerability of women during times of war is due not primarily to their sex, but rather to women's role and status in their communities (Chapter 10).

Zanetti first looks into mass rapes in World War II. An estimated 1.9 million women in eastern and central parts of Germany were sexually assaulted by Red Army soldiers during the conflict. Yet, at the Nuremberg Trials, rape and sexual abuse did not figure among the war crimes which the Charter explicitly qualified as 'crimes against humanity'. The same was true of the Tokyo Trials. Nor is rape explicitly mentioned in the 1949 Geneva Convention. The first Additional Protocol of 1977 includes rape as an illicit act, but does not list it as a serious breach. Not until the war in Bosnia-Herzegovina and the genocide in Rwanda, where sexual abuse was used as a method of humiliating an entire community and effecting 'ethnic cleansing', was rape finally included in the catalogue of 'grave breaches' of humanitarian law. Zanetti traces this evolution, examines its legal and humanitarian consequences, and investigates the impact of the international tribunals on the treatment of sexual violence in international humanitarian law. She argues that the very nature of the 'new wars' exacerbates the vulnerability of women. If the consequences of these wars are extremely hard for civilian population, they are especially harsh on women, whose social role already places them in a somewhat precarious position. When rape becomes an instrument of war, women are doubly victimized: as individuals and as symbols of their community. By raping women, soldiers seek to humiliate enemy men by demonstrating that they are not strong enough to protect 'their' women. They also stigmatize the women they have raped as 'impure' and often turn them into outcasts in their community. Finally, the chapter examines the protection of women under international humanitarian law, and certain modifications of this protection enacted by the International Criminal Tribunal for the Former Yugoslavia, the International Criminal Tribunal for Rwanda, and the International Criminal Court. Whether these developments in international law provide a fully adequate response to the vulnerability of women to sexual violence in wartime remains to be seen.

Most just war theorists hold that not only civilian life and limb, but civilian property too, ought to be immune from attack. Some international conventions forbid the destruction of private and public civilian property in war and occupation. But life is more important than property. Why should we think that civilian property ought to be protected from attack if by destroying it we can save human lives, whether civilian or military? And if so, just how strong should this protection be? Janna Thompson (Chapter 11) examines several answers to these questions. One is that of John Locke: we must respect property rights. Those who wage an unjust war may forfeit their lives, but defending ourselves against them does not entitle us to take or destroy their property. This will not convince those who doubt that property is a fundamental human right, but there are other reasons why belligerents should not attack civilian property. One is pragmatic: even in the midst of war, we need to think about peace to come at its end. The less destruction is caused to property in the course of war, the less difficult will it be to establish peaceful relations between the parties when the war is over. More to the point, we need to ask why property is important, and to attend to the central role that homes, farms, or businesses can play in the lives of individuals and families, and to the importance of other types of property to entire communities, and indeed to humanity. Most people do not value life as such, but rather life worth living. Such a life involves engaging in activities that depend on the existence of private or public property. Finally, there are weighty reasons for protecting 'cultural property'. Some such property is highly valuable and ought to be immune because of its importance to the members of a particular society or culture—for instance, a cathedral. But some cultural property is regarded as precious and deserving to be preserved because of its aesthetic value and significance to humanity. There is considerable disagreement about how much risk belligerents should accept in order to avoid harm to something of great aesthetic value. Nevertheless, Thompson argues that such value requires a high level of protection. There are, then, good reasons for holding that (some) civilian property should be immune from attack or appropriation in war, and that belligerents should avoid, even at some cost to themselves, destroying civilian property, whether private or public. To be sure, none of these reasons supports absolute protection of such property, or mandates that we treat its protection on a par with the protection of civilian life and limb.

An even more comprehensive treatment of civilian immunity in war might include further issues. One is the status and fate of children in war, and in particular in contemporary warfare: as an especially vulnerable part of the civilian population exposed to both 'collateral' and intentionally inflicted harm, and as minors commandeered or manipulated into joining military or paramilitary formations.[13] Another is terrorism. There are some references to terrorism in this book (in Chapters 1 and 6), but the subject warrants more extended analysis, in particular if we accept the widespread (but by no means universal) view that victimization of innocent people is a defining trait of terrorism.[14] Veronique Zanetti (Chapter 10) deals with mass rape as the most drastic consequence of women's vulnerability in war. But the issue of gender may also be approached from a different angle. R. Charli Carpenter has recently argued that today the principle of civilian immunity is often applied in a restrictive way, mediated by criteria of gender and age. Both belligerent parties and humanitarian organizations tend to conflate 'innocent civilians' with 'women and children', thus denying the protection of civilian immunity to adult male civilians, and in particular those of draft age.[15] Yet another issue is the deliberate destruction of a particular type of civilian property: buildings and sites of cultural and historical significance. The 'new wars' in particular, but some 'old wars' too, have been 'wars on architecture' as well as on people. That has involved much intentional and systematic destruction of places of worship, libraries, museums, and other buildings, whether as part and parcel of wars of extermination and 'ethnic cleansing', or as a method of terrorizing civilian population.[16] These topics had to be left out here. Nonetheless, I trust the book provides much food for thought for anyone engaging with the issues to do with the status and fate of civilians in war, and in particular in wars waged in our time.

---

[13] See Helen Brocklehurst, *Who's Afraid of Children? Children, Conflict and International Relations* (Aldershot: Ashgate, 2006).

[14] For a range of views on how terrorism should be defined and whether it can ever be morally justified, see I. Primoratz (ed.), *Terrorism: The Philosophical Issues* (Basingstoke and New York: Palgrave Macmillan, 2004).

[15] See R. Charli Carpenter, *'Innocent Women and Children': Gender, Norms and the Protection of Civilians* (Aldershot: Ashgate, 2006).

[16] See Robert Bevan, *The Destruction of Memory: Architecture at War* (London: Reaktion Books, 2006).

PART I

1

Civilian Immunity in War: Its Grounds, Scope, and Weight

IGOR PRIMORATZ

The immunity of civilians, or non-combatants, from deadly violence in war is enjoined by the centrepiece of the *jus in bello* prong of just war theory, the principle of discrimination. It is also a central tenet in consequentialist accounts of the morality of war, for it provides an obvious way of limiting killing, mayhem, and destruction in war. Even pacifists have good reason to give serious consideration to the issue of civilian immunity. Elizabeth Anscombe famously charged pacifism with obliviousness to the moral difference between killing soldiers and killing civilians in war, and argued that this makes pacifists—not in intent, but in effect—complicit in the rampant scepticism regarding moral constraints on the ways of waging war:

Pacifism teaches people to make no distinction between the shedding of innocent blood and the shedding of any human blood. And in this way pacifism has corrupted enormous numbers of people who will not act according to its tenets. They become convinced that a number of things are wicked which are not; hence, seeing no way of avoiding 'wickedness', they set no limits to it.[1]

The pacifist might bite the bullet and say that all killing, or all killing in war, is indeed absolutely, and equally, wrong. But a more discerning, and therefore more promising, response would be to try to find within the pacifist theory some way of distinguishing, whether in type or degree,

First published as Igor Primoratz, 'Civilian Immunity in War', *The Philosophical Forum*, 36 (2005), 41–58. Published by Blackwell Publishing. Reprinted by permission.

[1] G. E. M. Anscombe, 'War and Murder', in *Collected Philosophical Papers*, iii (Oxford: Blackwell, 1981), 57.

between the wrongness of killing soldiers and that of killing civilians, and thus come to terms with the idea of civilian immunity.

The theoretical importance of the subject needs no emphasis. Nor does its importance in practical terms. The principle of civilian immunity was considered one of the major achievements of moral progress from early modern times to the Great War, but has been under constant attrition ever since. At the beginning of the twentieth century, the ratio of military to civilian casualties in war was eight to one; by its end, that ratio was reversed, and is now one to eight.[2] The most salient characteristic of end-of-century wars—in the Balkans and in the Caucasus—was utter disregard of civilian immunity. Indeed, some find it difficult to call them 'wars', for they were, for the most part, onslaughts of armies and militias on defenceless civilian populations, with the aim of extermination and 'ethnic cleansing'.

In this chapter I want to discuss the grounds of the principle of civilian immunity in war, its proper scope, and its weight.

Rejecting Civilian Immunity

Before looking into the main ways of grounding the principle of civilian immunity and demarcating its proper application, I want to say something about a very different view on the subject: one that rejects the very idea of civilian immunity. One does not come across this view in philosophical debates about the morality of war, but rather in essays written by two thinkers who had no philosophical background but were much concerned with moral issues of the day. Interestingly enough, both had been at the receiving end of attacks of enemy air force on civilians and might have been expected to have some appreciation of the idea of civilian immunity.

The first is George Orwell. He had personal experience of the bombing of London by the *Luftwaffe*. Yet, in a column published on 19 May 1944, he wrote that the idea of constraining warfare by some such rule as civilian immunity, and indeed all talk of limiting or humanizing war, was 'sheer humbug'. He could not see why it was worse to kill civilians than to kill

---

[2] Mary Kaldor, *New and Old Wars: Organized Violence in a Global Era* (Cambridge: Polity, 2001), 8.

soldiers. While 'legitimate' warfare kills 'the healthiest and bravest of the young male population', a bomb dropped on a city kills a cross-section of the population—a preferable outcome, in Orwell's judgement, because

war is not avoidable at this stage of history, and since it has to happen it does not seem to me a bad thing that others should be killed besides young men. I wrote in 1937: 'Sometimes it is a comfort to me to think that the aeroplane is altering the conditions of war. Perhaps when the next war comes we may see that sight unprecedented in all history, a jingo with a bullet hole in him'. We haven't seen that yet ... but at any rate the suffering of this war has been shared out more evenly than the last one was. The immunity of civilians, one of the things that have made war possible, has been shattered. ... I don't regret that. I can't feel that war is 'humanized' by being confined to the slaughter of the young and becomes 'barbarous' when the old get killed as well. [...] War is of its nature barbarous, it is better to admit that. If we see ourselves as the savages we are, some improvement is possible ...[3]

Orwell's argument is one of distributive justice. At this stage of history, at least, war is inevitable, like a natural disaster, rather than a matter of someone's responsibility. It is therefore better—more just—that the suffering it brings should be distributed more evenly, rather than inflicted for the most part on healthy young men in the field.

Yet war is not at all, or at least not entirely, something that just happens to people, completely unrelated to human choice and responsibility. Orwell, too, knew this. If it were, one could not think it a good thing to see 'a jingo with a bullet hole in him'. What people choose to do and not do does matter. To be sure, if you advisedly help bring about war, you deserve to pay a price for it. But it is not obvious that you deserve to pay the *ultimate* price. And in any case, not all civilians are jingoes. But if so, there is something to be said for civilian immunity, after all.

The other author I want to cite is Hans Magnus Enzensberger. He, too, spent endless nights in a cellar, hoping to survive an air raid on his city. Yet he, too, has no time for civilian immunity. But his reasons are different from Orwell's:

I well remember the ... terror of air raids. And the grown-ups who cowered on the benches in the cellar, at whom these 'terror raids' were aimed; they

---

[3] S. Orwell and I. Angus (eds.), *The Collected Essays, Journalism and Letters of George Orwell* (London: Secker & Warburg, 1968), iii. 151–2.

were the 'innocent civilians.' [...] But it wasn't always like this. A strange transformation had occurred in the 'innocent civilians' who sat in the cellar while all around them phosphor bombs turned the city into a sea of fire. I remember how their eyes lit up every time the Führer spoke and let them know what he had in mind: 'a titanic and unprecedented struggle', a fight to the bitter end. [...] Without their enthusiastic support the Nazis could have never come to power.[4]

Wars always start with jubilant masses applauding the warmongers leading them. These leaders are often elected; sometimes their position is confirmed in subsequent elections. They, and the soldiers they send off to war, are acting as 'representatives of their society who feed on its rage, its cruelty, its lust for revenge'. If so, civilians are not really innocent, but rather responsible for what their military do to the other side. Accordingly, when attacked by the other side, they are merely facing the fatal repercussions of their own actions and omissions.[5]

On the face of it, there is something to this. Yet, at the same time Enzensberger's stance seems much too harsh on—indeed, cruel to—his fellow Germans. No doubt they or, more accurately, many of them, could properly be blamed on several counts. But is the fact that their eyes lit up and they cheered at rallies organized by the Nazi regime in wartime reason enough for them to be blown to pieces or incinerated in their cities and towns? Surely no thoughts and feelings in themselves can justify such extreme punishment. Nor can support for an unjust war, manipulated or coerced by a totalitarian state.

What of the claim that the government and the military are 'representatives' of their society? This, I take it, means that the killing and destruction that the military wreak on the enemy in the course of an unjust war somehow 'represent' what civilians in the rear are thinking, feeling, and saying. That certainly shows those civilians and their society in a very bad light. But again, surely that is not enough, in itself, to justify killing and maiming them, whether as deserved punishment or as a measure of military exigency.

Both Enzensberger's judgement of his compatriots and his sweeping rejection of the idea of civilian immunity, then, are wide of the mark.

[4] H. M. Enzensberger, *Civil War*, trans. P. Spence and M. Chalmers (London: Granta Books, 1994), 50.
[5] Ibid. 51.

A Useful Convention

The main division in ethical theory between consequentialism and deontology is reflected in the ethics of war in the divide between consequentialist accounts of the morality of war and just war theory. The consequentialist position on civilian immunity, as on everything else, is quite simple: we should go by consequences, and by consequences only. Civilian immunity ought to be respected, for respecting it has, on balance, good consequences.

Consequentialist thinkers usually present their view on civilian immunity against the background of a critique of attempts of philosophers and legal thinkers to account for civilian immunity in deontological terms. Having satisfied themselves that those attempts have been unsuccessful, they put forward the claim that civilian immunity has nothing to do with civilians' acts or omissions, guilt or innocence, responsibility or lack of it, but is merely a useful convention. It is useful, since it rules out targeting a large group of human beings, and thus helps reduce greatly the overall killing, mayhem, and destruction in war.

The consequentialist view of civilian immunity is exposed to objections on two counts: the protection it offers to civilians is too weak, and the ground provided for it indicates a misunderstanding of the moral issue involved. The protection is too weak, because civilian immunity is understood as but a useful convention. This makes it doubly weak. First, if it is merely a *useful* convention, if all its moral force is due to its utility, then it will have no such force in cases where it has no utility. This is a familiar flaw of consequentialism. It denies that moral rules have any intrinsic moral significance, and explains their binding force solely in terms of the good consequences of acting in accordance with them. Therefore it cannot give us any good *consequentialist* reason to adhere to a moral rule in cases where adhering to it will not have the good consequences it usually has, and where better consequences will be attained by going against the rule.[6] This means that we should respect civilian immunity when, and only when, doing so will have the good consequences adduced as its ground: when it will indeed reduce the overall killing, maiming, and destruction. On the other hand, whenever we have good reasons to believe that, by targeting

---

[6] I discuss this at length in my *Justifying Legal Punishment*, 2nd edn. (Atlantic Highlands, NJ: Humanity Books, 1997), 118–37.

civilians, we shall make a significant contribution to our war effort, thus shortening the war and reducing the overall killing and mayhem, that is what we may, and indeed ought to, do. Civilian immunity is thus made hostage to the vagaries of war, instead of providing civilians with iron-clad protection against them. This is not a purely theoretical concern. As Kai Nielsen has pointed out, systematic attacks on civilians in the course of a war of national liberation can make an indispensable contribution to the successful prosecution of such a war. That was indeed the case in Algeria and South Vietnam, and may well have been the case in Angola and Mozambique as well.[7]

Then again, if civilian immunity is merely a useful *convention*, that weakens it by making it hostage to the stance taken by enemy political and military leadership. They may or may not choose to respect the immunity of our civilians. If they do not, then, on the consequentialist view of this immunity, we are not bound to respect the immunity of their civilians. Being a convention, it binds only if, or as long as, it is accepted by both parties to the conflict. As an important statement of this view puts it, 'for convention-dependent obligations, what one's opponent does, what "everyone is doing," etc., are facts of great moral importance. Such facts help to determine within what convention, if any, one is operating, and thus they help one discover what his moral duties are.'[8] To be sure, even if no such convention is in place, but we have reason to believe that we can help bring about its acceptance by unilaterally acting in accordance with it and thereby encouraging the enemy to do the same, we should do that. But if we have no good reason to believe that, or if we have tried that approach and it has failed, our military are free to kill and maim enemy civilians whenever they feel they need to. Thus our moral choice is determined, be it directly or ultimately, by the moral (or immoral) choice of enemy political and military leaders. So is the fate of enemy civilians. The fact that they are civilians, in itself, counts for nothing.

This brings me to the final objection: the consequentialist misses what anyone else, and in particular any civilian in wartime, would consider the

---

[7] See K. Nielsen, 'Violence and Terrorism: Its Uses and Abuses', in B. M. Leiser (ed.), *Values in Conflict* (New York: Macmillan, 1981), 446–9.

[8] G. I. Mavrodes, 'Conventions and the Morality of War', *Philosophy and Public Affairs*, 4 (1974/5), 128.

crux of the matter. Faced with the prospect of being killed or maimed by enemy fire, a civilian would not make her case in terms of the disutility of killing or maiming civilians in war in general, or of killing or maiming her then and there. She would, rather, point out that she is a civilian, not a soldier; a bystander, not a participant; an innocent, not a guilty party. She would point out that she has done nothing to deserve, or become liable to, such a fate. She would present these personal facts as considerations whose moral significance is intrinsic and decisive, rather than instrumental and fortuitous, mediated by a useful convention (which, in different circumstances, might enjoin limiting war by targeting *only* civilians). And her argument, couched in personal terms, would seem to be more to the point than the impersonal calculation of good and bad consequences by means of which the consequentialist would settle the matter.[9]

The Defence View

Accounts of civilian immunity offered by adherents of just war theory acknowledge the personal nature of the relevant considerations. As Thomas Nagel puts it, they start from 'the principle that hostile treatment of any person must be justified in terms of something *about that person* which makes the treatment appropriate. Hostility is a personal relation, and it must be suited to its target.'[10] Just what is it about a person that makes him a legitimate target of deadly violence in war? What is it about an enemy soldier that makes him a legitimate object of our hostility and the deadly violence in which it is expressed, unlike an enemy civilian, who remains off limits?

Well, he is a soldier, a war is going on, and he is doing what soldiers do in war: he is waging war on us. We are defending ourselves. Or it may be that we are not under attack, but someone else is, and we have come to render aid. In any case, it is a matter of defence. Civilians are not attacking

[9] A consequentialist ethics of war might present civilian immunity as a useful *rule*, rather than a useful *convention*. That might make the second objection beside the point, but the first and third would still stand and, I trust, suffice.

[10] Thomas Nagel, 'War and Massacre', in *Mortal Questions* (Cambridge: Cambridge University Press, 1979), 64.

us or anyone else; there is no such thing as defence against civilians. They have a right not to be attacked. To attack them would mean to violate this right and commit grave injustice. How do we show that civilians have such a right? One could go about this in more than one way; but it seems to me that whatever argument one might construct at this point would be less compelling than the claim the argument was supposed to prove. As Michael Walzer rightly says, 'the theoretical problem is not to describe how immunity is gained, but how it is lost. We are all immune to start with; our right not to be attacked is a feature of normal human relationships.'[11] Civilians have done nothing to forfeit this right; therefore they have it, and must not be attacked. Soldiers have, by waging war on us, or on those to whose aid we have come; therefore they have forfeited this right, and may be attacked.

To be sure, this does not draw a hard and fast line between the two groups, and an array of questions immediately suggest themselves. Just who counts as a soldier, and who as a civilian? Is a military chaplain or medic a soldier and, accordingly, a legitimate target? Is a soldier, by virtue of being a soldier, a legitimate target at any time and in any circumstances? May he be shot while sleeping, rather than attacking us? Or when on leave, on his way to visit family back home? Then again, some civilians play an important role in the war being waged on us. The defence minister is a civilian. So is the scientist doing research required for the development of military technology, and the worker in an arms factory. Are they nevertheless protected, by virtue of being civilians?

In spelling out what might be termed the defence view of civilian immunity and soldiers' lack of it, one might say that the criterion for demarcating the two groups is: who is, and who is not, 'currently engaged in the business of war'.[12] Now 'currently' does not mean right this minute, and 'engaged in the business of war' does not mean only using some kind of arms in an attempt to kill us, or issuing commands to someone doing that. The 'business of war' is a complex collective activity and a prolonged affair. The soldier may be sleeping right now, but he will wake up later and resume his part in this business; therefore he is fair game even when asleep. The same applies to the case of a soldier on leave.

---

[11] Michael Walzer, *Just and Unjust Wars: A Moral Argument with Historical Illustrations* (New York: Basic Books, 1977), 145 n.
[12] Ibid. 43.

The political leaders of a country at war wear no uniform and do no fighting themselves; but it is they who make the decisions that others shall fight, and when, where, and how they shall do that. Therefore they, too, are legitimate targets. Workers in an arms or ammunition factory wear no uniform and do no fighting, but are nevertheless deeply involved in the business of war: without their products war could not be fought. Accordingly, an arms or ammunition factory and those working in it are legitimate targets too. The same applies to scientists doing research involved in the production of military technology.

War could not be fought without soldiers being fed either; yet workers in a food factory may not be attacked, even if all their produce goes to the army. For workers producing arms or ammunition are providing the means of fighting, and catering to soldiers as soldiers. Workers producing food are feeding soldiers as human beings, not as soldiers; they are catering to a need that humans have at all times, not only in war. The same is true of military chaplains and medics, however. They are in uniform, and we will be hard put to distinguish them from enemy soldiers proper; but whenever we can do so, we ought to refrain from shooting them.

This does not take care of all cases that might be thought borderline; some of them might prove quite hard. But we are not left without a clue in the face of such cases. Just as in criminal law we start from the presumption of innocence that the prosecution must rebut, so, when facing a dubious case in war, we should always start from the presumption of immunity, and attack only if we have succeeded in overturning this presumption and showing that the target is indeed part of the chain of agency in the attack we are fending off.

The defence view has several things going for it. It is an obvious view to take. Henry Shue makes this point forcefully. Civilian immunity 'is a reaffirmation of the morally foundational "no-harm" principle. One ought generally not to harm other persons. Non-combatant immunity says one ought, most emphatically, not to harm others who are themselves not harming anyone. This is as fundamental, and as straightforward, and as nearly non-controversial, as moral principles can get.'[13]

---

[13] Henry Shue, 'War', in H. LaFollette (ed.), *The Oxford Handbook of Practical Ethics* (Oxford: Oxford University Press, 2003), 742.

Of the main approaches to civilian immunity considered in this chapter, the defence view is closest to the understanding of this immunity in the laws and customs of war. The way The Hague and Geneva Conventions provide for the protection of civilians is in line with this view, although the scope of the category is wider: civilians are contrasted with combatants, and the latter are those, and only those, who openly carry arms, either at all times or at least at the time they are fighting or preparing to do so.[14] The defence view has been espoused by a number of philosophers, such as Elizabeth Anscombe, Thomas Nagel, Jeffrie G. Murphy, and Michael Walzer.[15]

These philosophers, too, use the word 'innocent'. But they make it clear that they are using it in a technical, rather than an ordinary sense. Its technical meaning is the meaning suggested by etymology: the innocent are *innocentes*, those not harming us. If we were to use it in some ordinary, morally rich sense, the class of those qualifying for protection would shrink drastically. In a modern war, and in particular in a modern war that is popular with the population, only children, the insane, and the aged and infirm, as well as the odd dissenter, would be truly innocent of the war. Almost everyone else would be in some way, to some degree, contributing to, or implicated in, the war effort. Moreover, to talk of innocence, and thereby also of guilt, is to be out of touch with the realities of modern war. While our medieval ancestors conceived just war as punishment of the guilty, modern war—when it has a just cause—is no longer fought in order to punish the guilty, but rather to fend off aggression. Accordingly, those protected from it are not those innocent in relation to aggression, but rather those not engaged in it.[16]

[14] See Colm McKeogh, *Innocent Civilians: The Morality of Killing in War* (Basingstoke: Palgrave, 2002), 131–40, and Ch. 3 in this volume.

[15] Anscombe, 'War and Murder', 53, 59–60; *idem*, 'Mr. Truman's Degree', in *Collected Philosophical Papers*, iii (Oxford: Blackwell, 1981), 67–9; Nagel, 'War and Massacre', 70–2; J. G. Murphy, 'The Killing of the Innocent', *Monist*, 57 (1973), 529–35; Walzer, *Just and Unjust Wars*, 42–4, 138–51.

[16] The above account of the defence view is couched in a way that presupposes a high degree of independence of the two prongs of just war theory (and any ethics of war), *jus ad bellum* (justice *of* war) and *jus in bello* (justice *in* war). This way of putting it implies that the principle of civilian immunity is equally binding on all soldiers, whether the war they are fighting is justified or not as a whole. When they fight in accordance with the principle, they kill enemy soldiers, but commit no murder. When they disregard the principle and kill enemy civilians, they commit murder. But the defence account can also be adopted by those who consider *jus ad bellum* and *jus in bello* to be much more closely linked, and argue that soldiers fighting for an unjust cause should not be doing so and that, accordingly, when they kill enemy soldiers whose cause is just, that is unjustified killing, i.e. murder. For although every

Could the tables be turned at this point on the adherents of the defence view? Might they be out of touch with the reality of modern warfare? The view of war as the preserve of those actually fighting it, with civilians as mere bystanders, is accurate as far as medieval and early modern warfare is concerned, but wide of the mark when it comes to modern wars. In medieval and early modern times the monarch was the sovereign, solely responsible for making decisions about war and peace. The military consisted of professional, paid soldiers. It fought on behalf of the monarch, a mere tool of his or her policies. Civilian population had no say in these matters; nor was it involved in any significant way in actual warfare. Indeed, there was no need for civilians to concern themselves very much with the course and outcome of war, as long as soldiers were at pains not to endanger civilian life, limb, and property while fighting. The court and the military, on the one hand, and the civilian population, on the other, were separate sections of society with very little in common. The former did not pursue their policies and wars on behalf of the latter, and the latter had no control over policy and warfare. Civilians were literally mere bystanders.

Since the French Revolution and the triumph of popular sovereignty and democracy, however, they are mere bystanders no longer. Sovereignty no longer belongs to the ruler, but rather to the people. The government is the agent of the people. The military carry out the policies of the government and thus, in the last analysis, of the people. More often than not, the military is not mercenary and professional, but rather a citizens' army, the people in arms. War is no longer a conflict between rulers, with their subjects looking on as bystanders, but a struggle among nations themselves. When governments make war, they always claim to be doing so on behalf of the people. When made by a democratic government, such a claim certainly needs to be taken seriously. When made by an undemocratic government, such a claim may be true, or it may be spurious. Be that as it may, civilians may be in a position to influence government decisions concerning war and peace, or to affect their implementation. Surely these facts have some bearing on the issue of civilian immunity. And they point beyond the understanding of this immunity solely in terms of defence.

---

murder is an extremely grave matter morally, not every such matter—not every murder—is morally grave in the same degree. To murder a person who is not fighting us, who is defenceless, and who cannot relate her death in some meaningful way to her own choices and actions, is morally worse than to murder a soldier who is fighting us with a just cause.

Responsible Bystanders

Looking beyond the defence view, one might grant that civilians are indeed bystanders, but add that they are not necessarily *mere* bystanders. This line of thought is examined in Kai Draper's paper 'Self-Defense, Collective Obligation, and Noncombatant Liability'.

Draper takes as his point of departure the claim made by a senior United States Air Force officer at a briefing during the First Gulf War that Iraqi civilians were not entirely innocent, and therefore were not entirely immune against lethal violence either, since 'ultimately the people have some control over what goes on in their country'.[17] Admittedly, Iraqi civilians took no part in the decision-making process that led to Iraq's aggression on Kuwait, or in the military aggression itself. As far as the actual aggression was concerned, they were bystanders: persons present at, but not involved in, the aggression. But they had some control over their government and military with regard to the aggression. They failed to prevent it, and thereby lost their immunity against deadly violence. When harming them serves a military purpose, they may legitimately be harmed.

It might be objected that as long as one does not authorize a morally wrong action or policy, takes no part in it, nor contributes to it, one remains a bystander. One's failure to prevent the action or policy does not undermine one's bystander status and the immunity that comes with it. But a closer look at the connection between being a bystander and having immunity from deadly violence shows that things are not quite as simple as the objection assumes.

Consider the following scenario. A is about to kill B, with no moral justification for doing so. C is a bystander who could, at no great cost to himself, prevent A from killing B. But C refuses to do so, without having a justification or excuse for that. B cannot save her life by killing A, but can do so by killing C. C's death will affect A in such a way that he will no longer want or be able to kill B.

In such a case, it seems to me, C is indeed a bystander. But he is not a *mere* bystander; he, too, is responsible for B's death, if B is killed. This responsibility is not quite the same as that of A, but is nevertheless

---

[17] K. Draper, 'Self-Defense, Collective Obligation, and Noncombatant Liability', *Social Theory and Practice*, 24 (1998), 57.

extremely serious. If, on the other hand, B saves her life by killing C, she will have done nothing wrong. She will not have violated C's immunity against deadly violence. C could and should have acted to prevent A from attacking B, and lost this immunity by failing to do so. *Responsible* bystanders, unlike mere bystanders, have no such immunity.

If so, the question to ask about Iraqi civilians during the First Gulf War, and about civilians in general, is this: can they, or some of them, be seen as C in the above scenario? For them to lose the immunity they have as civilians, it would have to be true that (1) they could indeed prevent the aggression at issue, (2) could do so at no great cost to themselves, (3) have a moral duty to do so, and (4) have no justification or excuse for not doing so.

These conditions are interrelated. Most obviously, 'ought' implies 'can': if I cannot do something, I cannot have a duty to do it. Then again, when the price bound up with doing one's duty passes a certain threshold, the duty no longer binds (putting aside duties that bind absolutely, if any). Finally, conditions (1) and (2) are jointly sufficient for generating condition (3). Draper cannot make up his mind on this, but it seems to me that, at least with regard to very serious harms, when one is facing the prospect of such harm being unjustifiably inflicted on another human being and is able to prevent that at no great cost to oneself, one has a moral duty to act; no previous undertaking to do so should be required.

Of course, no common citizen of Iraq could have prevented the country's aggression against Kuwait on his or her own. But it might be maintained that Iraqi civilians *collectively* should have acted to prevent it. If it is true that they could have prevented their country's aggression had they acted collectively to that purpose, that they would not have had to pay too high a price for so acting, that accordingly they as a group had a duty to do so, and that they had no justification or excuse for not doing so, then they are collectively at fault for failing to prevent the aggression. They make up a group of responsible bystanders. Moreover, their collective responsibility is distributive. It can be assigned to individual Iraqi civilians by means of some such principle as the one advanced by Draper: 'The failure of a group to act as it should can be blamed on all those members who, without exculpating [reason], were unwilling to take part in the group acting as it should.'[18]

---

[18] Ibid. 73.

Accordingly, when military exigency requires it, they may legitimately be attacked.

However, the circumstances of Iraqi civilians at the time of the First Gulf War were not at all like that. Spontaneous individual action had no hope of preventing the aggression on Kuwait. Even if a large number of individuals had chosen to act without co-ordinating their action with that of others, that would not have achieved this end. In order to stand a chance of preventing their country's aggression, Iraqi civilians would have had to act in a concerted, organized way to that purpose. Given the nature of the regime, that was clearly not feasible. Thus condition (1) for considering them responsible bystanders does not hold. Condition (2) does not hold either, and for the same reason. Given the nature of the regime, any vigorous public opposition to the attack on Kuwait, whether individual or collective, would have been bound up with a prohibitive price. Consequently, condition (3) was not satisfied: Iraqi civilians did not have a moral duty to prevent the aggression on Kuwait. They cannot be considered responsible bystanders, and were not fair game for the Allied military.

Is that but a specific case of circumstances that tend to prevail in countries at war? It seems so, at least as long as we are dealing with countries with authoritarian regimes. But the circumstances should be different in a democracy. When a democracy wages an unjust war, its citizens do not lack opportunities of co-ordinating and organizing their anti-war activities, and need not fear drastic response from the government to their actions. However, in such a case the prospect of success will be relevant, and indeed decisive. When their country is at war, whether just or unjust, people tend to rally around the flag, and to give strong, indeed uncritical support to the government and the military. This is true of a democracy, just as of a country ruled by an unrepresentative, undemocratic government, although, of course, citizens of a democracy should know better. And when a war, whether just or unjust, enjoys strong support by the vast majority of the population, attempts of a small, marginalized, disliked, and suspected bunch of dissenters at preventing or stopping it will be bound to fail. That will be reason enough, both in prudence and in morality, not to make such attempts.[19]

---

[19] To say that they need not try to prevent or stop a war is not to say that they need do nothing at all about it. There may well be a good case for protesting against it, although such protest will not

To be sure, circumstances may be different: the support for a war may not be so widespread and strong that dissent stands no chance of preventing the government from starting an unjust war, or stopping a war if it is already under way. In such a case, those who are in a position to undertake concerted action to that purpose do have a duty to do so, and can properly be considered responsible bystanders if they fail to discharge it. If so, may the military of the unjustly attacked country attack them too, if they hold that doing so would contribute significantly to defeating the aggression? A powerful practical consideration suggests that the answer is no. Enemy civilians who could be considered eligible for attack on the basis of the responsible bystander argument would virtually always live thoroughly intermingled with other enemy civilians who would not be eligible: those who mistakenly but excusably believe their country's cause to be just; those who know that the cause is not just, while mistakenly but excusably believing that there is no chance of affecting the events for the better; those who are not in a position to contribute anything to the opposition to the war, such as the sick and the very infirm; and, last but not least, minors. There is no way of making sure that in an attack on a civilian target, only the former are hit, while the latter emerge unscathed.

Therefore I concur with Draper that, as far as civilian immunity in war is concerned, the responsible bystander line of argument will have very little purchase on reality.[20] It will virtually never apply in the type of case that Draper considers: in countries similar in the relevant respects to Iraq at the time of the First Gulf War. For somewhat different reasons, it will virtually never provide moral justification for targeting civilians in the type of case he does not consider: in countries dissimilar in the relevant respects to Iraq at the time. Issues of civilian immunity in war should be approached and settled in terms of the defence view alone.

Is Civilian Immunity Absolute?

The defence view, then, provides the answer—all the answer we need—to the question of the ground of the principle of civilian immunity against

change the course of events. See T. E. Hill Jr., 'Symbolic Protest and Calculated Silence', *Philosophy and Public Affairs*, 9 (1979/80).

[20] Draper, 'Self-Defense', 78.

military attack in war, and to the question of the scope of this principle. But it says nothing about its weight. Is it an absolute principle, binding in every single case to which it applies, whatever the consequences of abiding by it? Or is it only a *prima facie* principle, although, of course, a very weighty one?

Given that the principle is construed as one of justice, and the immunity it grounds is understood as a right, one might want to say that it binds absolutely (at least in so far as it refers to *intentional* killing and maiming of civilians in war).[21] That would mean to say that civilians must never be attacked, whatever the military advantage of attacking them might be. They must not be attacked even if it is only by attacking them that a defeat in a just war can be averted. This may be thought a hard view; the military, in particular when on their last legs, will not be happy with this kind of ethical advice. But that is no argument against the absolutist position. What does point towards such an argument is the question: Just what kind of defeat in a just war would that be? What would it mean for the defeated?

This question is the point of departure of Michael Walzer's argument of supreme emergency. He considers the plight of Great Britain in early 1942. It seemed about to lose the war against Germany, and there was nothing its military could do about it, at least as long as they were fighting 'clean'. Moreover, Britain's defeat was not going to be yet another defeat of one country by another, entailing such things as loss of some territory, war reparations, political concessions, and the like. Britain was perceived as the only remaining obstacle to the subjugation of most of Europe by the Nazis. And the rule of the Nazis over most of Europe would mean genocide of at least one people, expulsion of a number of others from their lands, and something very much like enslavement for still others. In Walzer's words, 'Nazism was an ultimate threat to everything decent in our lives, an ideology and a practice of domination so murderous, so degrading even to those who might survive, that the consequences of its final victory were literally beyond calculation, immeasurably awful.'[22] Thus Britain was facing what Walzer calls a 'supreme emergency': an (a) imminent threat

---

[21] In this chapter I discuss civilian immunity in war against violence inflicted with *intent*, but say nothing about harming civilians without intent, but with *foresight*. The latter issue—which mainstream just war theory proposes to settle by means of the doctrine of double effect—is complex and important enough to merit separate treatment. See Chs. 3 and 6 below.

[22] Walzer, *Just and Unjust Wars*, 253.

of (b) something utterly unthinkable from a moral point of view, a moral disaster. In such an emergency, and in such an emergency only, one may act in breach of such a basic and weighty moral principle as that of civilian immunity, if that is the only way one can hope to prevent the disaster. Accordingly, Britain decided that it would no longer fight 'clean', and unleashed its air force on the civilian population of Germany. Over more than three years, almost to the last days of the war, the Royal Air Force, later joined by the United States Air Force, devastated many cities and towns in Germany, killed more than half a million civilians, and seriously injured another million. Now, as it happens, most of that was merely a war crime of immense proportions unredeemed and unmitigated; since after the defeats at El Alamein and Stalingrad, it was obvious that Germany was not going to win the war. But in its first year, in Walzer's judgement, the terror bombing of Germany was morally justified (albeit a war crime too). It was morally justified as the only possible response to the supreme emergency facing Britain in 1942.

What if it is only one country, rather than many, that is facing a threat of enslavement or extermination? Walzer holds that the argument of supreme emergency would still apply. He writes:

> Can soldiers and statesmen override the rights of innocent people for the sake of their own political community? I am inclined to answer the question affirmatively, though not without hesitation and worry. [...] ... It is possible to live in a world where individuals are sometimes murdered, but a world where entire peoples are sometimes massacred is literally unbearable. For the survival and freedom of political communities—whose members share a way of life, developed by their ancestors, to be passed on to their children—are the highest values of international society. Nazism challenged these values on a grand scale, but challenges more narrowly conceived, *if they are of the same kind*, have similar moral consequences.[23]

Walzer ends his chapter on supreme emergency by emphasizing that the rules of war in general, and the principle of civilian immunity in particular, may not be breached in the face of defeat *simpliciter*, but only in the face of defeat 'likely to bring disaster to a political community'.[24]

We need to proceed slowly, however. For what we have here are two different conceptions of supreme emergency. The threat is imminent in both, of course; otherwise there would be no emergency. But the nature

---

[23] Ibid. 254.   [24] Ibid. 268.

of the threat differs: it is one thing to meet the fate that the Nazis had in store for peoples they considered racially inferior, and another to have one's political community dismantled. By moving back and forth between these two types of supreme emergency under the ambiguous heading of threat to 'survival and freedom of a political community', Walzer is inviting us to extend to the latter the moral response appropriate to the former. But the invitation should be declined. While genocide, expulsion, or enslavement of an entire people does qualify as a moral disaster, its loss of political independence is, at most, a political disaster. If a political community to be dismantled lacks moral legitimacy, its demise might actually be a moral improvement. But even if a political community does have moral legitimacy, it is difficult to see how a threat to its 'survival and freedom' amounts to 'an ultimate threat to everything decent in our lives'. Therefore, it is also difficult to see how its military could be justified in waging war on enemy civilians in order to defend it.[25]

The suggestion that they might is yet another illustration of Walzer's tendency to endow the political community with much greater moral significance than it deserves, which comes to the fore in his discussion of such issues as terrorism and military intervention as well. He has been taken to task for this tendency by a number of critics, including, most recently, Tony Coady. But Coady also rejects the entire argument of supreme emergency, and insists that civilian immunity be adopted as an absolute moral principle. He supports his position with three arguments.

First, Coady argues that some moral prohibitions are so central to our entire moral experience, so deeply entrenched in it, that they 'function in our moral thinking as a sort of touchstone of moral and intellectual health'. The suspension of such a prohibition brings about 'an upheaval in the moral perspective'; its rejection leads to 'an unbalance and incoherence in moral thought and practice'. The prohibition of intentionally killing innocent people is one of them.[26]

I concur with Coady in granting the principle of civilian immunity some such centrality and weight in our moral thinking. I, too, find its *rejection* or

---

[25] Walzer's more recent discussion of supreme emergency is also plagued by this slippage; see his 'Emergency Ethics', in *Arguing about War* (New Haven and London: Yale University Press, 2004).

[26] C. A. J. (Tony) Coady, 'Terrorism, Just War and Supreme Emergency', in T. Coady and M. O'Keefe (eds.), *Terrorism and Justice: Moral Argument in a Threatened World* (Melbourne: Melbourne University Press, 2002), 19.

suspension unthinkable. But *overriding* it in a particular instance, when that is the only way to avert a moral disaster of the sort that Nazi rule over most of Europe would have meant, and when it is done with full awareness of the extremely high moral cost involved, is another matter. Overriding the principle in such a case does not mean that it should not be applied in every other case that falls short of moral disaster, or that it should not continue to function as a touchstone of moral sanity. Overriding it will amount to 'an upheaval in the moral perspective' only on the question-begging assumption that it must also be an absolute principle, to be followed even if the heavens fall.

Coady's second point is the rejection of the 'primacy of the political community' in Walzer's version of just war theory. I, too, reject that primacy. But this does nothing to undermine the supreme emergency argument when it refers, as it should, to a moral, rather than merely a political disaster.

Finally, Coady warns that 'admission of this exemption is likely to generate widespread misuse of it', and concludes that 'we surely do better to condemn [deliberate attacks on civilians] outright with no leeway for exemptions'.[27] The force of this type of argument varies with the circumstances in which it is deployed. In some cases it may carry great weight. In others its force, and indeed its relevance, may be much doubted. Think of a people facing the prospect of genocide, or of being 'ethnically cleansed' from its land, and unable to put up a fight against an overwhelmingly stronger enemy. Suppose we said to them: 'Granted, what you are facing is an imminent threat of a moral disaster. Granted, the only way you stand a chance of fending off the disaster is by acting in breach of the principle of civilian immunity and attacking enemy civilians. But you must not do that. For if you do, that is likely to generate widespread misuse of the exemption.' Could they—indeed, should they—be swayed by that?

I therefore prefer to think of civilian immunity as an *almost* absolute principle that spells out one of the central and most stringent requirements of justice as it applies to war, and recognizes an *almost* absolute right of the vast majority of civilians—namely, all those who cannot be considered 'currently engaged in the business of war'—not to be targets of deadly

---

[27] Ibid. 20.

violence. The right and the principle trump other moral considerations with which they may come into conflict, with one exception: that of a (narrowly understood) moral disaster.

A Note on Terrorism

I wish to conclude with a few words on the related question of the morality of (sub-state) terrorism. I have discussed civilian immunity in the context of war. But if what I consider the right position is accepted, that will have a bearing on the issue of terrorism.

The issue is related for several reasons. Political organizations and movements that resort to terrorism consider themselves to be at war. Although earlier versions of just war theory were meant to provide moral restraint on war in the traditional, narrow sense of military conflict between states, today the theory aims at application over a wider area of organized and sustained political violence, whether it is employed by states or by sub-state agents such as political groups and movements. And according to a widely shared understanding of terrorism, one of its defining traits is the use of violence against innocent people, rather than against the military, security services, and highly placed political officials.[28] Now, while the morality of terrorism is very much an open question when approached in terms of consequentialism, it is not an open question from the point of view of just war theory, as it inevitably offends against the principle of civilian immunity. Yet one might ask: could not an organization or movement engaged in a violent struggle against class oppression, colonial rule, or occupation by a foreign power, be facing circumstances in which terrorism is the only method of struggle available, and then justify its resort to it by the argument of supreme emergency?

If civilian immunity is indeed not an absolute, but rather an *almost* absolute moral principle, the answer to this question is: yes, it could. This should not be confused with the argument that terrorism is the only method of struggle available to the poor and powerless, the only way of levelling the playing field. For this argument, popular with apologists for terrorism, more often than not assumes that class oppression, or colonial

[28] See my 'What Is Terrorism?', *Journal of Applied Philosophy*, 10 (1990).

rule, or occupation by a foreign power, is in itself such a moral enormity that putting an end to it can justify the killing and maiming of innocent people. I do not subscribe to this assumption. I do not mean to deny that virtually every case of such a practice is a moral enormity; but I do not think that it is necessarily an instance of moral disaster such that its elimination would justify the use of terrorism. However, if a population were facing the prospect of genocide, or of being 'ethnically cleansed' from its land, then it would indeed be facing a true moral disaster. If terrorism were indeed the only way of fending off such a fate, then, and only then, a resort to terrorism by those fighting on its behalf might be morally justified.

2

Civilians and Soldiers

UWE STEINHOFF

I

Do civilians deserve immunity in war? If 'yes', why? If 'no', why not? And if the answer is 'it depends', what does it depend on? These questions cannot be answered without examining the status of non-civilians, the so-called combatants. What differentiates soldiers and combatants from civilians and non-combatants? Why are the former, presumably, non-innocent, and the latter not? How are we to make sense of 'non-innocence' and 'innocence' in armed combat at all? To answer these questions, we first discuss some of the most important theories in this field, before examining the implications of the analysis.

Let us begin with Elizabeth Anscombe. In her classic essay 'War and Murder' she rejects direct attacks (i.e., not including those covered by the principle of double effect) on the innocent as absolutely forbidden. Non-innocents, however, may be attacked. She writes:

Innocence is a legal notion; but here, the accused is not pronounced guilty under an existing code of law, under which he has been tried by an impartial judge, and therefore made the target of attack. ... This, however, does not mean that the notion of innocence fails in this situation. What is required, for the people attacked to be non-innocent in the relevant sense, is that they should themselves be engaged in an objectively unjust proceeding which the attacker has the right to make his concern; or—the commonest case—should be unjustly attacking him. Then he can attack them with a view to stopping them; and also their supply lines

This chapter is also being published, in an expanded form, as Ch. 4 of Uwe Steinhoff, *On the Ethics of War and Terrorism* (Oxford University Press, in press).

and armament factories. But people whose mere existence and activity supporting existence by growing crops, making clothes, etc. constitute an impediment to him—such people are innocent and it is murderous to attack them ... [1]

Her distinction between the innocent and the non-innocent corresponds to that between non-combatants or just combatants, on the one hand, and unjust combatants, on the other: that is, roughly between those who do not fight or who fight justly and those who fight unjustly. This correspondence is only 'rough', because it is not always entirely clear who exactly counts as a combatant and why. An influential attempt at clarifying this issue is provided by Jeffrie G. Murphy:

Combatants are those anywhere within the *chain of command or responsibility*—from bottom to top. ... The links of the chain (like the links between motives and actions) are held together logically and not merely causally, i.e. all held together, in this case, under the notion of who it is that is *engaged in an attempt* to destroy you. The farmer qua farmer is, like the general, performing actions which are causally necessary for your destruction; but, unlike the general, he is not necessarily engaged in an attempt to destroy you. ... The farmer's role bears a contingent connection to the war effort whereas the general's role bears a necessary connection to the war effort ... The farmer is aiding the soldier qua human being whereas the general is aiding the soldier qua soldier or fighting man.[2]

From this it follows that not only those fighting in the strict sense—those firing upon the enemy or carrying weapons in order to do so—may be attacked, but also those giving orders, presidents and ministers included. This view is supported by the laws of war.

As many critics have pointed out, this formulation is not nearly as unproblematic as it may first appear. To use an example from George I. Mavrodes, a farmer could be a well-educated and fanatical supporter of the Nazis and their war who, while watching over his farm, saves every penny to contribute to the war effort, lends his voice to Nazi propaganda, and does all this in the full knowledge of who the Nazis are and what they do (perhaps he has relatives working in the concentration camps or with the Gestapo). Conversely, an uneducated and naïve young man who knows little of what happens outside his village and nothing of what

---

[1] G. E. M. Anscombe, 'War and Murder', in Richard A. Wasserstrom (ed.), *War and Morality* (Belmont, Calif.: Wadsworth, 1970), 44 f.
[2] Jeffrie G. Murphy, 'The Killing of the Innocent', *Monist*, 57 (1973), 532–4.

the war is about could nevertheless be drafted to serve in the war effort although he detests the service and wishes nothing more than to be allowed to leave.

But he is 'engaged', carrying ammunition, perhaps, or stringing telephone wire or even banging away ineffectually with his rifle. He is without doubt a combatant, and 'guilty', a fit subject for intentional slaughter. Is it not clear that 'innocence', as used here, leaves out entirely all of the relevant moral considerations—that it has no moral content at all? [3]

As this example shows, a civilian—an alleged 'non-combatant'—may support soldiers *qua* soldiers and deliberately support the war and engage in an effort to destroy the enemy at least as much as do the soldiers themselves. Moreover, the farmer, in his support for the war effort, is obviously much *guiltier* in the moral sense than the villager. It's hard to assign much blame to the villager. Not so with the farmer.

Mavrodes concludes not that the immunity of non-combatants, which is already relativized by the acceptance of 'collateral damage', is further undermined by this example, but rather that this immunity must be interpreted differently: namely, as a useful *convention*.[4] The convention restricts the brutality of war in the interests of the warring parties. The fact that it is simply a convention does not mean that one doesn't have to abide by it. It is the convention in Germany to drive on the right-hand side of the road. Although it is not *of itself* moral to drive on the right (Australians are not immoral for driving on the left), it would indeed be immoral to drive on the left in Germany *because of* this convention (there would be a lot of accidents). It is thus a convention-dependent obligation, but no less obligatory for that. According to Mavrodes, the same is true of the principle of immunity for non-combatants.

The claim that this principle is a simple convention is often disputed. Richard Norman, for example, points out that Mavrodes also discusses the idea of a single-combat convention: the leaders of the warring nations would settle their differences in, well, single combat. Such a convention

---

[3] George I. Mavrodes, 'Conventions and the Morality of War', in C. Beitz, M. Cohen, T. Scanlon, and A. J. Simmons (eds.), *International Ethics: A Philosophy and Public Affairs Reader* (Princeton: Princeton University Press, 1990), 81.

[4] Ibid. 82 ff. Michael Green supports a similar approach in 'War, Innocence and Theories of Sovereignty', *Social Theory and Practice*, 18 (1992), 39–62. See also Gabriel Palmer-Fernández, 'Innocence in War', *International Journal of Applied Philosophy*, 14 (2000), 161–74. Neither author mentions Mavrodes.

would obviously further restrict the damage caused by war. Mavrodes himself admits that there is no chance of such a convention being adopted. Norman would like to know why not, and suggests, of course, that the principle of civilian immunity is adopted because it does have a convention-independent relevance.[5] However, one should not forget that war damage is not to be avoided *at any price*. Many find at least some things valuable enough to risk some degree of destruction. Mavrodes himself does not see this point clearly enough, as he describes the single-combat convention as attractive (though utopian). Yet the idea that, in a clash that would normally have led to war, 'whatever territory, influence, or other price would have been sought in the war'[6] should instead, on the basis of this new convention, simply be handed over to the winner of the single combat is not particularly attractive. What if the winning nation is out to rape, enslave, or murder the population of the other country? If one nation says to the other, 'We'd like to commit genocide on your population,' should the matter be settled by arm wrestling? Should the losing country then say, 'OK, go ahead,' with sportsmanlike resignation? And if the war is not over genocide or enslavement but 'merely' over a considerable restriction of freedom, is it honourable and *moral* simply to give up because one lost the arm-wrestling match rather than defend one's freedom with much stronger means and efforts? (This would also be the argument of many pacifists, who, rather than simply giving up for the sake of peace, advocate resistance by means which, while non-violent, nevertheless entail great sacrifice and loss.[7])

In short, the idea that the immunity of non-combatants is justified by its being a useful convention can't be dispensed with simply by pointing out that the single-combat convention could have been chosen—because the latter just *isn't* useful. But—one might object—if it comes down to defending yourself against certain unjust and unbearable consequences with everything you've got, why shouldn't the immunity of non-combatants be thrown out as well? It is perhaps useful to consider the comparison with 'fighting honourably' or 'fighting like a man'—concepts we know not just from westerns but perhaps also from the school playground (or even from personal experience), whereby one party to a combat gives the other 'a

---

[5] Richard Norman, *Ethics, Killing and War* (Cambridge: Cambridge University Press, 1995), 164 f.

[6] Mavrodes, 'Conventions', 82 f.

[7] Robert L. Holmes, *On War and Morality* (Princeton: Princeton University Press, 1989), ch. 8.

knuckle sandwich', as they say, but avoids more sensitive body parts. The analogous question here is: if one is prepared to break the other's nose, and to risk having one's own nose broken, why doesn't this preparedness extend to other parts? The answer is obvious. In a fight to defend or assert one's manhood, it would be counterproductive to allow that which is being defended to be hit and perhaps permanently damaged. He who fights to prove he's a man would still like to be one after the fight is over. In addition, the chances of resuming normal relations after the fight may well depend on neither party suffering lasting damage. Such concerns provide men who become involved in fights with good reason to adhere to rules against low blows, and to consider such conventions a matter of honour. (Such codes seem to exist even among hooligans.) These considerations can be applied to the case of war between nations. A battle to defend freedom and self-determination would be undermined if it involved damaging the nation's most valuable asset—its capacity to reconstruct itself after the war. As Michael Green puts it:

... Nations will wish to limit war so that the possibility of their nation being totally destroyed is minimized, or at least significantly reduced. Most will wish that enough of their country remain so that their country can be rebuilt and their way of life continued after hostilities. A nation will wish to preserve its cultural, educational, and religious sites, its reproductive capacity (traditionally represented by women and children), and its nonmilitary economic assets.[8]

Norman's second criticism of Mavrodes is also less than convincing. Norman suggests that rules justified by reference to rule-utilitarian considerations have the tendency to collapse into the (act-)utilitarian principle itself. If, in other words, the greatest utility of the greatest number would be served by breaking the rule, the utilitarian justification of the rule must also justify breaking it.[9] It must be seen, however, that in most cases following such a rule, and the attendant recognition and strengthening of the rule which serve to ensure that it will be followed in the future, serve human utility better than violating the rule. There are clearly extreme and exceptional cases in which the rule may be trumped simply by virtue of the magnitude of what is at stake, something that Norman's own position provides for.[10] This doesn't, however, refute the argument that these rules

---

[8] Green, 'War, Innocence', 57.   [9] Norman, *Ethics, Killing and War*, 165.
[10] Ibid., esp. 197 f.

serve in most cases as a firm anchor against short-sighted or less extreme utility considerations.

II

Thus, the principle of the immunity of non-combatants does make sense when considered as a convention. This does not mean, of course, that it can't be justified in some convention-independent way. Michael Green, however, offers an even more radical critique of this than Mavrodes. According to Green, the idea that civilians such as farmers are innocent is simply a relic of the Middle Ages, the outdated product of an antiquated, hierarchical model of political legitimacy:

Since the chain of authority on this view was from God to government to people, the people had no part to play in legitimizing, commanding, or controlling the activities of the government. Thus, their contribution to these were minimal and so was their responsibility for them. One cannot be held responsible for what one cannot and is not obligated to control.[11]

In this political paradigm, the principle of the immunity of non-combatants naturally seems plausible. According to Green, however, this principle is obsolete:

After the French Revolution, war was fundamentally different because political authority and thus responsibility were conceptualized in a fundamentally different manner. In the new paradigm, war became a conflict among nations and peoples involving the total mobilization of those nations.[12]

Green accuses defenders of the immunity principle—Walzer, Nagel, and Holmes, to name a few—of clinging to the medieval paradigm while publicly declaring themselves democrats. Otherwise, they would have drawn the right conclusions:

In a perfect democracy each and every person would be...fully responsible, because if the method of consent has been in operation, each has agreed to the decision reached by that method, or, if not that, to be bound by whatever decision was reached by that method. ... Within democratic theory, it is not clear that

---

[11] Green, 'War, Innocence', 41.   [12] Ibid. 43.

even children, the insane, and the mentally handicapped are innocent. These have guardians who represent their interests. These guardians are still bound by and to the general will of the society in which they find themselves in representing their interests. Thus, even if as a matter of fact political authorities are responsible for most wars and citizens are usually forced into being soldiers against their will, it is not clear that this absolves them from responsibility if they were responsible for letting themselves be put in circumstances in which they are so passive.[13]

Now, this may be more or less accurate as a characterization of totalitarian democracy à la Rousseau,[14] but the current paradigm is probably the liberal-democratic one. And the characteristic of *liberal* democracy is precisely that the individual is *not* required to accept whatever is collectively decided. Rather, such decisions are constrained by the space of individual rights. Green's reference to Locke, of all people, as supporting the idea of the responsibility of the whole populace,[15] including even critics and dissenters, is out of place or, worse, a misrepresentation. Let us examine what Locke himself wrote on the topic:

For the People having given to their Governors no Power to do an unjust thing, such as is to make an unjust War, (for they never had such a Power in themselves:) They ought not to be charged, as guilty of the Violence and Unjustice that is committed in an Unjust War, any farther, than they actually abet it; no more, than they are to be thought guilty of any Violence or Oppression their Governors should use upon the People themselves, or any part of their Fellow Subjects, they having impowered them no more to the one, than to the other.[16]

Green's criticism is thus rather excessive. A person is not automatically responsible for the crimes of her country simply because the country is a democracy. *On the other hand*, it is true that citizens of a democratic state aren't as obviously innocent of the crimes of war as were farmers or servants in the Middle Ages. *In this respect*, Green's critique does indeed

---

[13] Green, 'War, Innocence', 51 f.

[14] Tellingly, there are uncanny parallels with the undemocratic and entirely medieval writings of Francisco de Vitoria, a Dominican writing in the first half of the sixteenth century, who was of the opinion that '*the entire community can be punished for the sins of its king*. If a king starts an unjust war with another power, the other power to whom injustice has been done can…kill the subjects of the king, even if they are entirely innocent.' See Francisco de Vitoria, *Vorlesungen I (Relectiones): Völkerrecht, Politik, Kirche*, ed. Ulrich Horst, Heinz-Gerhard Ustenhoven, and Joachim Stüben (Stuttgart, Berlin, and Cologne: Kohlhammer, 1995), 139, §12.

[15] Green, 'War, Innocence', 51.

[16] John Locke, *Two Treatises of Government*, ed. Peter Laslett (Cambridge: Cambridge University Press, 2002), 388, §179.

affect the arguments of Walzer, Holmes, and others. Walzer in particular is quite distinctly concerned with absolving simple soldiers (including those of democratic states) as well as citizens of democracies of as much responsibility as possible—even if they fight in the war or support it enthusiastically.[17] As can be seen from the above quotation, this goes too far for Locke—and rightly so, as the arguments for distancing such individuals from moral guilt are rather thin. Of course, people are routinely indoctrinated, misinformed, and manipulated by governments; but in a democracy they *can* discover the relevant information, and in the face of the evils presented by war, they are indeed *required* to do so before patriotically trumpeting support for or otherwise taking part in an unjust war.[18] Walzer, in an outburst of paternalistic generosity which I can't quite reconcile with his supposed liberalism, clearly wants to leave the analysis of such information to the 'foreign policy elites' (amongst whom, I assume, he counts himself). Coates argues in the same vein:

... The individual citizen is rarely in a position to make an informed and responsible judgment about the justice or injustice of the war. The knowledge and expertise required to make a rational judgment of such key criteria as last resort, proportionality and prospects of success are almost always confined to a closed élite even in a democracy. Not only would it be imprudent to allow the public at large to exercise judgment, in this area, but the publication of the sensitive material that informed decision-making would require might jeopardize the security of the state. As a result, whereas in the case of the government the moral presumption must be against war, in the case of the individual citizen the moral presumption may be for war. In either case, of course, that presumption can be (and ought to be) overcome in the face of overwhelming evidence to the contrary.[19]

The last sentence is welcome, but doesn't quite suffice. First, many conservatives have argued that individual citizens are also not in a position to judge most other policies either (such as social security, nuclear power, the European Union, etc.). This suggests that a citizen is likewise not in a position to evaluate party platforms, the rationality of campaign

[17] Michael Walzer, *Just and Unjust Wars: A Moral Argument with Historical Illustrations*, 3rd edn. (New York: Basic Books, 2000), esp. 34–41, 296–303. Robert Holmes is of the same opinion. See Holmes, *On War*, 187 f., and Robert L. Holmes, 'Pacifism and Wartime Innocence: A Response', *Social Theory and Practice*, 20 (1994), 200 f.
[18] Cf. Jeff McMahan, 'Innocence, Self-Defense and Killing in War', *Journal of Political Philosophy*, 2 (1994), 214; Robert Nozick, *Anarchy, State, and Utopia* (New York: Basic Books, 1974), 100.
[19] A. J. Coates, *The Ethics of War* (Manchester: Manchester University Press, 1997), 141 n. 3.

promises, or the policies of candidates. In other words, if citizens can't be trusted to decide between war and peace, how can they be trusted to elect representatives or presidents? Coates's argument for a 'presumption for war' at the level of individual citizens hardly seems possible without a 'presumption against democracy' at the level of the 'elites'. Luckily, however, Coates's argument is entirely wrong. The 'key criteria' of 'last resort, proportionality and prospects of success' are hardly quantum physics; they are concepts which ordinary citizens use to make all kinds of decisions on a daily basis, and which they could therefore also use in deciding on war or peace. To do so, of course, they will require the necessary information. In particular, people will need information about specific difficulties and particular aspects which must be kept in mind when applying these concepts to questions of war and peace. Books like Coates's and others provide exactly this sort of information, and bring arguments and approaches to the table for discussion. Such books certainly require a certain level of concentration, persistence, and preparedness for discussion (and contradiction) in order to be profitable. To be understood, they may even require a dictionary—but certainly not a Ph.D. They do not present average citizens with an insurmountable obstacle.

In addition to such theoretical information, individual citizens require information about the actual or potential war. Coates believes that the publication of such information would jeopardize the security of the state. But why? In the case of *ultima ratio* (as also *causa justa*), this is entirely implausible. How could it jeopardize security if it became clear that non-military means could be used to reach the desired goal? (And how could it jeopardize security if it became clear that there was no reason at all to go to war? Wouldn't that rather improve security?) When discussing the likelihood of success and proportionality, the case may be different. Clearly, if precise details of attack strategies were discussed publicly, the opponent would have the opportunity to prepare for them. On the other hand, it's hard to imagine that the opponent wouldn't have prepared anyway, even without such discussions. He would, naturally, have given thought to the ways in which he could be attacked. Thus, the discussions which occur before a possible war—as opposed to the publication of actual tactics during a war—do not pose a major security risk. Only in exceptional cases would the military develop a brilliant strategy which no one else would have thought of and which would dramatically increase the chances of success (and perhaps proportionality too). And because this will happen only in exceptional cases, individual citizens have the right of 'presumption against the exception'; that is, they may assume that the government's rhetoric about an unbeatable secret plan is nothing more than propagandistic nonsense. In this context, one might wonder what Coates means when he says that it would be 'imprudent' to allow the citizenry to make judgements on such matters. Imprudent for whom? Possibly for the governing elite and their friends, who would no longer be able to serve their own private interests—but not imprudent for the populace at large. A populace willing to trust the assertions of government on questions of war and peace, rather than insisting on verifiable information, proof, data, and documents, might later face quite unpleasant surprises. For, as Coates concedes elsewhere, 'nothing benefits a ruler more than a good war. ... As a consequence the moral claims made for war need to be viewed with very considerable scepticism ... '[20]

This insight is hardly reconcilable with a moral presumption for war. Individual citizens have not only a right, but also a duty, to be sceptical. So, in a democracy, one cannot simply shrug off the responsibility that comes with supporting an unjust war.

III

Thus far we have seen that the distinction between combatants and non-combatants cannot be traced back to the distinction between the (ordinary language) concepts of moral guilt and innocence.

Robert K. Fullinwider suggests a different approach. The distinction between combatants and non-combatants is to be based not on the principle of punishment (which would have us protect the innocent and punish the guilty), but rather on the concept of *self-defence*. (Note that, following legal usage, I use the term 'self-defence' here to include cases of defending others.) According to this principle, direct aggressors would be legitimate targets of violence (and thus in the technical sense of the principle of self-defence 'non-innocent'), independently of any possible moral claims one might make against them. Individuals who are not

---

[20] Coates, *The Ethics of War*, 162.

themselves direct aggressors would be illegitimate targets, irrespective of whether they bear moral responsibility for the aggression. Let us take a closer look at Fullinwider's argument:

To set the scene, first consider an example. Jones is walking down a street. Smith steps from behind the corner of a nearby building and begins to fire a gun at Jones, with the appearance of deliberate intent to kill Jones. ... Jones is afforded no means of escape. Jones, who is carrying a gun himself, shoots at Smith and kills him. Jones is morally justified in killing Smith by the Principle of Self-Defense. Smith's actions put Jones' life directly and immediately in mortal jeopardy, and Jones' killing Smith was necessary to end that threat. From the point of view of self-defense, these facts about Smith's action are the *only* relevant ones. The moral justification of the killing rests on them alone given the legitimacy of self-defense.[21]

Fullinwider sketches a background story explaining Smith's attack on Jones: Smith's wife attempted to seduce Jones, but was rebuffed. In revenge, she told Smith that Jones had attempted to rape her. Smith, angry and incited to violence by his wife, then hunts for Jones in order to kill him. Or, as another story, let us assume that Smith owed gambling debts to the Mafia. The Mafia will write off his debts (which he cannot pay) only if he kills Jones. Smith, knowing what the Mafia will do to him if he cannot pay his debt, hunts for Jones. Fullinwider claims:

None of this background information alters the situation from the point of view of self-defense. ... Again, suppose that Smith's wife was standing across the street egging Smith on as he fired at Jones. Jones, though he justifiably shot Smith in self-defense, could not justifiably turn his gun on the wife in self-defense. Or suppose the mobsters were parked across the street to observe Smith. After killing Smith, Jones could not turn his gun on them (assuming they were unarmed). No matter how causally implicated the wife or the mobsters were in Smith's assault on Jones, in the situation it was only Smith who was the agent of immediate threat to Jones; the wife and the mobsters were not posing a direct and immediate danger. From the point of view of justifiably killing in self-defense, they are not justifiably liable to be killed by Jones; they are immune.[22]

He now applies these considerations to the case of war:

I claim that a nation may justifiably kill in self-defense. ... In a war, the armed forces of nation *A* stand to opponent nation *B* as Smith stood to Jones. It is

---

[21] Robert K. Fullinwider, 'War and Innocence', in Beitz *et al.* (eds.), *International Ethics*, 92.
[22] Ibid. 92 f.

against them that *B* may defend itself by the use of force. The active combatants, their arms, ammunition, war machines and facilities, are the legitimate targets of intentional destruction. Though *A*'s civilian population may support its war against *B* and contribute to it in various ways, they stand to *B* as Smith's wife or the mobsters stood to Jones. For the purpose of justifiably killing in self-defense and from that point of view, the civilian population is morally immune—it is 'innocent.'[23]

As the principle of self-defence is the most favoured way of justifying war, Fullinwider's solution to the problem of 'non-innocence' and 'innocence' in war seems at first especially elegant and fitting. There are, however, difficulties. Lawrence A. Alexander notes:

Fullinwider is correct that *after* killing Smith, Jones may not invoke the Principle of Self-Defense to then turn and kill the mobsters. *The threat to his life has been removed.* ... However, Fullinwider's hypothetical is inapposite when we are discussing whether noncombatants along with combatants may be killed in an ongoing war. ... Let us amend Fullinwider's hypothetical to make it relevant to the issue he is addressing. Suppose the situation is the same except that Jones has not yet killed Smith. May Jones invoke the Principle of Self-Defense to kill the mobsters instead of Smith if by doing so he will cause Smith to relent? Of course he may. If the mobsters had a gun trained on Smith and had ordered him to kill Jones, and he were about to comply, Jones not only could, but should, kill the mobsters rather than Smith if killing them would be no riskier than killing Smith and would remove the threat to Jones by removing Smith's motive for killing him.[24]

Alexander concludes that the principle of self-defence is not as capable of drawing the line between legitimate and illegitimate targets in the normal way, the way assumed by the laws of war. This is so, according to Alexander, because there are many non-combatants in war who, whether morally guilty or not, present a threat to the opposing nation. 'A combatant at a camp miles behind the lines is often less a threat than a noncombatant delivering arms and ammunition to combatants at the front.'[25]

Alexander's conclusion 'that the intentional killing of innocent non-combatants is not necessarily immoral if one accepts the Principle of

[23] Ibid. 94.
[24] Lawrence A. Alexander, 'Self-Defense and the Killing of Noncombatants: A Reply to Fullinwider', in Beitz *et al.* (eds.), *International Ethics*, 99 f.
[25] Ibid. 102.

Self-Defense' can be drawn, however, only when 'noncombatant' is defined as narrowly as Fullinwider seems to want.[26] As we saw, only 'active combatants, their arms, ammunition, war machines and facilities ... [are] legitimate targets of intentional destruction'. Under the laws of war, however, and in normal interpretations of just war theory, supply transports, in particular deliveries of munitions to combat units, are obviously legitimate targets, and those delivering the supplies are treated as combatants. They are, in Murphy's formulation, 'engaged in an attempt to destroy you'.

On the other hand, one can support Alexander's case with the earlier example of the Nazi farmer. We said that he is also engaged in 'an attempt to destroy you'. It seems, then, that we are back where we started. This circle can be avoided, however, if we attempt to shift our perspective away from the fixation on *actual* non-innocence and innocence (interpreted according to either a moral concept or the principle of self-defence) of potential targets, and focus instead on what the attacker can *know* of the guilt or innocence of potential targets, and with *what degree of certainty* he can know it. An infantryman or a helicopter pilot can surely recognize enemy soldiers, tanks, and munitions transports more easily than he can the disposition or financial transactions of a farmer. He can recognize the soldiers by their weapons and their behaviour, which demonstrate that they are engaged in an attempt to kill him or damage his country. Not so in the case of the farmer, and not, by the way, in the case of enemy radio or television propagandists either. Even if the latter were to broadcast continuously the words 'Let us bathe in the blood of our enemies', it is entirely unclear that destroying the radio tower or killing the journalists would lessen the danger. Enemy soldiers obey commands, react to threats, and would be inundated with propaganda even without radio or television, which would be targeted, rather, at the civilian population. To attempt to justify attacks on radio stations and journalists by reference to the principle of self-defence is under nearly all circumstances a laughable and shameful misuse of that principle. Such attacks are indeed intended as punishment, or as simple attempts to clear the airwaves for the attackers' own propaganda. He who punishes a public expression of opinion—or a

---

[26] Lawrence A. Alexander, 'Self-Defense and the Killing of Noncombatants: A Reply to Fullinwider', in Beitz *et al.* (eds.), *International Ethics*, 105.

call to arms against enemy soldiers, or even contrary views—with death himself deserves punishment. It's even worse when one considers that it's much harder to justify the killing of innocents (e.g., janitors in a radio station building) as a side-effect of an act of punishment in war than it is to justify it as a side-effect of an act of collective self-defence. In the latter case, under some circumstances one could say that the deaths of the innocents were acceptable as part of an attempt to save a larger number of innocents: that is, as the lesser of two evils. In the former case—killing as a side-effect of an act of punishment—that would be true only if the principle of self-defence (or the principle, set out below, of a justifying emergency) is *also* already applicable anyway. Only when, for example, the actions of enemy journalists do indeed result in deaths on one's own side can the potential deterrent effect of the punishment of such journalists prevent further deaths from journalistic propaganda in the present or future conflicts. The assumption that this condition is met, however, is unfounded. And putting punishing the guilty above protecting the innocent, although a concept from the Old Testament—and thus commended in some places—is morally perverse. It is not for nothing that the laws of war treat attacks upon radio stations as war crimes. This goes, too, for attacks on other civilian resources, and for the same reasons.

To conclude this list of different approaches, a fourth one, inexplicably overlooked in the literature, should be mentioned: namely, the concept of a *justifying emergency,* which is defined as follows in §34 of the German penal code:

Whosoever, in order to avert a not otherwise avoidable present danger to life, body, freedom, honor, property, or another legally protected interest, acts so as to avert the danger to himself or others, does not act illegally if, upon consideration of the conflicting interests, namely of the threatened legally protected interests and of the degree of the threatened danger, the protected interest substantially outweighs the infringed interest. This, however, is true only if the act is an appropriate means to avert the danger.

The decisive difference between self-defence and a justifying emergency is that the latter requires only present, and not otherwise avoidable, *danger* to justify an act, but not a present *attack.*

IV

We have surveyed four approaches to distinguishing the 'non-innocent' from the 'innocent', the legitimate from the illegitimate human targets in war: the *moral guilt theory*, the *convention theory*, the *self-defence theory*, and the *justifying emergency theory*. How do these approaches correspond to the concepts, borrowed from the laws of war, of immunity of civilians and non-immunity of soldiers? Well, the moral guilt theory clearly cannot explain the immunity of civilians or the non-immunity of just soldiers. The latter are innocent, and the former can be morally guilty. The self-defence theory concedes the immunity of civilians, but grants such immunity also to just soldiers—and also to unjust ones whenever they are not involved in a present attack (e.g., when they sleep, oil their weapons, repair their tanks, or march without firing). Clearly, on the premiss that ordinary citizens and soldiers don't know much, don't think much, and aren't bound to acquire information, both approaches correspond at least partially to the principles of the laws of war. These laws, as a conventional legal system, do not maintain that both parties are *morally allowed* to kill one another. Instead, they provide for the idea that soldiers may not be *punished* for killing enemy soldiers (e.g., in a POW camp during the war or by a tribunal after the war). That soldiers may kill one another without punishment can be conceded by the moral guilt and self-defence theories in those cases in which both sides are *excused* (whereby one side may even be right). On the other hand, the moral guilt and self-defence theories (as opposed to the conventional or legal ones) can be reconciled with the laws of war only up to a point. Whereas the laws of war excuse soldiers for fighting in the war so long as they behave according to the principles of *jus in bello* (i.e., so long as they do not slaughter civilians or torture prisoners), the moral approach does not: it requires soldiers also to adhere to the principles of *jus ad bellum*. Soldiers are moral agents, and as such they bear a responsibility for their actions that they cannot disavow. On an issue as important as whether or not to fight in a war, one has, as described above, a duty to make an informed and considered decision. Soldiers fighting on the unjust side who could have known that they were on the wrong side, and who could avoid fighting without great danger to themselves (e.g., by draft dodging, deserting, or intentionally missing when shooting at the enemy), are morally guilty even without killing civilians. For even the *soldiers* on the just side are (so long as they adhere to *jus in bello*) innocent.[27] If the soldiers on the unjust side kill these innocent soldiers, *they are committing criminally negligent homicide at least*. If these soldiers *know* that their side is in the wrong, *by killing enemy soldiers, they commit manslaughter or murder*.[28]

Naturally, the rule-utilitarian principle comes closest to the distinction in the laws of war. On the justifying emergency theory, in turn, the distinction between the non-innocent and the innocent, or between legitimate and illegitimate (human) targets, corresponds—*with respect to the unjust side*—largely to the distinction between combatants and non-combatants, but not entirely. Sometimes a grave and present danger to life, limb, or freedom cannot be avoided in any way other than by attacking civilians or non-combatants. The reference to the 'consideration of the conflicting interests, namely of the threatened legally protected interests and of the degree of the threatened danger' denies civilians absolute immunity.

All of these approaches have a valid moral principle at heart: namely, the principle of moral guilt, the rule-utilitarian principle, the principle of self-defence, and the principle of justifying emergency. The various approaches differ from the principles they are based on, however, in that each approach raises its respective principle to an absolute status, and uses it as the one and only measure for distinguishing between legitimate and illegitimate targets and acts. One correspondingly arrives at new approaches when one applies more than one principle. As we have seen, Anscombe's approach itself makes use of both the moral guilt principle and the principle of justifying emergencies—even if it claims not to. Fullinwider too, however sceptically, does allow for the possibility of connecting his favoured principle of self-defence with the moral guilt principle.[29] As stated above, though, all four principles are valid, and they interact with one another. For example, one of the legally protected interests which must be considered in the weighing process required by the principle of justifying emergency is that the innocent be free from punishment, and this, of course, leads to the principle of moral guilt, which serves to protect the innocent. Moreover, these principles can conflict, as the guilt principle and the self-defence principle did in the case of the innocent aggressor.

[27] Holmes, *On War*, 186.   [28] Cf. McMahan, 'Innocence', 209.
[29] Fullinwider, 'War and Innocence', 95–7.

Such conflicts arise at the level of severity and situation-relative priority, but not at the level of validity.[30] Both principles are valid standards for morally correct action. In other words, in the event of such conflicts, the 'overridden' principle gives way to the other, but only within certain bounds: up to this point, but no further! The continued validity of the guilt or innocence principle, even in the case of the innocent aggressor, can be seen in the fact that the application of force is allowed *only to the extent* that it is necessary to avert the danger (whereas in the case of a guilty aggressor the aggression may perhaps be 'paid back with interest', i.e., punished). The principle of self-defence, indeed, recognizes these limits explicitly, in that it does not allow for anything beyond what is necessary for defence. On the other hand, there is no such explicit recognition of the principle of self-defence within the moral guilt principle. This is normally the case in conflicts between principles. In view of such conflicts, as also with interactions between principles, it is necessary to *weigh* the principles with sufficient judgement, circumspection, and sensitivity to the particulars of the situation. That is, the morally correct action cannot be derived from the principles in the way in which the value of an unknown variable can be derived from a system of equations; it cannot be deduced as a conclusion from premises. Rather, it must be found on a case-by-case basis, in light of the particulars of the situation. This is not a matter of applying principles which are already determinate in rank and scope for each case; rather, the judgement must be made by interpreting the principles and the situation in such a way that the interpretation of the principles and the characterization of the situation influence each other. The morally relevant aspects of the situation are identified in light of the principles, and the principles are weighed in light of the morally relevant aspects of the situation.

In order, then, to evaluate the meaning and implication of these principles, and thus also the results of our analysis, it is important to keep this consideration—that the principles interact with one another, and that the particular interactions depend on the concrete situation—in mind. From this perspective, the rejection of the orthodox view set out above in favour of the moral view that soldiers on the unjust side, even if they adhere to the principles of *jus in bello*, are still morally guilty of murder when they kill opposing soldiers, is less radical in its practical implications than it might

---

[30] Cf. Robert Alexy, *Theorie der Grundrechte* (Baden-Baden: Nomos, 1985), 78.

seem to be at first glance. For there are strong *rule-utilitarian* grounds which limit the moral guilt principle significantly. As McMahan observes:

... There are no impartial institutions competent to determine which soldiers do deserve punishment and how severe a punishment they deserve. ... Even if the victor in a war is the side that fought in a just cause, it could not possibly administer punishment to large numbers of soldiers in an informed and impartial manner. And matters are of course much worse if it is the unjust side that emerges victorious. ... If the practice were sanctioned, [the victors] would doubtless be moved to seek vengeance, under the guise of punishment, against soldiers who had justifiably resisted their wrongful aggression. Finally, the expectation that ordinary soldiers would face punishment at the hand of their adversaries in the aftermath of war would deter either side from surrendering, thereby prolonging wars well beyond the point at which fighting might otherwise cease. The laws of war, therefore, have to diverge from the morality of war.[31]

This last sentence, however, postulates an unpleasant divergence that is unnecessary in our model. On the basis of the rule-utilitarian principle, itself a valid moral principle, adhering to the laws of war is *morally required*— though only up to a point, of course. The usefulness of the laws of war consists not only in their protection of soldiers from unjust punishment, but also in their protection of non-combatants—and indeed the very foundations necessary for the continued existence of the nation—from soldiers. But, one may argue, soldiers or fighters on one side don't keep their end of the bargain and violate the convention, then the other side doesn't have to either. Yet this attempt to justify attacks on civilians is still undermined by the principle of moral guilt. For civilians—in so far as they really are innocent—can't do much about the crimes of their soldiers. The *soldiers*, however, can. And they have broken not only the tacit agreement with the soldiers of the opposing side, but also their agreement with the *civilians* of the opposing side. It follows that these civilians are no longer required to keep out of the fight. Moreover, on the principle of self-defence, they may defend themselves and their property, family, and friends. Won't they, by taking up arms, become combatants and thus legitimate targets? Well, in the sense provided by the laws of war,

---

[31] McMahan, 'Innocence', 208 f. See also Hersch Lauterpacht, 'Rules of Warfare in an Unlawful War', in George Arthur Lipsky (ed.), *Law and Politics in the World Community: Essays on Hans Kelsen's Pure Theory and Related Problems* (Berkeley: University of California Press, 1953).

yes, but certainly not morally. For none of the fighters on the just side, from a moral perspective, is a legitimate target—this is the insight of the moral standpoint. Decisive, however, is the fact that the enemy soldiers can neither legitimately nor innocently attack civilians in arms (people, we may imagine, shooting at the enemy from their own homes). Their attack on the wider population is itself an obvious violation of *jus in bello*, and makes the soldiers *morally guilty* (unless, of course, they are forced at gunpoint to attack), while the civilians remain innocent, as in such a case the moral principles allow the violation of the normal laws of war. (It's not even clear that this would be a violation of the laws of war. The important point here is that, even if it were, it would be morally permissible under the circumstances.) The rule-utilitarian principle does not forbid people in such a situation to take up arms, and the moral guilt principle—and possibly even the self-defence and justifying emergency principles—give people a *right* to break the convention. This right *forbids* soldiers to prevent civilians from exercising it. And if the soldiers do not obey this, they not only contravene moral rules, they are also culpable—they are simple murderers. The only way of not continuing to commit murder would be to retreat.[32]

In this context, let us examine the following example. Various extended families, living in some archaic land, simply know that arguments between families will continue to erupt into armed conflict, but nevertheless wish to keep the damage arising from such conflicts within certain limits. In order to achieve this, the families agree that only men may be attacked, and that women and children may not attack anyone. One day, the men of family A attack family B, including the women and children. Because a majority of the men in family B have already been eliminated, some women and children pick up weapons and defend themselves. The men of family A respond to this by saying, 'You're breaking our convention, and are attacking us. Now we can kill you in self-defence.' This appeal to

---

[32] Walzer, *Just and Unjust Wars*, 187, claims that the distinction between combatants and non-combatants breaks down in every case of mass uprising. Green ('War, Innocence', 53) thinks, however, that Walzer assumes the generality of a distinction that is made questionable by exactly such cases. It seems to me, indeed, that not *every* uprising morally demands the retreat of the target of the uprising. It depends entirely on whom the uprising is directed at. If the uprising is against an occupier who spurns the principles of *jus in bello* and attacks the basic means of living of the population—i.e., who fights a war against the populace—then such a withdrawal is the only possible way of avoiding *further* crimes. 'Further', because such attacks on a population's means of living is itself already a crime.

self-defence is just as illegitimate as in the case where Smith, who first fires a shot that misses Jones, uses Jones's counterattack as an excuse to kill him 'in self-defence'. Of course, it's possible that many A-men attacked B-men only in the original attack. These A-men would, in my view, be perfectly entitled to fight the women and children in self-defence—but only in so far as they aren't responsible for creating the situation where they must defend themselves. An A-man, being shot at by women and children because his comrade next to him opened fire on them, can act in self-defence to cause them to cease fire—namely, by killing the comrade standing next to him. The A-men who knew that others would fire upon women and children, but who went along anyway, are also responsible for creating the situation. They have no right to self-defence—unless, of course, they've come along to hinder their comrades. When they see, however, that they have failed to persuade their comrades to desist, and that they can stop them only with violence, they must do so or—the morally inferior alternative—run away. Otherwise they lose the right to self-defence.

Contrary to popular opinion, then, not only must *jus in bello* be taken into account in *jus ad bellum*, but *jus ad bellum* must be taken into account in *jus in bello*. The aggressor and the defender cannot be placed on the same level, and the aggressor's breaches of convention cannot be treated in the same way as those of the defender. This is not a call for double standards; on the contrary, it follows directly from application of the same moral standard. The *same* moral norms and principles are valid for both sides, but in so far as the two sides *don't* behave in the same ways and *aren't* in the same situation, it follows that they are subject to different moral imperatives, and in some situations are bound by *conventions* to different degrees (though they are bound by moral principles to the same degree). This is also true for the convention of the immunity of non-combatants.[33]

---

[33] I have argued in particular that the principles presented and analysed here would, in some situations, interact in such a way as to trump the convention requiring that civilians wishing to maintain their immunity may not take up arms. But an even trickier question is whether the situation could be reversed: whether the immunity of non-combatants could be trumped so that direct attacks on civilians were allowed. I have discussed this question in Uwe Steinhoff, 'How Can Terrorism Be Justified?', in Igor Primoratz (ed.), *Terrorism: The Philosophical Issues* (Basingstoke: Palgrave Macmillan, 2004), 97–109.

3

Civilian Immunity in War: From Augustine to Vattel

COLM MCKEOGH

Two intellectual developments were important in the evolution of the principle of non-combatant immunity (PNCI). One was the abandonment by Grotius of the attempts since Augustine to justify killing in war by reference to guilt; this positive development opened the way to the modern PNCI. The second, which had a negative impact on the fate of civilians in war, was the development by Aquinas of what came to be called the principle of double effect. These two developments are in tension in that, as long as the excuse of double effect (or 'indirect attack') is admitted, the standard set by Augustine for the proper treatment of people in war has not yet been met.

Augustine's Justification of War

For most of its history, the primary concern of 'just war' thought has been to apply the concepts of guilt and innocence to the justification and limitation of war. For this reason, the history of the concept of civilian immunity in war cannot be separated from the history of the Western attempt to justify war. The evolution of the PNCI has been intertwined with the justification of the killing of combatants in war. Thus, the search for the roots of the PNCI must start in what might seem an unlikely place: the *ad bellum* thought of a 'just war' thinker, St Augustine, who had little to say about *jus in bello*.[1] There had been

---

[1] *Jus ad bellum* refers to law about the resort to war, while *jus in bello* refers to law about permissible means and methods of warfare once hostilities have commenced. Richard Kolb reports that both terms

centuries of Roman thought on *bellum justum* when the great Christian theorist and Father of the Church, St Augustine of Hippo (354–430), turned his attentions to it. Augustine justified war in much the same situations that the Romans had when he wrote: 'Just wars are usually defined as those which avenge injuries, when the nation or city against which warlike action is to be directed had neglected either to punish wrongs committed by its own citizens or to restore what has been unjustly taken by it.'[2]

To Augustine, war could still be waged in defence against an aggressor or to undo wrongs committed by another party (the circumstances in which the Romans had held war to be just). He permitted war in the same circumstances as the Romans, but he characterized it in a novel manner: to Augustine, it was loving punishment of a wrongdoer on God's behalf. This focus on sin is apparent in the *City of God* when he writes: ' ... It is the wrong-doing of the opposing party which compels the wise man to wage just wars; and this wrong-doing, even though it gave rise to no war, would still be a matter of grief to man because it is man's wrong-doing.'[3]

The punishment of sin is given as the motivation for war by Augustine when he writes elsewhere that

the real evils in war are love of violence, revengeful cruelty, fierce and implacable enmity, wild resistance, and the lust of power, and such like; and it is generally to punish these things, when force is required to inflict the punishment, that, in obedience to God or some lawful authority, good men undertake wars ...[4]

There were many strands to Augustine's justification of some wars as, at times, the right course of action for a Christian. First the war had to be *just*: there had to be a breach of faith or a breach of peace by a party that was thereby legally in the wrong. Secondly, the war had to be *good*: it had to preserve or create the social peace and order that was of benefit to

may date back no further than the early twentieth century; see Richard Kolb, 'Origin of the Twin Terms *Jus Ad Bellum/Jus In Bello*', *International Review of the Red Cross*, no. 320 (Sept.–Oct. 1997), 553–63.

   [2] Augustine, *Quaestiones in Heptateuchum*, 6. 10; quoted in R. S. Hartigan, *The Forgotten Victim: A History of the Civilian* (Chicago: Precedent Publishing, 1982), 29.

   [3] Augustine, *City of God*, bk. XIX, ch. 7, in *The Political Writings of St. Augustine*, ed. Henry Paolucci (Chicago: Gateway, 1962), 138.

   [4] Augustine, *Contra Faustum* XXII, in *Political Writings*, 164.

both Christians and non-Christians. But, thirdly, killing in war had to be an act of *love* and charity. War could only be good, just, and loving for two reasons. First, Augustine assumes a very close connection between the legal and the moral orders: the legal wrong done by the adversary is the just cause of the war, but this legal wrong is also proof of a moral wrong. That is, he assumes that a breach of law also involves a sin. A nation which violates the *legal* rights of another also breaks the *moral* law. In punishing the wicked on God's behalf, the Christian is upholding both the moral and the legal orders.

The second reason why war can be good, just, and loving is that Augustine assumes a very close link between the nation or tribe and the individual. He assumes that people on the side without just cause are guilty; it is therefore both loving and just to punish them for their wrongdoing. It is loving and charitable too to prevent them from committing further wickedness (by killing them if necessary). Those whom the just warrior harms and kills in war merit this treatment as a just punishment for their personal guilt.[5] All soldiers who fight on the unjust side share in both the legal and the moral wrong, and their guilt is the reason why each person on the enemy side can be killed. Indeed, not only combatants on the side without just cause may be killed as punishment for participation in legal wrongdoing and moral wickedness, but so may civilians. The most important figure in the foundation of 'just war' thought in Western culture did not address the issue of civilian immunity.[6] Indeed, there is no basis in Augustine's characterization of a 'just war' for any principle of non-combatant immunity. For if war is punishment of wickedness, then the civilian population may merit punishment no less than the combatants.

---

[5] As Hartigan puts it: 'For Augustine, who believed in an intimate relationship between individual and social morality, it is highly doubtful that an unjust nation will be populated by good or just citizens' (Hartigan, *Forgotten Victim*, 32). Another commentator sees Augustine's 'expanded notion of war guilt that can potentially include whole populations' as an idea that 'took root in Allied airmen responsible for the Combined Bomber Offensive against Germany' (Lt. Colonel Peter R. Faber, 'The Ethical-Legal Dimensions of Strategic Bombing during WWII: An Admonition to Current Ethicists', *Joint Services Conference on Professional Ethics*, xvii, Washington, DC, 25–6 Jan. 1996; <http://www.usafa.af.mil/jscope/JSCOPE96/faber96.html>.

[6] His rejection of revengeful cruelty, lust of power, and love of violence may be seen as a precursor to *jus in bello*, but the restriction applies as much to the killing of combatants as civilians. No distinction is made between the combatant and non-combatant segments of the enemy population; neither should be harmed wantonly, but both may be attacked if necessary for victory.

The Standard for Proper Treatment of the Person

Why did Augustine seek to justify war in this manner? It was because no other justification of war would meet the standards of Christianity. War was not to be justified in terms of the greater good alone; it was not enough to claim that war is a pre-condition of a peace and order that benefits all, or that it is a just punishment of nations. To Augustine, not only war, but the killing of people in war, was in need of justification. The killing of a person in war had to be an appropriate treatment of that person. In justifying war as loving and just, as well as good, Augustine sought to justify war as a proper treatment of the individual.

This is not surprising given the individualism of the Christian world-view. It is to the individual that Christianity addresses itself.[7] This emphasis on the separateness, the uniqueness, and the ultimate significance of each human being was to be strengthened by the Protestant Reformation and came to be central to liberalism, the dominant political creed of the modern era. This status of the human person affects how we ought to treat them; as a modern moral philosopher writes: 'whatever one does to another person intentionally must be aimed at him as a subject, with the intention that he receive it as a subject. It should manifest an attitude to *him* rather than just to the situation.'[8]

Such a focus on the individual does not forbid the harming of people or the taking of human life. It is possible to do harm to a person while still treating them as a person. Indeed, even the killing of a person can be a response to them as a person, and not just to the situation. There are at least four types of killing that meet this standard for the appropriate treatment of the individual. First is punitive killing: a person killed as punishment is still treated as a person, because punishment involves treating them as responsible for their own action. Second is preventative killing: if one kills another person in self-defence, in defence of others, or to prevent them acting in a certain way, then the reason for killing is connected to the

---

[7] Each of the Ten Commandments begins 'Thou shalt ...' or 'Thou shalt not ...'; the injunctions of Jesus are also rules to govern individual behaviour; the difficulty in using them as guidelines for the organization of society or its political structure is shown by the variety of political and social structures in the Christian world through history.

[8] Thomas Nagel, 'War and Massacre', in *Mortal Questions* (Cambridge: Cambridge University Press, 1979), 66.

person killed as an individual. They are killed because of the person they are, or the action they are doing. To stop someone from killing you by killing them is still to treat them as a person. Third is consensual killing: to kill someone with their consent is to treat them as a person (and their life as their own). An informed adult, *compos mentis*, can consent to death, or to the risk of death (examples of consensual killing include duels, voluntary euthanasia, assisted suicide, and violent sports). Fourth is charitable killing (such as involuntary euthanasia or mercy killing), in which the reason for killing a person is to do with the person.

Augustine's attempt to reconcile Christianity and war yielded a guilt-based justification of killing in war that met this standard. Indeed, it set that standard as the one to be met by all subsequent Christian justifications of war: killing in war was to be an appropriate treatment of the person killed. To Augustine, killing in a 'just war' met this standard because a just war was (by definition) one that punished the guilty for their wrongdoing as well as undoing the wrongful aggression or expropriation.

Augustine's justification of war was good in theory. Unfortunately, it did not fit reality very well. For the claims (first, that a breach of the law is also a sin and, second, that all on the side without just cause share in that sin and are deserving of punishment) are difficult claims to accept. Perhaps Augustine's argument may have made more sense then than now. Perhaps his claim that the defence of the legal order was also the defence of the moral order may have been more tenable in the Roman Empire of Augustine's own time. The wars between the Empire and the barbarian invaders were seen not as wars between competing orders, but as a struggle between order itself and anarchy. Furthermore, the Roman legal order was fast intertwining itself with the moral order of the Christian Church.

Perhaps Augustine's punitive model of a 'just war' was coherent too in the cavalry wars and feudal politics of medieval Christendom. Certainly his justification of war as punishment dominated official Church teaching for more than a thousand years. By the time Augustine was creating his justification of war, the Romans had abandoned their reliance on both infantry and conscription. The Roman army had become a volunteer force of cavalry, and the age of cavalry lasted for a thousand years. The wars waged by feudal societies in medieval Europe were wars fought primarily by knights, who also had some share in political power. It could be claimed that these combatants bore some responsibility for the decision to wage war and for the cause for which they fought. If so, then Augustine's notion of personal guilt for the unjust cause of one's side made some sense when applied to the medieval period.[9]

This justification of war as punishment gave no basis for the development of a PNCI. Indeed, it justified all necessary attacks on the unjust enemy, combatant and non-combatant. Its assertion of guilt on the part of all people on the side without just cause undermined the claims to immunity of civilians, for Augustine's assertion of guilt allowed all to be killed if it contributed to the victory of the side with just cause. Yet Augustine remains important for the development of the PNCI because in his justification of killing in war lies the ground for the claim of civilian immunity in war. The standard that Augustine set remained the one to be met: all people had to be treated appropriately in war.

The 'Peace of God'

Despite the dominance of Augustine's justification of war, calls for limitations on targeting in war were heard. From the 970s to the 1030s, peace movements, known to us collectively as the *pax Dei* or 'Peace of God', granted a protected status to certain categories of person and property in the Frankish realm. The gradual collapse of the traditional authority of the Holy Roman Empire had led to intensified warfare among princes, dukes, and knights fighting for land, peasants, and power.[10] This disorder and feuding often impacted on the Church and peasantry and on their property. Added to this were apocalyptic fears of the Last Judgement (as the thousandth anniversaries of the birth and crucifixion of Jesus drew near) which spurred a movement to purify the Church and society of Western Christendom.[11]

---

[9] Perhaps there was another type of war to which the idea of war as punishment could be applied with some coherence: the Crusades. Pope Urban II called for the First Crusade at the Council of Clermont in 1095, and the ensuing wars against Saracens and infidels could possibly be justified for punishment for heresy. This was a rare circumstance in which the claim could plausibly still be made that, not only a ruler, but also his agents and soldiers, merited death because of their own actions and wickedness (in holding to heresy or to a false religion).

[10] Thomas Head and Richard Landes (eds.), *The Peace of God: Social Violence and Religious Response in France around the Year 1000* (Ithaca, NY: Cornell University Press, 1992), 13.

[11] Ibid. 6.

The results were renewed prohibitions on clerical marriage and the sale of ecclesiastical offices, but also a quest to limit political violence which was to last into the 1030s.[12]

The protection of the Church and its resources was clearly a central theme of the Peace movement. Such crimes as theft of church property, assaults on clergy, and theft of animals from peasants were to be punished by excommunication. But the canons issued by this movement expanded the categories of person to which protection from attack in war ought to be given. The prohibition on the assault and arrest of unarmed clergy was extended to monks, later to nuns, and then to unarmed companions of clergymen, and even to widows and noblewomen travelling without their husbands. Later councils extended the principle until it encompassed all unarmed and non-combatant persons, and some early eleventh-century peace oaths gave protection to unarmed knights during Lent.

In this way, the canons of the 'Peace of God' movement foreshadow the emergence of the concept of the 'civilian'. A more precise social delineation of the combatant occurred as laity and clergy were granted protection from warrior violence. The conflation of women and children (excluded from war by the Romans in the name of honour) and clergy and monks (excluded by the Church from fighting wars) was the first step along the road towards a principle of non-combatant immunity. A second step towards a more general principle of non-combatant immunity was taken when those engaged in agriculture were added to the category of the immune. For as the category of protected people expanded, so the category of legitimate targets shrank towards combatants, and combatants alone. Thus the 'Peace of God' movement can be seen as an early manifestation of the pressures for the development of a principle of non-combatant immunity.

The Punitive Model Persists: Aquinas and Vitoria

But despite such pressures, Augustine's punitive model of war continued to dominate Christian thought into the second millennium. Eight hundred years after Augustine's death, Thomas Aquinas (1225–74) famously shifted

---

[12] Head and Landes (eds.), *The Peace of God* 280.

the basis of the state's authority from the suppression of the consequences of sin to the promotion of the common good; no longer were all rulers seen as having a divine mandate to rule; only those who promoted the common good had a right to the obedience of their subjects. In the *Summa Theologiae*, Aquinas explains how this responsibility of the ruler for the community allows him to use lethal force for the sake of the whole community, just as a physician could amputate a limb for sake of the body:

It is permissible to kill a criminal if this is necessary for the welfare of the whole community. However this right belongs only to the one entrusted with the care of the whole community—just as a doctor may cut off an infected limb, since he has been entrusted with the care of the health of the whole body.[13]

Oddly, given the originality and creativity of much else of his moral theology and political theory, Aquinas has little new to say about war. Indeed, given how significantly Aquinas's political theory differs from Augustine's, one would expect a very different treatment of the issue of war. Yet, when Aquinas comes to the moral justification of war, he does no more than restate the old Augustinian justification of war as punishment for legal and moral wrongdoings: 'a just cause is required, namely, that those who are attacked, should be attacked because they deserve it on account of some fault.'[14] Later in the *Summa* he justifies fighting against enemies on the basis of restraining them from further sinning:

It is lawful to attack one's enemies that they may be restrained from sin: and this is for their own good and the good of others. Consequently it is even lawful in praying to ask that temporal evils be inflicted on our enemies in order that they may mend their ways.[15]

Aquinas's justification of war, then, is simply a reiteration of the established Augustinian one. The just cause of war is some fault and sin committed by an adversary that needs to be punished and that renders him deserving of attack.

Why does Aquinas persist with this justification of war that no longer fitted reality (if it ever did)? Why does he perpetuate Augustine's fiction that all in the population whose leadership had done wrong shared in the

---

[13] Thomas Aquinas, *Summa Theologiae*, II. II, qu. 64, art. 3, trans. by Fathers of the English Dominican Province (London: Burns Oates & Washbourne, 1917–22).

[14] Ibid. qu. 40, art. 1.   [15] Ibid. qu. 83, art. 8, *ad* 3.

guilt? A justification of war on the basis of the common good would have gelled with the rest of Aquinas's political theory. It would also have fitted the changing reality of war. Yet Aquinas did not embark on that path, but instead retreated to the established Augustinian justification of war as punishment. For only that justification could meet the standards of the Christian religion. To kill innocent people, simply so that the good of society could be promoted, would be at odds with the moral foundations of Christianity.

It was changes in the technology and personnel of war, from the mid-1200s onwards, that had led to a growing mismatch between the established guilt-based justification and the military and political realities of European warfare. Longbows, crossbows, and pikes (as well as the rising cost of armour) all led to the decline of cavalry in European war from the thirteenth century and the re-emergence of infantry. Attempts to ban crossbows came to nothing, as did the attempt to ban mercenaries.[16] The result was that war in Europe was no longer waged by knights with social, political, and military responsibilities and powers. Augustine's characterization of war as punishment may never have fitted reality (even knights may not have borne sufficient responsibility and guilt so as to merit death as a punishment). But by the thirteenth century, the poor fit between the justification of killing in war on the basis of punishment and the reality of warfare was all the more glaring. With the move from knightly warfare towards mass armies and mercenarism, the grounds for the ascription of guilt to soldiers on the side without a just cause grew even weaker.

The pressures for civilian immunity in war continued, though the claim for civilian immunity remained a difficult one to make within the punitive model of war. One attempt to do so was made by Francisco de Vitoria (1486?–1546), the pre-eminent theologian and political theorist of sixteenth-century Catholic Europe.[17] Guilt and innocence remained the

---

[16] At the end of the eleventh century, Pope Urban II condemned the use of bows and crossbows against Christians. Four decades later, in 1139, the Second Lateran Council issued a canon anathematizing all those who used the crossbow or longbow in wars between Christians. The Third Lateran Council of 1179 confirmed the moral stigma on mercenaries, as well as the threat of excommunication that applied to them. These moves halted neither the adoption of the new technologies of war nor the spread of mercenarism.

[17] Francisco de Vitoria, *Political Writings*, ed. Anthony Pagden and Jeremy Lawrance (Cambridge: Cambridge University Press, 1994).

key concepts for Vitoria. The justification for killing combatants remained their guilt, but the immunity of civilians was to rest on their presumed innocence. This was to be achieved by presuming soldiers on both sides to be guilty while a war is being waged. While war was in progress, the questions of 'unjust cause', and the consequent guilt of those furthering it, could be put aside. Combatants on both sides might be presumed to be guilty of participation in an unjust cause (unless it was known otherwise) and killed (without murder being done).

The bearing of arms was thus only an indicator of guilt while a war was in progress and for as long as the issue of wilful participation in an unjust cause was still unsettled. Indeed, it might be found that both rulers and ruled on the side without just cause believed, in good faith, that they had justice on their side. If this were so, then they were wrong only because of invincible ignorance:

Note, however, that sometimes, nay, frequently, not only subjects, but princes, too, who in reality have no just case of war, may nevertheless be waging war in good faith, with such good faith, I say, as to free them from fault; as, for instance, if the war is made after a careful examination and in accordance with the opinion of learned and upright men. And since no one who has not committed a fault should be punished, in that case, although the victor may recoup himself for things that have been taken from him and for any expenses of the war, yet... it is unlawful to go on killing after the victory...[18]

Indeed, soldiers too may well be innocent (in the sense that they did not knowingly and wilfully participate in injustice and wickedness), and if this is so known, they must not be harmed unless military victory requires it: 'if there should even be a soldier who is clearly innocent, and our soldiers are able to let him go free, they must do so, whether during the war or after victory has been won...'[19]

Vitoria's assumption of the guilt of combatants on both sides (unless it was known to the contrary) and of the innocence of non-combatants on both sides (unless it was known to the contrary) would have had immense practical benefits. For it opened the way to firm *in bello* restrictions

---

[18] Francisco de Vitoria, *De jure belli*, 59, in *The Principles of Political and International Law in the work of Francisco de Vitoria*, intro. by Antonio Truyol Serra (Madrid: Ediciones Cultura Hispanica, 1946), 97.

[19] Bernice Hamilton, *Political Thought in the Sixteenth Century* (Oxford: Clarendon Press, 1963), 155.

on the targeting of civilians. The legitimate target was narrowed down from the entire population of one's adversary to its combatants alone. Vitoria's innovation allowed a distinction to be drawn between combatant and non-combatant members of the enemy population: only those who bore arms or engaged in fighting were to be presumed guilty in the absence of evidence to the contrary. Non-combatants on both sides (regardless of the justice of causes) were to be presumed innocent unless it could be shown that they knowingly and wilfully promoted injustice and wickedness. As such, non-combatants should not be killed, as the 'deliberate slaughter of the innocent is never lawful in itself'.[20] Innocence is a very powerful moral basis for non-combatants' immunity from targeting. To kill the innocent would be a serious breach of natural law.[21] Classes of people who must be presumed innocent until proven guilty were women, children, clerics, religious, foreign travellers, guests of the country, 'harmless agricultural folk, and also … the rest of the peaceable civilian population'.[22]

The strength of Vitoria's assumption lay in its practical benefits; its weakness was its theoretical incoherence (and even absurdity). He sought to create a strange half-way position between the Augustinian and modern models of war in which civilians were to be granted immunity, yet guilt remained the justification of killing in war. He attempted to ground a PNCI within the punitive justification of war, and could do so only by making bizarre claims about the probable guilt of combatants and the probable innocence of civilians. Vitoria allowed the guilt of combatants to be assumed because to require it to be ascertained would rule out war. Yet to kill combatants on the *presumption* of guilt is hardly defensible: later investigation would reveal innocent people to have been killed (indeed, this is a near certainty given his acceptance that even combatants fighting the side with just cause may have been fighting in good faith). Likewise, he allows the innocence of civilians to be assumed in the absence of any grounds for supposing civilians' responsibility for an unjust cause to differ from that of combatants. Vitoria's assumptions were thus no more acceptable than Augustine's assumption of moral wickedness on the part of the whole population of a party waging war without just cause.

---

[20] Vitoria, *De jure belli*, 35, in *Principles*, 88.   [21] Hartigan, *Forgotten Victim*, 87.
[22] Vitoria, *De jure belli*, 36, in James Turner Johnson, *Ideology, Reason and the Limitation of War: Religious and Secular Concepts 1200–1740* (Princeton: Princeton University Press, 1975), 196.

The End of the Punitive Model: Grotius

Augustine's punitive model of war was finally abandoned in the seventeenth century. It was no longer tenable in the modern era to justify war as the infliction of loving and divinely approved punishment on the wicked. The Reformation and the wars that followed it changed the political and intellectual context of war in Europe. Religious diversity was accompanied by a centralization of political authority and the development of large national states. The Thirty Years War ended with the Treaty of Westphalia that, by upholding the doctrine of state sovereignty, marked the start of the modern system of independent states. These states came to be served by professional standing armies, while new weapons, increasing the firepower of infantry, made war ever more destructive.

It was the founding figure of international law, the Dutch jurist and diplomat Hugo Grotius (1583–1645), who famously declared the punitive justification of war to be at an end. No longer, he asserted, could the fiction of enemy guilt be accepted: 'the law of nature does not allow inflicting reprisals, except on the actual persons who committed the offense. Nor is it enough that by a kind of fiction the enemy may be regarded as forming a single body.'[23]

The concepts of guilt and innocence, central to the attempt to justify war for more than a thousand years, were now abandoned. The enemy's desert of collective punishment was dismissed as a 'fiction'. Instead, the laws of war gained a new basis in natural law and international custom.[24] War was no longer the infliction of punishment on individuals, but a method of settling legal disputes between states when other methods have failed.[25]

---

[23] Hugo Grotius, *De Jure Belli ac Pacis*, trans. L. R. Loomis (Roslyn, NY: Walter J. Black Inc., 1949), bk. 3, ch. 11, sect. 16, p. 357.

[24] With the end of the punitive model died the only distinctly Christian justification of war. Once Augustine's focus on sin, guilt, and divine punishment had given way to a focus on state sovereignty and national interest, no longer would the Christian discussion of the rights and wrongs of war take place in terms fundamentally different from those of secular debate.

[25] Grotius instead based the right to kill in war on a natural right of self-defence: 'when our bodies are violently attacked with danger to our lives, and there is no other way of escape, it is lawful to fight the aggressor, and even to kill him. ... We must note that this right of self-defence derives its origin primarily from the instinct of self-preservation, which nature has given to every creature, and not from the injustice or misconduct of the aggressor. Wherefore, even though my assailant may be guiltless, as for instance a soldier fighting in good faith, or one who mistakes me for someone else, or a man frantic with insanity or sleeplessness, as we read sometimes happens, in none of these cases am I deprived of my right of self-defence ...' (*De Jure*, bk. 2, ch. 1, sects. 3–4, p. 73).

With the new characterization of war came the possibility of a PNCI, as no longer was civilian immunity ruled out by the *ad bellum* justification of war. Soldiers and civilians no longer shared the same status. Neither soldiers nor civilians were held to be guilty. The concepts of guilt, innocence, and punishment no longer applied to war on the *ad bellum* level.[26]

Grotius acknowledged that innocents comprised most of the enemy population in war. In doing so, he discarded the justification of war that had served Christendom for more than a thousand years. He also severed the link between just cause *ad bellum* and just conduct *in bello*: no longer did the justice of one's sovereign's cause have any implications for the rights of combatants (or non-combatants) in war. All combatants in war had equal status and the same right to kill. Even when the ruler was in the wrong, combatants could fight in his war without blame. Belligerent equality was achieved: *ad bellum* guilt, the very basis of Augustine's model of war, had no implications for the *in bello* level of Grotius's model of war. In short, guilt was no longer the reason why people might be killed in war.

Grotius described combatants as instruments when he distinguished the principal actors from those who carry out their orders. In war, he wrote, the principal is the sovereign authority, and the instruments are his subjects who willingly fight: 'When we say "instruments", we do not mean by it arms and things of that kind, but men who in action voluntarily make their wills dependent on another's will.'[27]

More than a hundred years later, the Swiss jurist Emmerich de Vattel (1714–67) adopted the metaphor and made it central to the modern era's characterization of the combatant:

The sovereign is the real author of war, which is made in his name and at his command. The troops, both officers and soldiers, and in general all the persons

---

[26] They did apply to war on the *jus in bello* level: actions done *in* war could be the basis for claims of guilt and desert of punishment of individual soldiers. But the *jus ad bellum* goal of the war itself would not.

[27] Grotius, *De Jure*, bk. 1, ch. 5, sect. 3, p. 69. Augustine had used this metaphor in connection with both executioners and warriors ('one who owes a duty of obedience to the giver of the command does not himself "kill"—he is an instrument, a sword in its user's hand' (*City of God*, 32)). Aquinas had used it to illustrate that the judge, and not the executioner, is to blame for the killing of an innocent man ('nor is it he who slays the innocent man but the judge whose minister he is' (*Summa Theologiae*, II. II, qu. 64, art. 6)). Neither Augustine nor Aquinas, however, made the notion of instrumentality central to their characterization of the combatant or to their justification of killing in war, as Vattel did.

by whom the sovereign carries on war, are only instruments in his hands. They execute his will and not their own.[28]

Vattel held combatants to be mere instruments of their states with no responsibility for the justice or injustice they furthered. Even when they killed in an unjust cause, combatants were not guilty of murder (in marked contrast to Augustine, who saw all killing on the battlefield by soldiers on the side without just cause as murder). For Vattel, the ruler alone bears responsibility for the injustice of war. When the cause of war is unjust, 'the sovereign alone is guilty' for the 'bloodshed, the desolation of families, the pillaging, the acts of violence'; his 'subjects, and especially the military, are innocent', for they killed and destroyed 'not of their own will but as instruments in the hands of their sovereign'.[29] In Vattel's characterization of combatants as instruments, combatants are no longer responsible for the lethal acts they perform. They do not have to enquire into the justice of their cause, and they do not have to be satisfied that they serve a good cause.

This characterization of the combatant as instrument of the state is the view that underlay the developments in the laws of war in the twentieth century. It is the basis of the principle of belligerent equality, and a consequence of the divorce of just conduct *in bello* from just cause *ad bellum*. It is grounded on a forthright acknowledgement that the justification of punitive killing does not apply to combatants (they are as innocent as civilians of *ad bellum* injustice). Yet it permits combatants to be killed at any time in war even when the justification of preventative killing does not apply. This is because of the customary acceptance in the Western world that members of armed forces may in war be treated as instruments, both by their own commanders and by their enemy's. The members of armed forces may have volunteered or (if pressed to join) at least acquiesced in being treated, not like individual human beings, but as instruments. In hostilities their lives may be taken as the means to a military or political objective. Combatants need not be engaged in an act of combatancy to be thought legitimate targets: as long as they are not *hors de combat*, they

---

[28] Emmerich de Vattel, *The Law of Nations, or the Principles of Natural Law Applied to the Conduct and to the Affairs of Nations and of Sovereigns* (1758), trans. Charles G. Fenwick (Washington: Carnegie Institute, 1916), bk. 3, sect. 6, p. 237.

[29] Ibid. bk. 3, sects. 184, 187, pp. 302–3.

may be killed in war even when they are not engaged in a combatant act and when there is nothing about the soldier as a person which makes hostile treatment justified. They have given up their right to be treated as persons (their right not to have their lives taken as a means to some end), and they have simultaneously been absolved of culpability for the killing they commit. So combatants are doubly depersonalized: they need not be guilty in order to be killed, and they do not incur guilt by killing. They are depersonalized when they are killed for reasons not to do with them as persons, and also when they are not held responsible for the killing they commit. In favour of this characterization of the combatant is that it established a sortal distinction between combatants and non-combatants. Issues of involvement, responsibility, and guilt (all scalar concepts) were avoided by the PNCI's focus on formal role. No assessment was required of a person's responsibility for the resort to war or contribution to the war effort. Issues of involvement, responsibility, or guilt were avoided, as they would require a judgement by the attacker of the victim's degree of involvement or responsibility (the sort of flexible assessment that the laws of war have sought to avoid).

Civilian Immunity

Grotius's assertions that natural law does not sanction punishment except of those who have done wrong, and that the enemy cannot be conceived as a single body are rightly famous. For with them, Grotius dismissed the punitive model of war. It was only with the abandonment of the attempt to base a justification of war on the concepts of guilt and innocence that the PNCI could develop. Grotius's dismissal of the punitive model of war allowed a principle of non-combatant immunity to be established with a firm foundation in law and justice. Immunity was to be given to all non-combatants; not only women and children, but all 'men whose way of life is opposed to warmaking', were to be immune from targeting in war (in the latter category he placed clergy, religious, agricultural workers, merchants, and 'other workmen and artisans, whose callings demand peace, not war').[30]

---

[30] Grotius, *De Jure*, bk. 3, ch. 11, sects. 10–12, p. 355.

Vattel followed Grotius in claiming immunity for all those who are not in the business of fighting, regardless of age or gender. 'Women, children, feeble old men and the sick' and also 'ministers of public worship and men of letters and other persons whose manner of life is wholly apart from the profession of arms' are categorized by Vattel as 'enemies who offer no resistance, and consequently the belligerent has no right to maltreat or otherwise offer violence to them, much less to put them to death'. He continues that 'as they do not resist the enemy by force or violence, they give the enemy no right to use it towards them'.[31] Thus, the immunity of these non-combatants is based on justice as well as humanity and charity. Justice, says Vattel, does not permit us to use violence against those who do not use force against us. It is wrong to kill civilians, not because harming them is unnecessary, but because they are not themselves engaged in harming others. For both Grotius and Vattel, then, the foundation of the claim for civilian immunity was justice. Justice requires that non-combatants be spared. Justice permits us to kill those who are guilty and those engaged in harming us; non-combatants are neither. Given this, justice requires that those not directly involved in trying to harm us be spared.

The Principle of Double Effect

For both Grotius and Vattel, the PNCI was a principle that could yield to the requirements of military success: civilians were to be immune only as military circumstances permitted. To understand why, one must look again at Aquinas's writings on killing and at another idea that came to be important for the concept of non-combatant immunity in Western thought. This is the 'principle of double effect', which appears in Aquinas's discussion of self-defence.[32] Self-defence played no part in Augustine's attempt to justify killing in a 'just war'; indeed, Augustine rejected killing in self-defence (to take the life of another human being purely so as to

---

[31] Vattel, *Law of Nations*, bk. 3, ch. 8, sects. 145–6, pp. 282–3.
[32] Though it has its roots in Aquinas, systematic usage of the principle did not occur until the sixteenth century. See Joseph Mangan, 'An Historical Analysis of the Principle of Double Effect', *Theological Studies*, 10 (1949), 41–61; James F. Keenan, SJ, 'The Function of the Principle of Double Effect', *Theological Studies*, 54 (1993), 294–315.

postpone our own death by a few more years betrayed, he thought, an undue attachment to the things of this world). Aquinas, in contrast, wished to legitimate the measured use of force in self-defence which he saw as the natural reaction of a living organism (and which therefore could not be bad). In discussing this issue of 'whether it is lawful to kill a man in self-defence', he utilized what has come to be known as the principle of double effect:

Nothing hinders one act from having two effects, only one of which is intended, while the other is beside the intention. Now moral acts take their species according to what is intended and not according to what is beside the intention ... Accordingly the act of self-defence may have two effects, one is the saving of one's life, the other is the slaying of the aggressor. Therefore this act, since one's intention is to save one's own life, is not unlawful, since it is natural to everything to keep itself in being, as far as possible ... But as it is unlawful to take a man's life, except for the public authority acting for the common good, as stated above, it is not lawful for a man to *intend* killing a man in self-defence, except for such as have public authority ...[33]

As elaborated by later moral theologians, this principle of double effect came to mean that one is not to blame for the indirect consequences (or side-effects) of one's actions as long as certain conditions are met. The first is that the action is in itself either morally good or morally indifferent. The second concerns intentionality: one must intend only the good effect of one's action, and not the bad one. The third condition is that the two effects be causally independent: the bad effect (in Aquinas's example, the killing of an attacker) must not be the *cause* of the good effect (the saving of one's life); it must be only a by-product of the good effect. The fourth condition is proportionality: the human good done must be proportionate to the human bad done. The principle of double effect, then, permits killing where it is the foreseen but unintended side-effect of doing good, where the bad does not lead to the good, and where the good outweighs the bad.

It is to this principle that Grotius refers when he holds that civilians are not to be killed in war except when that killing was necessary to defence or when that killing was collateral: 'an enemy, though he may be fighting a lawful war, does not have a true and inherent right to kill innocent persons,

---

[33] Aquinas, *Summa Theologiae*, II. II, qu. 64, art. 7.

clear of any blame for the war, except as a necessary measure of defence or *as a result of something not a part of his purpose.*'[34]

Grotius lays great emphasis on civilian immunity in war. However, the rule against attack on civilians is not absolute. The words 'a result of something not a part of his purpose' is Grotius's phrase for the principle of double effect: innocent civilians may be killed when it is an unintended, though foreseen, side-effect of an act necessary to achievement of the aims of the war. He thus allows what modern international humanitarian law calls 'indirect attack' on civilians: 'A ship filled with pirates, or a house with brigands, may be bombarded even though in that same ship or house there are a few children, or women, or other innocent persons, who are endangered by the attack.'[35]

In such cases, the principle of tactical proportionality still holds as Grotius makes clear when he cautions that

we should beware of things which happen and which we foresee may happen beyond what we intended, unless the good which is the aim of our act is much greater than the harm we fear, or unless, when the good and the harm are equal, the expectation of good is much stronger than the fear of harm, which is a question to be left for prudence to reflect on. But, as always, in case of doubt we should favour, as safer, the course that protects the other person's interest more than our own.[36]

For Vattel too, the prohibition on killing civilians in war could be overruled by the end for which the war is fought. If the defence of lives or property required it, then the prohibition on killing civilians might be ignored. Ultimately, like Grotius, Vattel allows all necessary means in pursuit of a just cause:

When the end is lawful, he who has a right to pursue that end has, naturally, a right to make use of all the means necessary to attain it … a sovereign has the right to do to his enemy whatever is necessary to weaken him and disable him from maintaining his unjust position; and the sovereign may choose the most efficacious and appropriate means to accomplish that object, provided those means be not essentially evil and unlawful, and consequently forbidden by the law of Nature.[37]

In order to justify war in a Christian manner, Augustine had relied on a convenient fiction that all in the population whose leadership had done

---

[34] Grotius, *De Jure*, bk. 2, ch. 26, sect. 6, p. 267; italics added.
[35] Ibid. bk. 3, ch. 1, sect. 4, p. 271.   [36] Ibid.
[37] Vattel, *Law of Nations*, bk. 3, sects. 136, 138, pp. 279–80.

wrong shared in the guilt. Only with the rejection of this idea could the way be opened to a PNCI in modern thought. But Aquinas introduced an idea that was to dilute that immunity of civilians in war, the claim that one can escape blame for the foreseen side-effects of one's actions. Applied to war, it makes civilian deaths (as a foreseen consequence of a military act) morally permissible as long as they are not intended, not directly productive of the military goal, and proportionate to the good sought.[38] In war, the principle of double effect is often invoked to excuse the killing of civilians as a consequence of an attack on a military target. Yet the principle does not apply to such a situation as well as it does to some others (such as the 'craniotomy case' in which a medical procedure is performed to save the life of a pregnant woman at the cost of that of her unborn child). There are at least three difficulties in applying the principle of double effect (PDE) to the killing of civilians in war.[39]

First, the PDE requires that the good end sought be proportionate to the harm done. In an attack on a military target in which (it is known) civilians will be killed, what is the good end that is to be proportionate to the harm that is the killing of civilians? Is it the saving of combatant lives that would otherwise be lost if such an attack did not take place, or if alternative means were used to the same tactical end? It is not (and in any case, civilians ought not to be killed as a side-effect of an action to save one's own combatants, for combatants may be treated as instruments, but civilians remain persons; it is not the case that two combatant lives saved outweigh one civilian life lost). Rather, the attack on the military target is only an intermediary step, a means to the end of victory in the war. Its

[38] Some commentators would describe as a 'fiction' the notion that we cannot intend a harmful effect of our action which we foresee *will* happen. For Richard Hull there must be 'some likelihood that a harm will not occur if foresight is to mean anything other than intention'. In a similar vein, Judith Lichtenberg argues that, for there to be a difference in moral culpability between the collateral killing of civilians and the direct killing of civilians, there must be a difference in the probability and magnitude of civilian deaths between the two cases. If the same number of civilians is just as likely to die in both cases, then the wrongness of the acts is the same. Camillo Bica too concludes that where the death of an innocent person is 'the foreseen though unintended effect of an act and *as probable* an occurrence as is the intended effect', an injustice has been committed. See Richard Hull, 'Deconstructing the Doctrine of Double Effect', *Ethical Theory and Moral Practice*, 3/2 (2000), 195–207; Judith Lichtenberg, 'War, Innocence and the Doctrine of Double Effect', *Philosophical Studies*, 74 (June 1994), 347–68; Camillo C. Bica, 'Another Perspective on the Doctrine of Double Effect', *Public Affairs Quarterly*, 13/2 (Apr. 1999), 131–9.

[39] For more on this, see the final chapter of Colm McKeogh, *Innocent Civilians: The Morality of Killing in War* (Basingstoke: Palgrave, 2002).

worth cannot be assessed without reference to the *ad bellum* end for which the war is waged by that party to the conflict. Yet, if the focus is switched from the tactical to the strategic level, then the end for which civilians are killed collaterally is not so clearly good or right; indeed, one party to the conflict firmly believes that end to be wrong or bad (in other cases to which the PDE is applied, the good end is clear: in the performance of a craniotomy, it is the saving of a woman's life; so too when a bystander pulls a lever to divert a run-away trolley on to a track where it will kill only one person rather than five: five lives are saved and only one lost).[40]

Secondly, not only is the goodness of the ultimate end in doubt; so too is the probability of attaining it. Again, this distinguishes war from other cases: in the craniotomy and trolley cases, the good or right end that is sought *can* be attained. The surgical intervention will save the woman's life at the cost of her pregnancy; pulling the lever will save five lives and lose only one. The probability of attaining the good end is much lower in war. Chance, as Clausewitz asserted, is essential to the nature of war; in war, no good at all may come from the harm that is done. In fact, no good at all will come from the harm that is done by one side—the side that loses; at least one side sacrifices the lives of civilians for no good or right outcome: civilians killed collaterally by the losing side are, ultimately, killed for nothing.

There is a third difficulty in applying the PDE to tactical operations in war that cause civilian deaths. This is that the sum of civilian deaths in such tactical engagements can exceed the maximum believed to be proportionate to the war's end. This is because war is a serial killer, a chain of violent events. Prior to each tactical operation in war, the question facing the military command concerns only the civilian deaths expected from the proposed future engagement. The PDE asks whether the *next* loss of civilian life would be outweighed by the expected good end. Past non-combatant deaths are past; civilians' lives already lost are out of the equation. If the expected good end has taken longer to achieve than initially

---

[40] The 'trolley' is a widely discussed case in recent philosophical literature; see Judith Jarvis Thompson, 'The Trolley Problem', in her *Rights, Restitution and Risk* (Cambridge, Mass.: Harvard University Press, 1986), 94–116; Frances Kamm, 'Non-consequentialism, the Person as an End-in-Itself, and the Significance of Status', *Philosophy and Public Affairs*, 21/4 (Fall 1992), 354–89, and *idem*, 'The Doctrine of Triple Effect and Why a Rational Agent Need Not Intend the Means to his End', *Proceedings of the Aristotelian Society*, suppl. vol. 74 (2000), 21–39.

anticipated, a disproportionate number of civilian lives may already have been lost. Yet the question facing the military command remains whether the loss of civilian life anticipated in the next operation is outweighed by the expected contribution to the war's end of the tactical operation. The anticipated loss of civilian life in each tactical event will nearly always be outweighed by the strategic good that is the *ad bellum* end of the war. But because war is a chain of such events, the cumulative loss of civilian life can become disproportionate to the strategic end of the war.

Conclusion

Two medieval ideas that were important in the history of the PNCI have been examined: the punitive justification of killing in war and the principle of double effect. Though it dominated Western thought for a millennium, the attempt to justify killing in war as punishment for wrongdoing failed. For that wrongdoing is on the strategic or *ad bellum* level; the implications of it for the individuals who fight war cannot be satisfactorily established. In war, the issue of *ad bellum* wrongs and rights often cannot be settled. Even if issues of just cause *ad bellum* could be settled, it is rarely the case that those fighting for an *ad bellum* wrong can be said to incur guilt for so doing. In the age of the nation-state, patriotism and state propaganda undermine the possibility of impartial assessment of one's country's cause by the individual combatant, lessening individual responsibility for participation in wrongdoing. Even if participation in that *ad bellum* unjust cause is thought to have legal and moral implications at the level of the individual combatant, it still needs to be established that this responsibility is sufficient to warrant the use of lethal force against the wrongdoer. Wrongdoing may be serious, but not serious enough to justify death: justice does not permit all necessary actions to prevent or undo the injustice. Even if death were a just punishment, it would not be death by such cruel means as war offers: by blast wounds, blood loss, burning, asphyxiation, exposure, and burial alive.

Though it was only with the abandonment of the attempt to apply the concepts of guilt and innocence to the justification of killing in war that a PNCI could emerge, Augustine's justification of killing in war remains important. For it was his attempt to justify killing in war by reference to love and punishment that authoritatively established the standard to be met in the treatment of people in Western Christendom. The standard that Augustine set 1,600 years ago, that all people be treated appropriately in war, remains to be met as long as there are held to be circumstances in which one can escape blame for the non-accidental killing of people who have done nothing to make such treatment of them appropriate.[41] What is called for is a PNCI which prohibits not only the intentional killing of civilians, but also the negligent or non-accidental killing of them. For as long as innocent civilians are killed non-accidentally, war is violence against people, not as individuals, but as members of categories, such as nationality, institutional role, and territorial location. Such violence can be justified, not by reference to the acts or attributes of those harmed, but only as a means to an end. People are killed, not because of who they are or what they are doing, but because of the situation. To kill people who have done nothing to deserve it, so that some good or right end may come about, is something that Western thought has long condemned and sought to prohibit.

---

[41] As regards combatants, the standard for appropriate treatment of people is met as long as those occupying the role of combatant have consented (or, if conscripted, at least acquiesced) to fill that role. Combatants killed preventatively are treated justly; those killed non-preventatively are justly treated if they have consented (or acquiesced) to such treatment. The non-preventative killing of unwilling conscripts (or those too young to consent) does not meet the standard of appropriate treatment.

4

Civilian Immunity in War: Legal Aspects

DAVID KRETZMER

Introduction

The duty to distinguish between combatants and civilians is the most fundamental principle of the law of armed conflict, or international humanitarian
law (IHL), as it is now generally called. Under this principle, parties to
an armed conflict must distinguish between combatants and civilians, and
between military and civilian targets. Combatants and military objects may
be the object of an attack; civilians and civilian objects may not. Parties in
an armed conflict are also duty-bound to take measures of precaution to
spare the civilian population, civilians, and civilian objects.

When taken in isolation, the principles of distinction and precaution
would appear to forge an impressive legal basis for protection of civilians in
war. However, even if these principles were fully respected in practice, they
would not provide complete legal immunity from attack for civilians. For,
while it is forbidden to make civilians or civilian facilities the *object* of an
attack, it is not necessarily unlawful to conduct an attack when it is highly
probable, or even certain, that civilians will be killed or injured. Under the
principle of proportionality, when the direct target of an attack is a military
object, the fact that civilians might be killed or injured will not make that
attack unlawful, unless the expected loss to civilians would be excessive
in relation to the direct and concrete military advantage anticipated from
the attack.

The principles of distinction, precaution, and proportionality are the
focus of this essay. Before discussing these principles, it is essential to clarify
a few premises on which the discussion rests.

Sources of norms relating to civilian immunity

The most important instruments of international law relating to civilian immunity are Geneva Convention IV Relative to the Protection of Civilian Persons in Times of War of 1949 (GCIV) and Additional Protocols to the Geneva Conventions of 1977 (API and APII). GCIV was the first attempt to draw up a treaty whose sole purpose was protection of civilians during armed conflict. It is largely restricted, however, to the situation of civilians who find themselves in the hands of a party to an armed conflict, whether in the territories of parties to the conflict or in occupied territory, and generally does not cover rules of combat. This lacuna was amended by API, which contains detailed provisions relating to protection of civilians in situations of combat.

Adherence to the Geneva Conventions is universal, and all states are therefore bound by their provisions. While most states have ratified or acceded to the Additional Protocols, a significant number of states have refrained from doing so, and are consequently not bound by their provisions. Nevertheless, it is generally considered that most of the provisions in these Protocols relating to conduct of hostilities reflect customary international law that binds all states.

Sphere of application

IHL applies whenever an armed conflict occurs, whether or not a state of war has been recognized by the parties. Since adoption of the 1949 Geneva Conventions, certain of the rules of IHL apply not only to 'classic' wars between states (armed conflicts of an international character), but also to armed conflicts between the armed forces of a state and organized armed groups, and even to armed conflicts between different organized armed groups occurring in the territory of a state (armed conflicts not of an international character).

The norms of IHL apply to all parties to the conflict, irrespective of the rights or wrongs of the initial resort to force. Following the fundamental distinction between *ius ad bellum* (the law regulating the right to resort to armed force) and *ius in bello* (the law that regulates the way in which armed force may be used in a conflict), once an armed conflict exists, the same rules apply to an aggressor and to a state exercising its inherent right to self-defence. The illegality of the initial resort to force does not taint with illegality everything the aggressor does in the course of the ensuing armed conflict. Nor does the inherent right of a state to defend itself excuse it from the duty to do so according to the norms of IHL. Under Common Article 2, the 1949 Geneva Conventions come into play in 'all cases of declared war or of any other armed conflict which may arise between two or more of the High Contracting Parties, even if the state of war is not recognized by one of them'. In such conflicts, namely inter-state conflicts, the threshold of violence required for an armed conflict to exist is low. While minor border clashes between states may not constitute armed conflicts, the International Criminal Tribunal for the Former Yugoslavia has held that an 'international armed conflict exists whenever there is a resort to armed force between States'.[1]

The majority of armed conflicts in today's world are not classic inter-state conflicts. They are internal conflicts between state authorities and armed groups in their territory, or between different organized armed groups. In some cases, such conflicts extend beyond the borders of one state and may involve a conflict between a state and a transnational or international armed group. The traditional law of war did not apply to internal conflicts (unless a state of belligerency with insurgents was recognized by the state involved). The 1949 Geneva Conventions took the first major step in changing this situation. Under Common Article 3 of those Conventions, certain fundamental principles of the law of armed conflict are to be applied in cases of internal armed conflict in the territory of a state. These principles must be respected by all parties to such conflicts. They apply not only to state actors, but to non-state actors who are parties to the conflict. According to the International Court of Justice, these principles reflect 'minimum considerations of humanity' that apply universally to all armed conflicts, however they are categorized.[2] First and foremost amongst these principles is the prohibition on violence to life and person of those not taking an active part in hostilities.

Traditional international law distinguishes between two armed conflict situations: hostilities and occupation of enemy territory. Occupation of enemy territory is usually a function of hostilities. However, following cases during World War II in which occupation of territories by the

[1] See Case No. 160, ICTY, *Prosecutor* v. *Tadic*, Jurisdiction Appeal, para. 70.
[2] International Court of Justice, *Military and Paramilitary Operations in and Against Nicaragua*, Decision of 28 June 1986, *ICJ Reports* (1986), 1, at para. 218.

Wehrmacht did not meet with armed resistance, under Common Article 2 (2) the Geneva Conventions apply 'to all cases of partial or total occupation of the territory of a High Contracting Party, even if the said occupation meets with no armed resistance'.

International human rights law in armed conflict

The law of armed conflict was originally perceived as a branch of law that regulates the relationship between states involved in armed conflict. Its object was to limit the use of force employed against the enemy. It was not concerned with the relationship between a state and its own nationals. This approach is reflected in the definition of 'protected persons' in GCIV, which excludes nationals of the party in whose hands they find themselves.

Following World War II and the Holocaust, a new branch of international law, international human rights law (HRL), has developed alongside IHL. The main innovation of international human rights law was the internationalization of the relationship between states and all individuals subject to their jurisdiction. The focus of international human rights law is the rights of the individual *vis-à-vis* the state, and not on the relationship between states.

While HRL was still in its infancy, the prevailing view was that IHR and IHL have separate spheres of application. IHL applies during armed conflict to the relationship between a state and the combatants and civilians of the enemy; HRL applies at all times to the relationship between a state and those it governs 'on the home front'. In recent years this convenient division has collapsed. The International Court of Justice (ICJ) opined that the norms of HRL apply at all times and places, although in a situation of armed conflict IHL constitutes *lex specialis*, which may be relevant in interpreting and applying the human rights norms.[3]

The Principle of Distinction

The principle of distinction forms the corner-stone of international humanitarian law. It mandates a distinction between combatants and civilians, and

---

[3] International Court of Justice, *Legality of the Threat or Use of Nuclear Weapons*, Advisory Opinion of 8 July 1996, *ICJ Reports* (1996), 226, at paras. 24–5. Also see International Court of Justice, *Legal Consequences of the Construction of a Wall in the Occupied Palestinian Territory*, Advisory Opinion of 9 July 2004, International Legal Materials, 4.3 (2004), 1009.

between military and non-military targets. Although it was not until adoption of the Additional Protocols to the Geneva Conventions in 1977 that this principle was codified in an international treaty, it has been recognized by the ICJ as one of 'the intransgressible principles of international customary law'.[4]

Article 48 of API defines the principle of distinction, terming it the 'basic rule' in protection of civilians against hostilities:

In order to ensure respect for and protection of the civilian population and civilian objects, the Parties to the conflict shall at all times distinguish between the civilian population and combatants and between civilian objects and military objectives and accordingly shall direct their operations only against military objectives.

The basic rule is followed by more detailed provisions. Thus, article 51 declares:

1. The civilian population and individual civilians shall enjoy general protection against dangers arising from military operations. To give effect to this protection, the following rules, which are additional to other applicable rules of international law, shall be observed in all circumstances.
2. The civilian population as such, as well as individual civilians, shall not be the object of attack. Acts or threats of violence the primary purpose of which is to spread terror among the civilian population are prohibited.

As the bedrock of civilian immunity this provision merits careful analysis.

Definition of civilians

A civilian is any person who is not a combatant.[5] In case of doubt about a person's status that person shall be regarded as a civilian.[6] The civilian population comprises all persons who are civilians.[7]

As categorization of a person as a civilian is a function of the definition of a combatant, it is necessary to examine this definition. Before doing so, however, it is important to appreciate the full implications of classifying a person as a combatant, rather than as a non-combatant or civilian.

---

[4] ICJ, *Legality of the Threat or Use of Nuclear Weapons*, para. 79. For the historical antecedents of the principle and its status prior to adoption of the Additional Protocols, see Louise Doswald-Beck, 'The Value of the 1977 Geneva Protocols for the Protection of Civilians', in Michael A. Meyer (ed.), *Armed Conflict and the New Law: Aspects of the 1977 Geneva Protocols and the 1981 Weapons Convention* (London: British Institute of International and Comparative Law, 1989), 137; Judith Gail Gardam, *Non-Combatant Immunity as a Norm of International Humanitarian Law* (Dordrecht, Boston, and London: Martinus Nijhoff, 1993), 16–27.

[5] API, art. 50 (1).   [6] Ibid.   [7] API, art. 50 (2).

Being a combatant in an international armed conflict has implications on three levels:

a. Combatants have the privilege to fight and are therefore immune from prosecution for fighting according to the laws of armed conflict (but not for violating those laws).
b. If apprehended by the adversary, combatants enjoy the status of prisoners of war.
c. Unless they are *hors de combat*, combatants may legitimately be targeted by the adversary.

Civilians do not enjoy the privileges of combatants: they may be prosecuted for fighting and do not enjoy prisoner-of-war status if apprehended. On the other hand, they are not legitimate targets.

In customary international law a combatant is anyone who is a member of the armed forces, and a civilian is therefore anyone who is not a member of the armed forces.[8] Alongside members of the regular army, members of the armed forces include members of armed groups belonging to a party to the conflict, provided they are commanded by a responsible commander, wear a fixed distinctive sign recognizable at a distance, carry their arms openly, and conduct their operations in accordance with the laws and customs of war.[9] They also include inhabitants of a non-occupied territory who, not having had time to form themselves into regular armed units, take up arms to resist an invading force, provided they carry arms openly and respect the laws and customs of war.[10]

API extends application of the law relating to international armed conflicts to armed conflicts which peoples are fighting against colonial domination and alien occupation and against racist regimes in the exercise of their right of self-determination.[11] Consequently, members of armed forces of such peoples, which are under responsible command, are regarded as combatants, even if the people are represented by a government not recognized by the adverse party to the conflict.[12] This controversial innovation has been rejected by a number of states, which have refrained from joining API. The API provisions on this issue are not regarded as part of customary

---

[8] International Committee of the Red Cross, *Customary International Humanitarian Law* (Cambridge: Cambridge University Press, 2005) (hereafter *ICRC Study*), rule 3.
[9] API, art. 50 (1) together with GCII, art. 4, A 2.
[10] API, art. 50 (1), together with GCIII, art. 4, A 6.   [11] API, art. 1 (4).   [12] API, art. 43.

law, and states that are not parties to API are not bound by the broader
definition of combatants. Whether the implications of non-applicability of
API are that 'API non-state combatants' are to be regarded as civilians or
as 'unlawful combatants' is one of the more contentious issues in IHL. Its
implications will be discussed below.

Scope of immunity from attack

Civilians' immunity from being the object of attack, offensive or defensive,
is a function of their lack of privilege to take part in fighting, not of
their lack of moral responsibility for the armed conflict.[13] If civilians are
responsible for a war of aggression, they may face criminal responsibility for
the crime of aggression, but this responsibility must be dealt with through
international criminal law, and not by targeting those civilians.

Not being allowed to participate in hostilities, civilians do not threaten
the enemy and may therefore not be targeted. It stands to reason that if
civilians fail to respect their lack of privilege to engage in fighting, they
may lose their immunity. Accordingly, the protection from attack enjoyed
by civilians does not apply to civilians who take a direct part in hostilities.[14]

Forfeit of immunity from attack by taking a direct part in hostilities raises
a number of questions:

a. What comprises 'taking a direct part in hostilities'?
b. For how long is the immunity forfeited?

Taking direct part in hostilities

In the law of armed conflict the term 'hostilities' is used in different
contexts. Sometimes it refers to the general situation of armed conflict
between parties; at others to the more specific situation of active combat.
In the present context, the term 'hostilities' refers to combat activities.

The ICRC *Commentary on the Additional Protocols* claims that 'hostile
acts should be understood to be acts which by their nature and purpose
are intended to cause actual harm to the personnel and equipment of the

---

[13] It is therefore abundantly clear that even if one accepts the argument (made by Seumas Miller
in Chapter 5) that there may be groups of civilians who should lose their immunity because of their
responsibility for the armed conflict, under the prevailing norms of IHL such civilians enjoy immunity
from being the object of attack.

[14] Art. 51 (3) of API and *ICRC Study*, rule 6.

armed forces'.[15] This definition would seem to be too narrow, as acts against civilians of the adversary—such as a terrorist attack on civilians—would not be included. At the very least, it would therefore seem that acts intended to cause harm to civilians, or civilian objects, of the adversary, are also included, provided they have a nexus to the armed conflict. Acts of force unconnected with the armed conflict are not included.[16]

A distinction must be drawn between hostilities and the war effort. Active participation in the war effort does not of itself constitute participation in hostilities, even if it is more crucial to military success than some activities of combatants.[17] Civilian workers in a munitions factory, civilians who supply food to the army, and civilians who broadcast messages of support for the armed forces, may be actively helping the war effort, but they are not taking part in the hostilities.

Participation in hostilities must be direct. Actually taking part in combat is obviously covered. But what of support for those involved in combat? How is one to regard civilians who provide logistical support for the fighting forces? What about civilians who perform tasks that in many cases are performed by members of the armed forces, such as providing transport for troops moving to the front?

There is little agreement on these questions.[18] The *ICRC Commentary* attempts to draw the line somewhere between active participation in military operations and participation in the war effort. It states that '[d]irect participation in hostilities implies a direct causal relationship between the activity engaged in and the harm done to the enemy at the time and the place where the activity takes place'.[19]

The *ICRC Commentary*'s requirement of a causal relationship between the actions of civilians and actual harm to the enemy is highly problematical.

[15] See ICRC, *Commentary on the Additional Protocols to the Geneva Conventions*, ed. Yves Sandoz, Christophe Swinarski, and Bruno Zimmerman I (Geneva: ICRC, 1987) (hereafter *ICRC Commentary*), para. 1942.

[16] See International Humanitarian Law Research Initiative, *Working Paper, Direct Participation in Hostilities under International Humanitarian Law*, prepared by Jean-François Quéguiner, available at <http://www.ihlresearch.org/ihl/feature.php?a=42> (visited 3 Aug. 2005). Also see Michael N. Schmitt, '"Direct Participation in Hostilities" and 21st Century Armed Conflict', in Horst Fischer *et al.* (eds.), *Crisis Management and Humanitarian Protection: Festschrift für Dieter Fleck* (Berlin: BWV, 2004), 505.

[17] *ICRC Commentary*, para. 1945.

[18] See A. P. V. Rogers, *Law on the Battlefield*, 2nd edn. (New York and Manchester: Juris Publishing, 2004), 10–12.

[19] *ICRC Commentary*, para. 1679.

Other commentators have argued for a wider view of 'direct participation'. It has been claimed that acts aimed at protecting military targets must be included, and also that if a person's acts as a civilian contribute more to the war effort than that person's service in the military, those acts should be regarded as direct participation in hostilities. According to another view, the crucial test is whether a civilian's activities are an essential and indispensable ingredient of the military actions.[20]

In modern warfare civilians are extensively involved in many activities connected with conduct of hostilities. In recent conflicts private military companies (PMCs) have been employed to perform a range of tasks, which include training military personnel in use and maintenance of weapons, building military installations, supplying weapons and food to soldiers at the front, transportation, and guarding civilian installations or military weapons stores.[21] Employees of such firms are not members of the armed forces, and therefore are not combatants. There is a wide diversity of opinion as to when they should be regarded as taking a direct part in hostilities.[22] It has been argued that the general test is whether the activities of the civilian personnel are integrated into combat operations. 'In this context, integration is becoming an uninterrupted, indispensable part of an activity such that the activity cannot function without that person's presence and combat operations are any military activities that are intended to disrupt enemy operations or destroy enemy forces or installations.'[23]

In some cases, such as the US action in Iraq, PMCs have been employed to perform security tasks alongside the armed forces,[24] such as protecting civilian and military installations, military convoys, and military personnel. When such personnel should be regarded as taking a direct part in

[20] The different views are presented in *Working Paper, Direct Participation*.
[21] The role of such corporations in modern-day armed conflicts is discussed in P. W. Singer, *Corporate Warriors: The Rise of the Privatized Military Industry* (Ithaca, NY, and London: Cornell University Press, 2003).
[22] See *Working Paper, Direct Participation*; Michael N. Schmitt, 'Humanitarian Law and Direct Participation in Hostilities by Private Contractors or Civilian Employees', *Chicago Journal of International Law*, 5 (2005), 511; Rogers, *Law on the Battlefield*, 11–12.
[23] See Michael Guillory, 'Civilianizing the Force: Is the United States Crossing the Rubicon?', *Air Force Law Review*, 51 (2001), 134. But see Rogers, *Law on the Battlefield*, 10–12, who argues for a narrow view of 'taking a direct part in hostilities' and would not include driving an ammunition truck to supply enemy armed forces.
[24] See Anthony Dworkin, *Security Contractors in Iraq: Armed Guards or Private Soldiers?* Crimes of War Project, at <www.crimesofwar.org/onnews/news-security.html> (visited 3 Aug. 2005).

hostilities is a grey area.[25] Some writers hold that in guarding civilian or military installations, PMCs are merely performing a 'policing function' and are not directly participating in hostilities.[26] One respected writer argues that guarding a military installation does not of itself constitute direct participation in hostilities, but that the position would change 'if the civilian guards tried by force to prevent attacks on, or attempts to capture, the military installation by members of the opposing armed forces'.[27] Another view is that guarding a military installation, or military personnel, against enemy attack *per se* constitutes direct participation in hostilities.[28]

What about military planning, intelligence gathering and analysis, and security-related decision making during an armed conflict? Are civilian officials in a Ministry of Defence who are involved in strategic planning during an armed conflict directly participating in hostilities? And what about cabinet ministers who give the military the go-ahead to carry out a certain military campaign? It would seem that a distinction must be drawn here between functions and decisions on the general strategic level and operational or tactical decisions. General strategic analysis does not constitute direct participation in hostilities; analysis of potential targets, or other intelligence information, which is provided to combat units as the basis for their combat activities, probably does.[29] Similarly, decisions of a strategic nature made by political leaders do not constitute direct participation in hostilities; involvement of a Prime Minister or Minister of Defence in tactical planning of military operations does constitute such participation.

The status of suspected transnational terrorists is another issue that has caused some controversy. Terrorists do not generally meet the definition of combatants in an international armed conflict. Some states have argued, however, that they should be regarded as 'unlawful' or 'unprivileged' combatants, who lose the immunity of civilians from attack, although they do not enjoy the privileges of lawful combatants. While some prestigious experts share this view,[30] both the ICRC and other experts contest the

---

[25] See *Working Paper, Direct Participation*; Rogers, *Law on the Battlefield*, 10–12.
[26] *Working Paper, Direct Participation*. See also Rogers, *Law on the Battlefield*, 12.
[27] Rogers, *Law on the Battlefield*.   [28] See Schmitt, 'Humanitarian Law', 538.
[29] But cf. Rogers, *Law on the Battlefield*, 11–12, who argues that assessing aerial photography for likely targets does not constitute direct participation.
[30] See Yoram Dinstein, *The Conduct of Hostilities under the Law of International Armed Conflict* (Cambridge: Cambridge University Press, 2004), 29.

very existence of a separate category of 'unlawful combatants'.[31] According to their view, terrorists must be seen as civilians who take a direct part in hostilities. The implications of this distinction is discussed below.

Loss of immunity

Article 53 (1) of API states that the immunity of civilians from attack is removed only 'for such time' as the civilians are taking part in the hostilities. The *ICRC Study* includes the time frame of article 53 (1) as part of the norms of customary international law.[32] It is nevertheless doubtful whether this is indeed the case.[33] The API position, which has been termed 'the revolving door approach',[34] has been severely criticized, especially when it relates to terrorists or other 'unlawful combatants' (as opposed to civilians who take a one-time 'accidental' part in hostilities).[35] Proponents of a wider view argue that immunity for civilians should be forfeited 'whenever they become offensive—that is, whenever they take action against military forces or their fellow citizens'.[36] Immunity from attack of a civilian taking direct part in hostilities should be removed, it has been argued, until such time as he or she makes 'an affirmative act of withdrawal', which could be by extended non-participation.[37] A further view is that becoming a member of a guerrilla group or armed faction involved in attacks against enemy forces constitutes direct participation in hostilities, and that the immunity from attack is lost as long as participation in the activities of the group or faction continues.[38]

If the narrow view regarding forfeit of immunity adopted in API is accepted, the distinction between the notion of an 'unlawful combatant' and a civilian who takes direct part in hostilities becomes crucial. Combatants may be targeted as long as they are not *hors de combat*; civilians only for such time as they are actually taking direct part in the hostilities. If members of

---

[31] See Antonio Cassese, *International Law*, 2nd edn. (Oxford: Oxford University Press, 2005), 420–3.
[32] *ICRC Study*, rule 6.   [33] See Schmitt, 'Humanitarian Law', 535.
[34] See W. Hayes Parks, 'Air War and the Laws of War', *Air Force Law Review*, 32 (1990), 118–20.
[35] See K. W. Watkin, *Combatants, Unprivileged Belligerents and Conflicts in the 21st Century*, HPCR Background Paper (Jan. 2003), <http://www.ihlresearch.org/ihl/pdfs/Session2.pdf> (visited 3 Aug. 2005).
[36] See Anne-Marie Slaughter and William Burke-White, 'An International Constitutional Moment', *Harvard International Law Journal*, 43 (2002), 13.
[37] Schmitt, 'Humanitarian Law', 536.   [38] See Rogers, *Law on the Battlefield*, 11–12.

terrorist groups are regarded as 'unlawful combatants', they may be targeted at any time, as if they were combatants; if as civilians, only when actually involved in carrying out a terrorist attack.

Threats of violence

Civilians are immune not only from being the object of attack but also from threats of violence. Like the immunity from attack, this immunity is limited. It applies only to threats the primary purpose of which is to spread terror among the civilian population. Threats to use unlawful violence will clearly meet this test. A party to an armed conflict may not threaten to bomb the cities or other civilian centres of the adversary. However, even if they were to spread terror among civilians, threats to destroy the army of an adversary, or even to use highly destructive, but lawful, weapons in an attack on military targets, would not be unlawful unless it could be proved that spreading terror among the civilian population was their primary purpose.

Reprisals

According to traditional norms of conduct in war, reprisals—i.e., performance of acts that are normally unlawful as an enforcement measure in response to unlawful acts of an adversary—were regarded as standard conduct. In reaction to attacks on one's own civilian population, attacks were mounted against the civilian population of the adversary. Under the influence of HRL, which focuses on protection of the individual rather than on state sovereignty and state interests, IHL no longer rests on reciprocity. The fact that State A's adversary has violated the rules of IHL does not give State A licence to do so. In accordance with this approach, API expressly prohibits reprisals against the civilian population, or civilians, against objects indispensable for the survival of the civilian population, and against works or installations that contain dangerous forces, if the attack may release such forces resulting in severe losses to the civilian population. This prohibition is phrased in absolute terms, knowing no exceptions. Military necessity does not serve as justification for a reprisal against civilians.

The absolute prohibition on reprisals is one of the more controversial provisions of API, from which a number of states saw fit to dissociate themselves. On accession to API, the United Kingdom expressly reserved the right to use reprisals against civilians of an enemy which had made serious and deliberate attacks on the UK's civilian population, if, after warnings to the enemy to stop the attacks went unheeded, it considered that such reprisals were necessary for the sole purpose of compelling the enemy to stop the attacks.

In light of the contrary attitude of some states, the *ICRC Study* found it 'difficult to conclude that there has yet crystallized a customary rule specifically prohibiting reprisals against civilians during the conduct of hostilities'.[39] On the other hand, it found it equally 'difficult to assert that a right to resort to such reprisals continues to exist'.[40] It concluded that at the very least there is a trend in favour of prohibiting such reprisals.

Starvation of civilians

The prohibitions derived from the principle of distinction extend beyond direct military attacks on civilians to other measures directed against the civilian population. Starvation of the civilian population as a method of warfare is explicitly prohibited under API. Furthermore, it is forbidden to attack or destroy objects, such as foodstuffs, that are indispensable to the survival of the civilian population. The *ICRC Study* claims that while the total prohibition on starvation of civilians was new at the time API was adopted, 'since then [it] has hardened into a rule of customary international law'.[41]

The specific prohibition on starvation of the civilian population, either directly or indirectly, challenges the legitimacy of certain traditional methods of warfare, such as a naval blockade or siege of a town. If the very purpose of the blockade or siege is to starve civilians, it would obviously be unlawful. But the purpose of a naval blockade is to prevent the enemy from receiving supplies necessary to carry on hostilities, and the purpose of a siege may be to cause a military force (such as a garrison in a defended town) to surrender. Will the fact that civilians are affected make the blockade or siege unlawful? It would seem that while in adopting the API provision forbidding starvation of the civilian population states did not intend to change the law that allows naval blockade,[42] there

---

[39] *ICRC Study*, 523.   [40] Ibid.   [41] Ibid. 186.
[42] *ICRC Commentary*, paras. 2092–7.

was every intention to outlaw siege of a town that leads to starvation of the civilians therein, even if its direct object is to force surrender of a military force.

The total ban on sieges of towns that lead to the starvation of civilians has been criticized as unrealistic.[43] The argument is that as long as the military force that places the siege allows civilians to leave the besieged town, it cannot be held responsible for their situation if they refuse to do so, or even if they are prevented from doing so by the defending military force. The *ICRC Study* supports the approach that a siege is lawful if civilians are allowed to leave the besieged town or if the besieging party allows passage of essential foodstuffs and other essential supplies.[44] This alternative path of action derives from a general obligation on parties to a conflict to allow and facilitate rapid passage of humanitarian relief for civilians in need.[45]

Civilian objects

Immunity from being the object of attack extends to civilian objects. As in the case of civilians themselves, the definition of civilian objects is a negative one. All objects that are not military objects are civilian ones.

The definition of military objects has long been controversial.[46] Military installations, such as military bases, ammunition factories, or military communications centres obviously pose no difficulty. However, other facilities may serve military purposes too. When should they be regarded as military objects? According to article 52 (2) of API legitimate military targets are objectives 'which by their nature, location, purpose or use make an effective contribution to military action and whose total or partial destruction, capture or neutralization, in the circumstances ruling at the time, offers a definite military advantage'. It may be argued that this definition is so wide that it could cover practically any installation. For it is not only the nature of the object that makes it a military object; the location of an entirely civilian construction, such as a bridge, may make it a legitimate object of attack if it meets the two-prong test of API: that it makes an effective contribution to military action and its destruction would offer a definite military advantage.

---

[43] See Dinstein, *Conduct of Hostilities*, 135.
[44] *ICRC Study*, 188.   [45] API, article 70 (2); *ICRC Study*, rule 55.
[46] See Rogers, *Law on the Battlefield*, 58–64.

The present use of a civilian facility like a school may make it a military objective; so may its intended further use (its purpose). Under the API test, dual-use facilities—i.e., facilities that serve both military and civilian needs, such as power stations and electric grids—may also be legitimate military targets.

What about facilities whose destruction may harm the war-sustaining effort of the enemy, such as television or radio stations that do not serve a direct military function, but are used by the regime to maintain civilian support for the war? Are such facilities legitimate military targets? US military manuals give a positive answer to this question, but many commentators have challenged this view.[47] The prevailing view would seem to be that the effect that destruction of a civilian facility will have on the war-sustaining effort of the enemy does not *per se* make it a legitimate target.

One of the exceptions to the notion that dual-use facilities may be legitimate military targets relates to foodstuffs and other objects indispensable for the survival of the civilian population. It is forbidden to destroy these, whatever the motive. Even if foodstuffs necessary for the survival of the civilian population are also used to feed the military, they may not be destroyed. API expressly states that the exception to the prohibition on destroying such items exists only if they are used by the enemy as sustenance *solely* for the members of its armed forces. When items necessary for survival of the civilian population are used in direct support of military activities, actions against these objects shall not be taken which may be expected to leave the civilian population with such inadequate food or water as to cause its starvation or force its movement.

Another exception to the legitimacy of attacking military objects relates to installations containing dangerous forces. According to article 56 (1) of API such works or installations—namely, dams, dykes, and nuclear power plants—or other military targets in the vicinity of such works or installations, may not be attacked 'if such attack may cause the release of dangerous forces and consequent severe losses among the civilian population'. This prohibition does not apply when the said works or installations are used in regular, significant, and direct support of military operations and the attack is the only feasible way to terminate such support (article 56 (2) of

---

[47] See Dinstein, *Conduct of Hostilities*, 87.

API). It is doubtful whether the prohibition itself is part of customary international law.[48]

Indiscriminate attacks

Immunity of civilians against attack is strengthened by a prohibition on indiscriminate attacks. According to article 51 (4) of API, indiscriminate attacks are

a. those which are not directed at a specific military objective;
b. those which employ a method or means of combat which cannot be directed at a specific military objective; or
c. those which employ a method or means of combat the effects of which cannot be limited as required by this Protocol; and consequently, in each such case, are of a nature to strike military objectives and civilians or civilian objects without distinction.

An attack which treats as a single military objective a number of clearly separated and distinct military objectives located in a location containing a similar concentration of civilians or civilian objects is also regarded as indiscriminate (article 51 (5) (a)).

Under the API test, use of certain weapons may be inherently illegal, even if it has not been specifically proscribed by treaty. This was one of the arguments raised against any use of nuclear weapons in the *Nuclear Weapons* case. The International Court of Justice refused to opine whether use of nuclear weapons would always be unlawful, although it emphasized that 'methods and means of warfare, which would preclude any distinction between civilian and military targets...are prohibited'.[49] This is now regarded as a norm of customary international law.[50]

While there may be weapons, such as nuclear bombs of the types dropped on Hiroshima or Nagasaki, whose use is inherently unlawful, absent specific treaty prohibitions, whether use of a particular weapon

---

[48] Ibid. 93–4; Christopher Greenwood, 'Customary Status of the 1977 Geneva Protocols', in Astrid J. M. Delissen and Gerard J. Tanja (eds.), *Humanitarian Law of Armed Conflict and Challenges Ahead: Essays in Honour of Frits Kalshoven* (Dordrecht, Boston, and London: Martinus Nijhoff Publishers, 1991), 95.

[49] ICJ, *Legality of the Threat or Use of Nuclear Weapons*, para. 95. In this case Judge Higgins was more explicit when she stated that 'a weapon will be unlawful *per se* if it is incapable of being targeted at a military objective': ibid., Separate Opinion of Judge Higgins, para. 92.

[50] *ICRC Study*, rule 71.

would be lawful will in most cases depend on the circumstances. If the particular circumstances do not allow for use of the weapon in a manner that discriminates between the lawful military target and civilian objects, its use will be unlawful.

Proportionality

In IHL proportionality addresses the issue discussed by philosophers as 'double effect' and by military spokesmen and others as 'collateral damage'. The principle is phrased in article 51 (5) (b) of API as a prohibition on targeting a legitimate military objective 'when the expected incidental loss of civilian life, injury to civilians, damage to civilian objects, or a combination thereof, would be excessive in relation to the concrete and direct military advantage anticipated'.

The centrality of the proportionality principle in *ius in bello* is beyond contention. How the principle is to be applied in practice is far less clear. As the special committee established by the Special Prosecutor of the ICTY to examine allegations of war crimes by the NATO forces in the Kosovo campaign noted:

It is much easier to formulate the principle of proportionality in general terms than it is to apply it to a particular set of circumstances because the comparison is often between unlike quantities and values. One cannot easily assess the value of innocent human lives as opposed to capturing a particular military objective.[51]

The principle of proportionality relates not only to cases in which harm to civilians or civilian objects is a possible consequence of attacking a military object, or a consequence which was not, but should have been, foreseen; it also covers cases in which commanders of the attacking force are perfectly aware that civilians will certainly be killed, or civilian objects damaged. Even in such cases the attack will be lawful if the civilian loss or damage is not excessive in relation to the concrete and direct military advantage anticipated. The implication is that civilian immunity in the law

---

[51] *Final Report to the Prosecutor by the Committee Established to Review the NATO Bombing Campaign Against the Federal Republic of Yugoslavia*, <http://www.un.org/icty/pressreal/nato061300.htm> (last accessed 10 Aug. 2005), para. 48.

of armed conflict is far from absolute: in some cases an attack may be undertaken even though the death or injury of civilians is a certain and inevitable outcome.[52] This is reflected, of course, in the way the principle of distinction is phrased in API: article 51 prohibits making civilians the object of an attack.

Some philosophers have challenged the acceptability of a principle which permits military action even when the death or injury of civilians is a certainty or near certainty.[53] In the law of armed conflict, however, based as it is on the need to find a fine balance between military necessity and humanitarian considerations, there seems little choice but to adopt this principle. A rule which made a military object an illegitimate target if the attacking commanders knew that civilians would be killed or injured in the attack would allow the enemy to acquire immunity for its military installations by placing them in residential areas, or by using human shields. Admittedly, such actions by the enemy would be unlawful, but the obligation to respect IHL does not depend on reciprocity.[54] A party to an armed conflict is not excused from 'playing according to the rules' because its adversary has broken them. Under article 51 (8) of API, violation of the obligation of one party not to use civilians to shield military objects or to impede military operations does not free its adversary of its obligations towards civilians, including respect for the principle of proportionality.[55]

There are two sides to the scale of proportionality. On the one side is the concrete and direct military advantage anticipated from the attack; on the other, the expected incidental loss of civilian life, injury to civilians, damage to civilian objects, or a combination thereof. It is only when the latter is excessive in relation to the former that the attack will be regarded as disproportionate.

It is obviously impossible to quantify the two sides of the scale. Nevertheless, a number of points merit emphasis. First, the test refers to the anticipated advantage and expected loss, thus making it clear that whether

---

[52] This theme is developed by Colm McKeogh in Chapter 3.

[53] See Colm McKeogh, *Innocent Civilians: The Morality of Killing in War* (Basingstoke: Palgrave, 2002), 169–73.

[54] *ICRC Study*, rule 140.

[55] It has been forcefully argued that placing the responsibility on the attacker, rather than on the defender who exposes the civilians to danger, is a departure from the accepted laws and customs of war: Parks, 'Air War', 173–9.

the test has been met must not be judged with the benefit of hindsight. What counts is the information that the commanders of the attacking force had, or should have had, when the attack took place. Second, it has sometimes been argued that causing extensive civilian damage is prohibited, whatever the military advantages may be.[56] There does not seem to be much support for this view. The question is always whether that loss or damage was excessive, in relation to the military advantage, and not whether it was extensive.[57] When the anticipated military advantage is great, extensive civilian loss and damage may not be excessive. Third, the API provision speaks of the concrete and direct military advantage anticipated. On ratifying or acceding to API, many states declared that they understood this to refer to the advantage anticipated from the attack considered as a whole, and not from isolated or particular parts of the attack. This idea is reflected in article 8 (2) (b) (iv) of the Rome Statute on the International Criminal Court (ICC). In defining the crime involved in launching a disproportionate attack, this article refers to the 'concrete and direct overall military advantage anticipated'. As mentioned above, violation by the adversary of its obligation to protect its own civilians does not free the other side's army of its obligations under IHL, including respect of the proportionality test. It has, nevertheless, been argued that in making the balance under this test, whether the defenders are deliberately exposing civilians or civilian objects to attack is one of the factors that may be taken into account.[58] One writer has even argued that civilians working in military objects, such as munitions factories, should not be included among the civilian losses calculated as part of the proportionality test.[59]

Precautions

Precautions in attack

Parties involved in an armed conflict are obliged to take measures of precaution so as to avoid harm to civilians and damage to civilian objects.

[56] *ICRC Commentary*, para. 1980.
[57] See Dinstein, *Conduct of Hostilities*, 121–2; Rogers, *Law on the Battlefield*, 21.
[58] See Rogers, *Law on the Battlefield*, 21–3.   [59] See Parks, 'Air War', 174–6.

First, there is a general obligation to take constant care in conduct of military operations to spare civilians and civilian objects. More specifically, according to article 57 of API, military commanders must take the following measures:

1. in planning an attack they must do everything feasible to verify that the objectives to be attacked are neither civilians nor civilian objects;
2. in the choice of means and methods of attack they must take all feasible precautions with a view to avoiding, and in any event to minimizing, incidental loss or civilian life, injury to civilians and damage to civilian objects;
3. they must refrain from deciding to launch any attack which would not be compatible with the principle of proportionality.

If it becomes apparent that the planned object of attack is not a military object, or that it will not be compatible with the principle of proportionality, the attack must be cancelled or suspended. This duty applies not only to the commanders in charge of the attack, but to those executing the attack too. Thus, for example, if a pilot who has been given an order to carry out an attack on a military target sees that in fact the target is a group of civilians, he is bound to refrain from attacking.

Article 57 (3) of API, states that 'when a choice is possible between several military objectives for obtaining a similar military advantage, the objective to be selected shall be that the attack on which may be expected to cause the least danger to civilian lives and to civilian objects'. Admittedly, this duty applies only when attacking the targets is expected to obtain a similar military advantage, a judgement which is often difficult to make in battle conditions. Nevertheless, inclusion of the duty in API serves to underline the importance placed on active precautions to avoid or minimize civilian losses.

The duty to take precautions has implications not only as regards choice of targets, but as regards choice of weapons, and even timing of attacks.[60] In modern-day warfare, with its high-precision weapons, it is incumbent on a party with such weapons at its disposal to choose them when use of other, less precise weapons would increase the risk of civilian casualties.[61] Some writers have even suggested that states with

---

[60] See Dinstein, *Conduct of Hostilities*, 126–8.   [61] See Rogers, *Law on the Battlefield*, 19.

more advanced weapons systems are duty-bound to employ them in
all circumstances. The problem with this approach is that it introduces an
element of legal discrimination between parties involved in armed conflicts.
Those with sophisticated weapons are bound to use them; those without
them (even if they could have acquired them, but chose not to do so) may
use other weapons.[62]

Choice of timing may be a crucial step that does much to avoid, or at least
minimize, civilian casualties. When use of sophisticated guided weapons
does not make accurate targeting of military objects possible, attacking at
night might not meet the demands of precaution. In other circumstances,
such as an attack on a munitions factory in which civilians work during
the day, attacking at night might limit civilian casualties. The Israel Air
Force attack on the Osiraq nuclear reactor in Iraq was carried out on a
Sunday when the expected number of civilian workers on the reactor site
would be minimal.[63] The Israeli government also claimed that its reason
for attacking the reactor long before it became operational was to avoid the
highly damaging release of radioactive substances that would have occurred
had the attack been carried out after the nuclear reactor was working.[64]

The duty of commanders to take precautions before attack requires them
to acquire adequate intelligence information on potential targets that will
allow them to assess both whether they are indeed military objects and
whether collateral damage to civilians or civilian objects is likely. While
commanders will often have to rely on information supplied to them by
intelligence sources, they cannot rely blindly on such information. If they
have doubts about the accuracy of the information, they must request
additional information.

One of the more problematical measures of precaution required of a
party is to give effective warning in advance of any attack which may
affect the civilian population. Such a warning could be incompatible with
the element of surprise that may be an essential ingredient of a military
operation. For this reason, article 57 (2) (c) of API qualifies the duty to
warn with the phrase 'unless circumstances do not permit'. This obviously
seriously weakens the warning obligation.

---

[62] See Dinstein, *Conduct of Hostilities*, 126–7.
[63] See Timothy L. H. McCormack, *Self-Defense in International Law: The Israeli Raid on the Iraqi Nuclear Reactor* (New York: St Martin's Press; Jerusalem: The Magnes Press, 1996), 109.
[64] Ibid. 105.

Precautions against the effects of attacks

GCIV relates only to protection of civilians of the enemy (or of states which do not have diplomatic relations with a belligerent state). It is not concerned with rules relating to the measures that a state involved in an armed conflict must take to protect its own civilians. This lacuna was rectified by API.

Article 51 (7) of API prohibits a party in an international armed conflict from using the presence or movements of the civilian population or individual civilians so as to render certain points or areas immune from military operations, in particular in attempts to shield military objectives from attacks or to shield, favour, or impede military operations. Parties may not use their own civilians, or those of the enemy, as human shields. Furthermore, parties must endeavour 'to the maximum extent feasible' to remove civilians and civilian objects under their control from the vicinity of military objectives and to avoid locating military objectives within or near densely populated areas. They must also take precautionary measures to protect civilians and civilian objects under their control from the dangers resulting from military operations. These provisions are strengthened by article 8 (2) (b) (xxiii) of the Rome Statute, which includes as a war crime '[u]tilizing the presence of a civilian or other protected person to render certain points, areas or military forces immune from military operations'.

Failure of a state to take measures to protect its own civilians never releases its adversary from its obligations towards civilians. By locating a munitions factory in a residential area, a state does not achieve immunity from attack for that factory. However, its adversary cannot simply ignore the existence of civilians in the vicinity when attacking the factory.[65] The factory remains a legitimate military target, but in deciding whether to mount an attack the attacking force will be bound by the principle of proportionality.

Occupied Territory

Territory is regarded as occupied under international law when it comes under the effective control of a hostile army. Such control implies denial of

---

[65] API, art. 51 (8).

the former regime's capability to exercise its powers in the territory. The occupying power is obliged to fill the gap. While it is still bound by all the norms regarding civilian immunity discussed above, the occupying power also acquires further 'governmental' duties towards the civilian population in the occupied territory. First and foremost amongst these is the duty to restore and ensure public safety and civil life, laid down in article 43 of the Hague Regulations.

GCIV contains a number of provisions that are highly relevant in ensuring the immunity of civilians in occupied territory from threats to their lives or other forms of abuse. Article 27 states:

Protected persons are entitled, in all circumstances, to respect for their persons, their honour, their family rights, their religious convictions and practices, and their manners and customs. They shall at all times be humanely treated, and shall be protected especially against all acts of violence or threats thereof and against insults and public curiosity.

Women shall be especially protected against any attack on their honour, in particular against rape, enforced prostitution, or any form of indecent assault.

Consistent with the status of an occupying power as the force with effective control over the occupied territory, article 27 goes much further than provisions relating to conduct of hostilities. Most of those provisions are negative in character: they prohibit certain types of acts which are likely to harm civilians. Article 27 obliges the occupying power not only to respect the listed fundamental rights of protected persons, but to actively protect them 'against all acts of violence or threats thereof and against insults and public curiosity'. The occupying power must ensure that its own forces do not violate the right to life and other rights of protected persons; it must also protect them against violence by other actors, whether state actors or private actors. If the occupied territory is attacked by another state, the occupying power is duty-bound to protect civilians there from the dangers of the attacks.

Alongside the general provision in article 27, GCIV contains more detailed specific provisions designed to ensure protection of the civilian population in occupied territory. Article 31 prohibits moral or physical coercion against protected persons, especially in order to obtain information from them or from third parties. Occupying forces are prohibited from taking any measure of such a character as to cause the physical suffering or extermination of protected persons in their hands (article 32). Protected persons may not be punished for offences they have not personally committed, and all measures of intimidation or terrorism are prohibited (article 33). Article 34 expressly prohibits reprisals against civilians in occupied territory.

Non-International Armed Conflicts

Armed conflicts not of an international nature are not subject to the detailed regulation to which international armed conflicts are subject under contemporary instruments of international law. Nevertheless, in the issues that concern us in this chapter, there would seem to be little difference between the norms relating to civilian immunity between international and non-international armed conflicts. Common Article 3 of GCIV expressly prohibits 'violence to life and person, in particular murder of all kinds, mutilation, cruel treatment and torture', as well as outrages on the dignity of persons not taking an active part in hostilities. Some of the provisions of API relating to civilian immunity appear in Additional Protocol II (APII), which applies to conflicts of a non-international character in which the non-state actors have control over part of the territory of the state 'as to enable them to carry out sustained and concerted military operations and to implement this Protocol'. Thus, article 13 (1) of APII prohibits making civilians who do not take a direct part in hostilities the object of attacks; article 13 (2) prohibits threats whose purpose is to spread terror among the civilian population; article 14 forbids starvation of civilians as a method of combat and destruction of objects indispensable for the survival of the civilian population. APII does not, however, contain provisions prohibiting attacks on civilian objects or indiscriminate attacks. Neither does it mandate measures of precaution or refer to the principle of proportionality. Notwithstanding these lacunae, the recent *ICRC Study* found that state practice accords to all these norms of conduct the status of customary international law in non-international armed conflicts.

The main problem in applying norms relating to civilian immunity in non-international armed conflicts is that in such conflicts there is no recognized status of combatants. Combatants are not defined, with the consequence that civilians are not defined either. Two opposing views exist on the implications of this lacuna. Some experts claim that there is simply no such thing as a combatant in non-international armed conflicts (at least as far as non-state actors are concerned); there are only civilians who take an active part in hostilities and those who don't. The opposing view is that use of the term 'civilians' in instruments dealing with non-international armed conflicts, such as APII and the Rome Statute, necessarily means that there must also be 'non-civilians', or combatants. While such persons do not enjoy the privileges enjoyed by combatants in international armed conflicts, for the purposes of attack they are to be regarded as combatants.

Both views are problematic. By denying the existence of combatants, the first view would seem to undermine the special protection enjoyed by civilians according to APII and implicit in the Rome Statute. If all persons are civilians, talk of civilian immunity is meaningless. The second view faces the problem of identification. In international armed conflicts, combatants must wear a fixed distinctive sign recognizable at a distance. As phrased in GCIII, this requirement seemingly applies only to armed groups and not to the armed forces of the state, but the view of most experts is that under customary international law it applies to armed forces too.[66] In the absence of provisions relating to combatants in non-international armed conflicts, there is obviously no such requirement, making it difficult for military forces of the state to distinguish between combatants and civilians, except when persons are actually fighting. If we draw the conclusion that persons are combatants only when taking part in fighting, we eliminate the difference between combatants and civilians, since the latter may also be attacked when they are taking an active part in hostilities.

Finally, it must be noted that while there is still some debate over the application of international human rights norms in all situations of international armed conflicts (especially in combat situations), there can be little doubt that a state's obligations under international human rights instruments continue to apply when there is an internal armed conflict in the state, subject always to the power of the state to derogate from some of these obligations. Application of these norms would seem to strengthen the protection afforded to civilians likely to be affected by the armed conflict. This should lead us to the conclusion that the norms relating to civilian

---

[66] See, e.g., Dinstein, *Conduct of Hostilities*, 36; Ingrid Detter, *The Law of War*, 2nd edn. (Cambridge: Cambridge University Press, 2000), 136. And cf. Cassese, *International Law*, 410.

immunity in non-international armed conflicts are at the very least as strong as those that apply in international conflicts.

Enforcement and Remedies

The primary responsibility for compliance with norms relating to civilian immunity rests on parties to armed conflicts. In the traditional case of international armed conflicts, this responsibility rests on the states involved in the conflict. They are responsible for acts committed by members of their armed forces, even if they were acting outside their authority and contrary to military orders. States have a duty to take measures to ensure compliance with IHL and to take appropriate action against those members of their armed forces who violate its norms.

In the field of HRL, there has been impressive progress in establishment of international institutions for monitoring compliance by states and granting remedies for violations, when the organs of the responsible state fail to do so. These institutions include the Human Rights Committee, the European Court of Human Rights, and the Inter-American Court of Human Rights. There has been no parallel development in the field of international humanitarian law. No institutionalized mechanism exists for monitoring state compliance with IHL and for granting a remedy to victims of IHL violations.

In some cases, acts which comprise violations of IHL norms may also constitute violations of a human rights treaty to which the particular state is a party, with the consequent jurisdiction of an international human rights court or treaty body to grant a remedy against the state involved. However, international human rights courts have at times refused to accept that alleged breaches of IHL carried out in the course of an international armed conflict could also involve breaches of human rights obligations subject to their jurisdiction. In the *Bankovic* case, family members of civilians who were killed in the NATO bombing of a television station in Belgrade during the NATO campaign over Kosovo tried to bring a case against the European members of NATO before the European Court of Human Rights. They argued that the attack had violated the victims' right to life, protected under article 2 of the European Convention of Fundamental Rights and Liberties. The Court dismissed the case for lack of jurisdiction, ruling that the persons killed were not in the jurisdiction of the defendant states at the time of the bombing and that, consequently, the European Convention did not apply to them.[67]

As opposed to mechanisms for providing remedies for violations of state responsibility, there have been dramatic developments in enforcement of personal liability for violations of IHL. These merit consideration.

It has always been accepted that severe violations of the law of armed conflict could result in criminal liability under the domestic law of the states involved. After World War I an attempt was made to establish a tribunal which would try members of the defeated German army for war crimes; but this did not get off the ground, and jurisdiction was left in the hands of the German legal system, which was responsible for holding the so-called Leipzig Trials. The breakthrough in internationalizing liability and jurisdiction for war crimes came after World War II, when the victorious powers established the Nuremberg and Tokyo tribunals to try members of the enemies' armies and political leadership for war crimes, crimes against humanity, and the crime of aggression. The guiding idea was that by committing particularly grave breaches of the law of armed conflict, the accused had incurred liability under international law, and that an international tribunal could try them for their crimes.

The 1949 Geneva Conventions classify violations of certain of their provisions as 'grave breaches'. States parties are obligated to enact legislation to provide effective penal sanctions against individuals who have committed such breaches, or ordered them to be committed. While the Conventions rely on domestic courts to try persons accused of grave breaches, they establish universal jurisdiction of these courts. States are obliged to search for persons alleged to have committed such breaches, irrespective of their nationality and whether or not there is a nexus between the crime and the particular jurisdiction. The underlying principle is *aut dedere aut judicare* (prosecute or extradite).

Following the atrocities perpetrated in the conflict in the former Yugoslavia, the UN Security Council established an *ad hoc* international criminal tribunal to try persons charged with committing war crimes, crimes against humanity, and acts of genocide there. A similar tribunal was later established to try persons accused of such crimes in Rwanda.

---

[67] *Bankovic and others* v. *Belgium* (2001), 11 BHRC 435.

In July 1998, the Rome Statute of the ICC was adopted, and the ICC came into being when the Statute entered into force four years later. As opposed to the *ad hoc* Yugoslavia and Rwanda tribunals, the ICC is a permanent international tribunal for trying persons charged with war crimes, crimes against humanity, acts of genocide, and aggression.

Violations of the norms relating to civilian immunity play a prominent part in the acts defined either as 'grave breaches' of the Geneva Conventions, or as 'war crimes' and 'crimes against humanity' in the Rome Statute. Under GCIV, wilful killing of civilians, their torture or inhuman treatment, including biological experiments, or wilfully causing them great suffering or serious injury to body or health, are all grave breaches. So is unlawful transfer or confinement of civilians. Individuals who commit grave breaches, or order them to be committed, are liable to criminal punishment. The Convention does not address rules of conduct towards civilians in combat situations, and does not deal with the principle of proportionality. Violation of this principle is therefore not listed as a grave breach. This gap was mended in API, which states expressly that launching an attack that does not conform to the proportionality principle is a grave breach of the Protocol, one that incurs criminal liability.

All grave breaches of the Geneva Conventions are recognized as war crimes under the Rome Statute. The Statute also adds the following as specific war crimes:

> intentionally directing attacks against the civilian population as such or against individual civilians not taking direct part in hostilities (article 8 (2) (b) (i));
> intentionally directing attacks against civilian objects, that is objects which are not military objectives (article 8 (2) (b) (ii));
> intentionally launching an attack in the knowledge that such an attack will cause incidental loss of life or injury to civilians or damage to civilian objects ... which would be clearly excessive in relation to the concrete and direct overall military advantage anticipated (article 8 (2) (b) (iv)).

International criminal jurisdiction for violations of IHL norms relating to civilian immunity does not cover all potential violations of norms pertaining to this immunity. The jurisdiction of the ICC is complementary jurisdiction. Primary jurisdiction lies in the hands of domestic courts of the parties involved in armed conflicts. It is only when the domestic courts are unwilling or unable to exercise jurisdiction that the ICC acquires jurisdiction. Furthermore, under the Rome Statute the jurisdiction of the ICC is 'limited to the most serious crimes of concern to the international community as a whole'. The Court has jurisdiction 'in respect of war crimes in particular when committed as part of a plan or policy or as part of a large-scale commission of such crimes'. The term 'in particular' leaves open the possibility of prosecuting a person before the ICC for an isolated grave breach of the Geneva Convention, such as the unlawful killing of one civilian, if that person's national courts are unwilling or unable to try him. However, such a crime would not necessarily be regarded as one of the most serious crimes of concern to the international community, and even if it were, it is highly unlikely that the jurisdiction of the ICC would be invoked. Even after establishment of the ICC, the vast majority of cases in which persons are alleged to have violated the rules of IHL relating to civilian immunity will remain solely in the hands of national legal systems.

Experience shows that states are not exactly over-zealous in prosecuting members of their own forces suspected of violations of IHL. Resort to universal jurisdiction by courts of uninvolved states is also rather rare. The result is a huge enforcement deficiency, which leads to wide-scale impunity for violators of civilian immunity. The main aim of establishing the ICC was to reduce the scale of impunity for war crimes and crimes against humanity, not only by bringing persons to trial before the ICC itself, but by creating an incentive for states to prosecute. It is still too early to know whether or not that aim will be achieved.

5

Civilian Immunity, Forcing the Choice, and Collective Responsibility

SEUMAS MILLER

In this chapter I explore the implications of notions of collective moral responsibility for civilian immunity in war. I do so in the context of a human rights-based just war theoretical account of the moral justification for waging war. Specifically, I argue that there are two neglected categories of civilians that ought not to enjoy civilian immunity in war. The first category consists of the members of civilian groups who have a share in the collective moral responsibility for non-life-threatening rights violations, yet are not morally responsible for the *enforcement* of these rights violations. Such persons are neither combatants nor their leaders; nor do they necessarily assist combatants *qua* combatants, as do, for example, munitions workers. The second category consists of members of civilian groups who are collectively morally responsible for culpably refraining from assisting those who have a moral right to assistance from them. Once again, such persons are neither combatants nor their leaders; nor do they necessarily assist combatants *qua* combatants. Note that these two categories overlap in so far as there are members of civilian groups who are guilty of certain non-life-threatening rights violations by virtue of culpably refraining from assisting the rights-bearers in question.

In the first section of the chapter I consider the moral justification for the killing of human beings in the context of a rights-based account of the just war; in the second section, the conditions under which waging war is morally justified. In the third and fourth sections my concern is with (respectively) non–life-threatening rights violators and culpable non–attackers.

Moral Justification for the Use of Deadly Force

In relation to moral rights, two distinctions are salient here. Human rights can be distinguished from institutional rights, and negative rights from positive rights. Human rights, as opposed to institutional rights, are rights possessed by virtue of properties one has *qua* human being.[1] So the right to life is a human right. By contrast, the moral (and legal) right that a police officer might have to arrest an offender is an institutional right. Negative rights are rights that one has not to be interfered with by others. So the rights not to be killed and not to have one's freedom restricted are negative rights. By contrast, the right to have sufficient food to keep one alive is a positive right; it is a right to assistance from others, if such assistance is required and can be provided.

As is well known, both of these distinctions are problematic in various ways. Indeed, the very notion of a moral right is itself problematic. Nevertheless, for the purposes of this chapter, I am going to assume that there are human rights, and that these rights include at least some of the ones typically referred to as positive rights.

Moreover, I am also assuming the following properties of human rights. Human rights generate concomitant duties for others: e.g., A's right to life generates a duty on the part of B not to kill A. And human rights are justifiably enforceable: e.g., if A has a right not to be killed by B, and if B attempts to kill A, then B can legitimately be prevented from killing A by means of coercive force, including, if necessary, the use of deadly force.

While there is an enforceable human right to life, killing another person can be morally justified only in very restricted circumstances. The basic such circumstance is that of self-defence.[2] However, self-defence is not the only justification for taking the life of another person. It is widely accepted that each of us has the right to kill in defence of the lives of others. I am

---

[1] For one recent account of human rights that is consistent with the view on offer here see James Griffin, 'First Steps in an Account of Human Rights', *European Journal of Philosophy*, 9 (2001), 306–27.

[2] See my 'Killing in Self-defence', *Public Affairs Quarterly*, 7 (1993), 325–40.

morally entitled to kill someone attempting to kill my spouse if this is the only means of prevention.

Indeed, some roles such as that of police officer or soldier are such that the occupant of the role might be morally *obliged* to kill in the defence of the lives of others. Here the moral rights and duties constitutive of the role are derived in large part from the moral point or end of the role—e.g., to protect the lives of citizens of the state in question. Note that any such end is itself subject to moral scrutiny and evaluation. If the end in question—or its pursuit in some context—turns out to be morally unacceptable, then the putative rights and duties derived from it may not in fact be *moral* rights and duties; or at least, may not be so in that context. So soldiers engaged in a war of conquest on behalf of a psychopathic authoritarian leadership might cease to have a right to kill enemy soldiers, or an obligation to protect their current leaders. Such was the case with Hitler in the World War II.

Elsewhere I have argued that killing in order to defend one's own life, or the life of another, is morally justified on the grounds that each of us has a right to life, and (under certain conditions) attackers forfeit their right to life (or, at least, their right is suspended). We are entitled to defend that right to life by killing an attacker under three conditions.[3] First, the attacker is intentionally trying to kill someone—either oneself or another person—and will succeed if we do not intervene. We are not entitled to shoot dead an attacker whom we know is threatening us only with (say) a replica of a gun. Secondly, we have no way of preserving our own or the other person's life other than by killing the attacker. For example, we are not able to flee to safety. Thirdly, and more problematically, our attacker does not have a decisive, morally justifiable reason for trying to kill. For example, it may be that a legally appointed executioner has a decisive, morally justifiable reason for carrying out the death penalty in the case of a serial killer, but that the serial killer does not have a decisive, morally justifiable reason for trying to kill the executioner in self-defence supposing the opportunity arises.

Having outlined an account of killing in self-defence or in defence of the life of others, let me now consider a different, or at least expanded,

[3] J. J. Thomson offers a more restricted set of conditions for justified killing in self-defence. See her 'Self-defense', *Philosophy and Public Affairs*, 20 (1991), 283–310. For criticisms, see my 'Judith Jarvis Thomson on Killing in Self-defence', *Australian Journal of Professional and Applied Ethics*, 3 (2001), 69–75.

kind of moral justification for killing: namely, killing in defence of rights other than the right to life.

In speaking of killing in defence of rights other than the right to life, one would obviously not want to include *all* moral rights, or at least *all violations* of all moral rights. For example, property rights are arguably moral rights, but for (say) a police officer to kill someone to prevent them stealing a handbag would be morally unacceptable. So the question becomes: 'Are there any moral rights, apart from the right to life, the protection of which would justify the use of deadly force?' Candidates for such rights might include a right not to be severely physically or psychologically damaged. Perhaps rape, serious child molestation, and grievous bodily harm are actions the prevention of which might justify use of deadly force. Candidates would also include the right to various freedoms, including freedom of thought and freedom of individual and—especially in the context of war—freedom of *collective* action, e.g., national self-government.

What of positive rights? Henry Shue has argued for the existence of what he terms 'basic moral rights'.[4] Such basic moral rights are not restricted to so-called negative rights; rather, they include some so-called positive rights, such as the right to subsistence. Moreover, these positive rights include ones that go beyond the right to life. For example, a person has a positive right not to live in a permanent condition of serious malnutrition or debilitating disease, if these conditions are alterable. Accordingly, deadly force might be justified in some circumstances in which someone is refraining from providing for the basic material needs of someone else.[5]

Let us now consider a simple example to test our intuitions for the claim that sometimes the use of deadly force to enforce positive rights is morally justified.

Consider a destitute African person who is dying of HIV AIDS, and who goes to a pharmaceutical company demanding drugs to enable him to live. Assume further that the pharmaceutical company is a state-subsidized entity, which is subsidized because it has as one of its clearly stated institutional purposes to provide cheap life-preserving drugs to the needy,

---

[4] Henry Shue, *Basic Rights* (Princeton: Princeton University Press, 1996).

[5] This claim is not be confused with the familiar claim and counter-claim as to whether there is or is not any moral difference between acts and omissions; nor should it be confused with the claim and counter-claim as to whether killing and letting die stand to one another as harming and not aiding in cases in which less than life is at stake.

albeit within the parameters of commercial viability. When the AIDS sufferer is refused the drugs, on the grounds that he must pay for the drugs a high price—rather than an affordable lower price—he threatens to kill one by one the owner-managers of the company responsible for the high price, unless and until he is provided with the drug at an affordable price. Assume further that although the owner-managers know that it would be commercially viable to sell the drug at the affordable lower price, they engage in the corrupt practice of selling it at the high price in order to ensure the resulting enormous profits for themselves. Assume, too, that providing this AIDS sufferer with the drugs would not be at the expense of some other (more affluent) AIDS sufferer.

Intuitively, the AIDS sufferer's action seems morally justified, given that this action was the only way to preserve his life, since in this corrupt society there is no legal means of ensuring that the company meets its obligations. For he had a positive right to be assisted, and the 'bystander' (or, rather, 'bystanders', but to simplify I will use the singular) was refraining from carrying out his institutional and moral duty to respect that right. Moreover, the 'bystander' is forcing the choice between two evils: if he handed over the drugs, no lives would be lost; but by refusing to do so, he is forcing the AIDS sufferer to choose between the life of the 'bystander' and his own life.[6]

By 'forcing the choice' I do not mean to imply that the bystander caused the threat to the AIDS sufferer's life; in my example he did not. Nevertheless, the 'bystander' has freely undertaken an institutional role in the state-subsidized company to assist AIDS sufferers, and in effect is paid a salary to do so. He has thereby intentionally put himself under an institutional obligation to assist, and therefore the AIDS sufferer has a reasonable expectation that he will be assisted. Moreover, given the threat to the life of the AIDS sufferer, this institutional obligation is also a weighty moral obligation; so the 'bystander' has put himself under a weighty moral obligation to assist. Indeed, the AIDS sufferer now has a moral right to be assisted. Further, there are no countervailing moral reasons for the 'bystander' not to assist; his only reason for not doing so is greed.

---

[6] See Philip Montague, 'Self-defense and Choosing between Lives', *Philosophical Studies*, 40 (1981), 207–19; my 'Killing in Self-defence' and my 'Self-defense and Forcing the Choice between Lives', *Journal of Applied Philosophy*, 9 (1992), 239–45.

Given that the 'bystander' has intentionally put himself under this weighty moral obligation to assist the AIDS sufferer, and is nevertheless refusing to discharge his obligation, the 'bystander' has intentionally eliminated the morally preferable option that the AIDS sufferer both had a moral right to, and would have chosen if it had been available (as he had good reason to expect it would be). Therefore, the 'bystander' is morally responsible for the fact that the AIDS sufferer has now to choose either to allow himself to die or else to kill, or threaten to kill, the 'bystander'. In short, the 'bystander', by culpably eliminating the morally preferable option, is forcing the AIDS sufferer to choose between two morally undesirable options.

Now assume that the AIDS sufferer chooses to kill, or threaten to kill, the 'bystander', rather than allow himself to die. In choosing to preserve his life over that of the 'bystander', the AIDS sufferer can point to a morally relevant difference: viz., the 'bystander' is the one forcing the choice between lives; but for the 'bystander's' refusal to act, both agents would live. The fact that the 'bystander' is forcing the choice between lives constitutes the moral justification for the AIDS sufferer killing the bystander.

This notion of forcing the choice functions as a moral justification for the AIDS sufferer's action by virtue of the 'bystander' being partially and indirectly responsible for his own death. For the 'bystander' partially caused the AIDS sufferer to act as he did, in the sense that he culpably forced the choice between lives, and thereby not only brought it about that the AIDS sufferer had to choose between their two lives, but also gave a moral discount to his own life. So the 'bystander' both created the choice of options confronting the AIDS sufferer, and provided the moral reason for the AIDS sufferer to choose one over the other. In this sense—and notwithstanding that the AIDS sufferer was directly responsible for the death of the 'bystander'—the 'bystander' was partially and indirectly responsible for his own death.

Evidently, this kind of case involving the AIDS sufferer is analogous to cases involving negative rights, such as the right not to be killed or the right not to have one's freedom interfered with. Moreover, the AIDS sufferer's action would be morally justified in some cases in which less than life was at stake. This would be so, for example, if the AIDS sufferer could live without the drugs, but would live a life of intolerable suffering as a consequence of his affliction.

So deadly force can be used, at least in principle, to enforce some positive rights, including, presumably, rights to subsistence, as well as to enforce negative rights, such as freedom or the right not to be killed.

Here I am assuming the usual principles of proportionate and minimally necessary force; deadly force should be used only as a last resort, and loss of life kept to a minimum. So if, for example, the AIDS sufferer could cause the government to intervene on his behalf, or cause the managers to hand over the drug by mere threats, then he should do so.

Moreover, as is the case with negative rights, third parties—at least in principle—have rights, and indeed duties, to use deadly force to ensure that positive rights such as subsistence rights are respected.

Consider a modified version of the above HIV AIDS scenario. In this modified version the AIDS sufferer is a young African boy dying in his bed, and it is his father who threatens the pharmaceutical managers with deadly force—indeed, he kills one of the owner-managers to get the drugs to save his son. Moreover, the father's action would be morally justified in some cases in which less than life was at stake. This would be so if—as in the previous version of this scenario—the AIDS sufferer could live without the drugs, but would live a life of intolerable suffering as a consequence of his affliction.

I conclude that under some conditions third parties might be morally entitled to use deadly force to enforce duties to assist. Let us now turn to the question of the moral justification for waging war.[7]

Just Wars

I am not restricting the use of the term 'war' to wars between nation-states. Wars waged by non-state agents, such as revolutionary wars and even wars against a state, or a number of states, waged by terrorist organizations, such as al-Qaeda, might count as wars. However, I am assuming that wars are waged by corporate entities that are also political entities. So 'wars' between rival criminal organizations, or the 'war' on drugs are not wars in this sense. Moreover, I am also assuming that the relevant

---

[7] See Michael Walzer, *Just and Unjust Wars: A Moral Argument with Historical Illustrations* (New York: Basic Books, 1977).

actions of corporate entities can be explicated in individualist terms. Here I note my own analysis of corporate actions in terms of the notion of a layered structure of jointly performed actions.[8] (See next section.) The account I favour is as follows.[9] Note also that I am providing only a (rough approximation) of a *sufficient* condition for waging war. (Each of these conditions is a necessary part of the sufficient condition. I am not claiming that each of these conditions is a necessary condition for waging war *tout court*.)

Corporate entity[10] A—e.g., a nation-state—is morally entitled (though not necessarily morally obliged) to wage war against corporate entity B—e.g., a second nation-state—if (though not *only if*):

1. B is attacking, or is about to attack, A, or B is otherwise engaged in widespread and serious violation of the human rights of members of A.

2. A wages war in self-defence, or to the end of bringing about the cessation of B's violation of members of A's human rights.

3. A has a reasonable chance of defending itself and/or ending these violations by waging war.

4. It is probable that if A wages war, the consequences, all things considered (in terms of human rights violations and the ability to exercise rights), will be better than if A does not.

5. There is no alternative non-violent method by means of which A could defend itself and/or prevent B's violation of A's rights, and do so within a reasonable period of time and without incurring an unreasonable cost to those deploying these non-violent methods (and to their supporters and any neutral or innocent parties).

6. A only uses an extent of violence that is necessary and proportionate to the end(s) in question.

7. A directs violence only at rights-violators (and those who assist rights-violators *qua* rights-violators), and only uses types and a degree of

violence that are morally appropriate and proportionate to the actions of those rights-violators.

Consistent with the opening section of this chapter, the notion of human rights in use here includes not only so-called negative rights, such as the right not to be killed or to have one's freedom restricted, but also some so-called positive rights, notably, subsistence rights. Recall too that I am assuming that human rights are enforceable; that is, it is in principle justifiable to use coercion, and indeed deadly force, to ensure that human rights are respected.

Notice that the above definition says nothing about the legitimacy of the leadership of A. Here I prefer to sidestep this difficult issue—especially in the context of revolutionary wars and the like—by simply speaking of the conditions under which corporate entity A is justified in engaging in war.

Notice also that the above definition is couched in terms of self-defence; it says nothing explicitly about the right of third parties to intervene on behalf of persons whose human rights are being violated. By 'third parties' I mean here other nation-states, or at least other political corporate entities.

However, since the wars in question are fought by corporate entities that comprise in part a civilian population, it is implicit in the above definition that some individuals are, at least in part, acting as third parties, or at least acting in order to protect others. I take it that in a just war of self-defence combatants use deadly force to protect the human rights of the civilians of the state that they are defending. As such, combatants are third parties. Moreover, they are third parties who have an institutional role responsibility to defend the rights of others. Naturally, it is also true that combatants in such a war are also protecting their own human rights, including their right to life.

Moreover, I support the view that war is under certain conditions—e.g., humanitarian intervention—justifiably waged by third parties in the sense of political corporate entities. However, this issue is not my concern here.

I am advocating a human rights-based conception of the justification for waging war. However, such a human rights-based conception is not necessarily inconsistent with a relatively restricted conception of the role of a combatant. In particular, it is consistent with a conception according to which a soldier's first duty is to the citizens of the state to which he or she belongs; the duty consists in the protection of *the human rights of the citizens of his or her own state.* Indeed, this conception of the role of a combatant is in an important respect narrower than the implicit, and sometimes explicit, role conception often envisaged by governments, in particular: namely, that the role of the soldier is to use deadly force, or the threat thereof, in the *interest* of the nation-state, or other political corporate entity. I reject the view that nation-states are entitled to go to war simply to protect their interests, given that the interests in question do not essentially (directly or indirectly) consist in the protection of the human rights of their citizens.

Notice further that the above definition makes the requirement that only morally legitimate methods of waging war be used (*jus in bello*) one of the conditions for engaging in war (*jus ad bellum*).[11]

Moreover, *contra* the standard legalist paradigm associated with Walzer,[12] it also seems to me that if a war is unjust by virtue of failing a *jus ad bellum* condition(s), then this has implications for the morality of the actions of the combatants fighting this unjust war. Specifically, soldiers fighting an unjust war ought not to be killing anyone.[13] So there is a clear moral difference between soldiers fighting a just war and the aggressors that they are fighting.

In the relevant kinds of case, there are only *two* options confronting the leaders and combatants who are about to wage a just war: either wage war or permit human rights violations. Moreover, the fact that these are the only options is due to the aggressor state (or other political corporate entity); the aggressor is forcing the choice between two evils.[14] For the aggressor is in effect ruling out a third option—the morally preferable option—namely, the aggressor's cessation of the rights violations (or threat thereof) or cessation of hostilities (or peaceful surrender). That is, the aggressor rights-violator is not only culpable in relation to the rights violations the aggressor is also culpable in virtue of attempting to prevent the defender from performing its duty to prevent these rights violations; and indeed, the aggressor is morally responsible for forcing the defender to choose between the two evils. This being so, as we saw earlier, there

---

[11] C. A. J. Coady, 'The Leaders and the Led: Problems of Just War Theory', *Inquiry*, 23 (1980), 286.
[12] Walzer, *Just and Unjust Wars*.
[13] Igor Primoratz, 'Michael Walzer's Just War Theory: Some Issues of Responsibility', *Ethical Theory and Moral Practice*, 5 (2002), 221–43.
[14] See Montague, 'Self-defense and Choosing between Lives', and my 'Killing in Self-defence' and 'Self-defense and Forcing the Choice between Lives'.

is a sense in which the aggressor is *indirectly and in part* responsible for the suffering the aggressor receives at the hands of the defender.

The above claims regarding the difference in moral status of combatants fighting a just war and those fighting an unjust war is consistent with it being the case that the lethal actions of the combatants fighting an unjust war might be excusable in the light of, for example, their reasonable, albeit false, belief that they are in fact fighting a just war.

This difference in moral status between combatants fighting a just war and those fighting an unjust war is also consistent with there being important moral differences between different cohorts of combatants fighting an unjust war. Clearly, combatants fighting an unjust war who respect civilian immunity and, for example, do not torture enemy combatants have a higher moral status—other things being equal—than combatants fighting an unjust war who do not respect civilian immunity and who follow the practice of torturing enemy combatants. The existence of this moral difference is sufficient to demonstrate, if it needed demonstration, that the moral (un)acceptability of actions within a war is not fully determined by the justice of the war conceived exclusively in terms of considerations of *jus ad bellum*—i.e., excluding *jus in bello* considerations.

At any rate, given my stance on these issues, it is appropriate simply to build the *jus in bello* requirement into the definition of *jus ad bellum*, as I have done.

Having provided an account of the general conditions under which the use of deadly force is morally justified, and (more specifically) of one, complex, sufficient condition—including as constituent conditions the *jus in bello* conditions—under which war is morally justified, let me now turn directly and in detail to two categories of civilians that I will argue ought not in fact to enjoy immunity in war.[15]

Civilian Immunity and Human Rights Violations

In this section I want to explore the moral notion of civilian immunity in relation to the category of civilians who are morally responsible for

---

[15] See J. G. Murphy, 'The Killing of the Innocent', *Monist*, 57 (1973), and G. Palmer-Fernandez, 'Civilian Populations in War, Targeting of', in R. Chadwick (ed.), *Encyclopedia of Applied Ethics* (New York: Academic Press, 1998), i. 509–25.

the rights violations that in large part justify the waging of war. The specific category I want to focus on is the category of non-life-threatening rights violations. In the section following this one, I turn to a category of civilians who are culpable, but who are not morally responsible for *actions* that constitute rights violations; their sins are sins of omission rather than commission. It will turn out that these two categories overlap in so far as there are members of civilian groups who are guilty of certain non-life-threatening rights violations by virtue of culpably refraining from assisting the rights-bearers in question. However, for ease of exposition, my focus in this section will be on rights violations that are acts, as opposed to omissions.

In a just war, enemy *combatants* can be legitimate targets on at least two grounds. First, they might be a subset of the *rights-violators* in respect of whom the war is being fought. This would be the case in a war of self-defence against an enemy hell-bent on genocide: e.g., the largely Tutsi army fighting against the Hutu army and its militias in Rwanda in 1996.[16]

Secondly, enemy combatants are legitimate targets if they are attempting to *enforce* a policy of rights violations. For example, the government in apartheid South Africa embarked on a policy of removal of so-called black spots: that is, moving black people out of designated white areas into impoverished black 'homelands'.[17] This policy was a form of so-called racial or ethnic cleansing, and as such was a violation of human rights.[18] However, the role of police and military personnel was one of enforcement of the policy; the policy *in itself* did not necessarily consist of the use of coercive or deadly force. For it is conceivable that such a policy could have been implemented by some means other than coercive force—e.g., by fraud.

Accordingly, on the above outlined rights-based theoretical account of the just war, civilians—as opposed to combatants—are legitimate targets, if (but not necessarily only if): (a) they are morally responsible for *the human rights violations*, or threatened rights violations, that justify the waging of

---

[16] See Fergal Keane, *Season of Blood: A Rwandan Journey* (London: Viking, 1995).
[17] F. Wilson and M. Ramphele, *Uprooting Poverty: The South African Challenge* (Cape Town: University of Cape Town Press, 1988).
[18] The policy did not necessarily, or in fact, involve large-scale murder of the persons being removed, as happened in, e.g., Bosnia in the days of Milošević and his Bosnian Serb allies.

war, and/or (b) they are morally responsible for the *enforcement* of rights violations.

Such civilians would include politicians, or other non-military leaders, who are responsible for the rights violations, or the enforcement thereof, in the sense that in the context of a chain of command they were the relevant *authority* that directed that the human rights violations be carried out, or that they be enforced.[19] Such civilians would also include persons who, while not necessarily part of any formal chain of command, nevertheless were responsible for the rights violations (or the enforcement thereof) in that they planned them, and saw to it that other persons performed the rights violations (or the enforcement thereof). Here, the latter are instruments, but not necessarily subordinates, of the former. The former are the principal agents without necessarily being in authority. For example, an ethnic leader might pay an army of mercenaries to engage in ethnic cleansing without being in a relation of authority to the mercenaries.

I take it that civilians who belong to either of the above resulting four categories (authorities or other principal agents of the rights violations, or of the enforcement of the rights violations) are—at least in principle—legitimate targets.

Thus far I have distinguished between rights violations and the enforcement of rights violations. Moreover, earlier I distinguished between positive rights and negative rights, and between life-threatening rights violations and non-life-threatening rights violations.[20] Some violations of negative rights, such as the right to freedom, might not be life-threatening. And some violations of positive rights, such as the right to subsistence, might be life-threatening.

It is easy to see why the use of deadly force in response to life-threatening rights violations might be morally justified. However, the use of deadly force in response to non-life-threatening rights violations is more problematic—especially when such use of deadly force is on a scale properly describable as engaging in war. For it is typically assumed that life is more important than other goods to which people have rights. So it

[19] Murphy, 'Killing of the Innocent', 532 f.

[20] Elsewhere I have used a somewhat wider notion than that of life-threatening rights violations: viz., rights violations that constitute the destruction, or threaten the destruction, of the self: e.g., torturing someone to the point that they lose their mind but remain alive. This wider notion is actually the one I need here, but for purposes of simplification I will talk in terms of life-threatening rights violations.

is harder to justify the use of deadly force in relation to non-life-threatening rights violations than it is in relation to the violation of life-threatening rights violations.

Accordingly, I will now address the question of the legitimacy of directing deadly force at a particular class of civilians: namely, persons responsible for non-life-threatening rights violations. So I am not speaking of persons responsible for life-threatening rights violations. Nor am I speaking of persons responsible for *enforcing* non-life-threatening rights violations (or for enforcing life-threatening rights violations).

The use of deadly force against persons responsible for life-threatening rights violations is typically self-defence or defence of the lives of others. (And in the case of life-threatening rights violations that are violations of positive rights, it is self-preservation, or preservation of the lives of others.) But what of the use of deadly force in response to non-life-threatening rights violations?

The use of deadly force in response to those who are *enforcing* non-life-threatening rights violations seems straightforward enough. For such enforcers are themselves using, or are threatening to use, deadly force in response to any attempt on the part of those whose rights are being violated to escape their fate. So the morally unjustified use of deadly force is being met with deadly force. This is not killing in self-defence; rather, it is killing in defence of rights other than the right to life. Nevertheless, it is the use of deadly force against combatants—combatants seeking to enforce non-life-threatening rights violations. And I take it that often in wars of conquest combatants fighting on behalf of the aggressor nation-state are seeking to enforce non-life-threatening rights violations, such as violations of the right to freedom—e.g., the right to freely perform various forms of collective political action. Accordingly, were the members of the state (whose rights to free collective action are under threat) to cease to resist, then their lives would cease to be at risk.

At any rate, the use of deadly force against such combatants seems justified on the basis of the accumulated moral weight of three considerations: (1) the deadly force is used in order to bring about the cessation of non-life-threatening rights violations, or the removal of the threat thereof, e.g., national self-determination; (2) the deadly force is used in response to the morally unjustified use of deadly force by the would-be enforcers of these non-life-threatening rights violations; (3) the would-be enforcers of these non-life-threatening rights violations are the ones forcing the choice between the two evils of waging war or permitting serious and widespread rights violations.

Moreover, in the light of our earlier discussion, the use of deadly force against civilians who have authority over such combatants enforcing rights violations, or with respect to whom the combatants are instruments, also seems morally justifiable, at least in principle.

However, this does not settle the question of whether it would be morally justifiable to use deadly force against civilians who are responsible for non-life-threatening rights violations, yet are not responsible for the enforcement of these rights violations. Consider in this connection public officials who plan and administer a policy of forced removals (racial or ethnic cleansing), but who might not have any role or authority in relation to the enforcement of the policy. Are such officials legitimate targets?

Here it is important to distinguish types of case. The typical situation involves the existence of some *collective end*:[21] e.g., the removal of people from their homes to an impoverished tract of land, or the occupancy and control of some other nation-state.

Ends such as the removal of people from their homes to an impoverished tract of land, or the occupancy and control of some other nation-state, are collective ends, since their realization requires a large number of different individual persons to perform distinct tasks in the service of a common end—indeed, to occupy a variety of different institutional roles in the service of a common end. There are planners, administrators, enforcers (combatants), leaders, and so on, engaged in a collective project: e.g., to dispossess a people, or to win a war of conquest. Given that the collective end in question constitutes a violation of rights (albeit a non-life-threatening rights violation), the participants in this collective project are morally culpable; they are collectively morally responsible for wrongdoing.

As is the case with individual responsibility, we can distinguish three senses of *collective* responsibility. I do so in relation to *joint* actions.

Roughly speaking, two or more individuals perform a joint action if each of them intentionally performs an individual action, but does so with the true belief that in so doing they will jointly realize an end which each of them has—i.e., a collective end in the sense defined above.

---

[21] In my *Social Action*, ch. 2, I offer an account of the notion of a collective end.

Agents who perform a joint action are responsible for that action in the first sense of collective responsibility: viz., *natural* (collective) responsibility. Accordingly, to say that they are collectively responsible for the action is just to say that they performed the joint action. That is, they each had a collective end, each intentionally performed their contributory action, and each did so because each believed the other would perform his contributory action, and that therefore the collective end would be realized.

If the occupants of an institutional role (or roles) have an institutionally determined obligation to perform some joint action, then those individuals are collectively responsible for its performance, in our second sense of collective responsibility. Here there is a *joint* institutional obligation to realize the collective end of the joint action in question. In addition, there is a set of derived *individual* obligations; each of the participating individuals has an individual obligation to perform his or her contributory action. (The derivation of these individual obligations relies on the fact that if each performs his or her contributory action, then it is probable that the collective end will be realized.)

What of the third, target sense of collective responsibility, collective *moral* responsibility? Collective moral responsibility for outcomes which are intended, or otherwise aimed at, is a species of joint responsibility. Accordingly, each agent is individually morally responsible, but conditionally on the others being individually morally responsible; and this interdependence in respect of moral responsibility exists because the action of each is performed in the service of a collective end. This account of one central kind of collective moral responsibility arises naturally out of the account of joint actions. It also parallels the notion of individual moral responsibility.

Thus we can make the following claim about moral responsibility:

If agents are collectively—naturally or institutionally—responsible for the realization of an outcome, and if the outcome is morally significant, then—other things being equal—the agents are collectively morally responsible for that outcome, and can reasonably attract moral praise or blame, and (possibly) punishment or reward for bringing about the outcome.

Here we need to be more precise about what agents who perform morally significant joint actions are collectively morally responsible for. Other things being equal, each agent who intentionally performs a morally significant *individual* action has *individual* moral responsibility for the action. So in the case of a morally significant joint action, each agent is *individually* morally responsible for performing *his contributory* action, and the *other* agents are *not* morally responsible for his individual contributory action. But, in addition, the contributing agents are *collectively* morally responsible for the outcome or *collective end* of their various contributory actions. To say that they are collectively morally responsible for bringing about this (collective) end is just to say that they are *jointly* morally responsible for it. So each agent is individually morally responsible for realizing this (collective) end, but conditionally on the others being individually morally responsible for realizing it as well.[22] Actually, the picture is more complicated than this, since each individual (say) enforcer is jointly morally responsible for a proximate collective end (say, winning a particular naval battle), which end is a means to the ultimate collective end (say, winning the war as such).

In many cases, enforcement is not only a means to a collective end—to the violation of non-life-threatening rights—it is integral to that end. This is obviously the case in wars of conquest. But it is also the case in our South African forcible removal example. The policy of the elimination of black spots in apartheid South Africa was a policy that in part consisted of enforcement: i.e., of use of force, or the threat thereof. Therefore, non-enforcers such as public officials who planned and administered this policy are not only morally responsible (jointly with others) for the non-life-threatening rights violations; they are also morally responsible (jointly with the enforcers) for the use of force. To this extent, they are analogous to military planners in respect of a war of conquest. Naturally, the degree of moral responsibility may differ. For example, combatants might have a greater share of the collective responsibility than those who merely assist combatants *qua* combatants—e.g., munitions workers.

However, arguably, there are cases in which enforcement is not integral to the collective end that consists of a non-life-threatening rights violation. Consider a variation on our forcible removal example. In our new scenario blacks in apartheid South Africa are falsely told that they are being

---

[22] So I am suggesting that *collective* moral responsibility can be understood in these cases as *joint* moral responsibility. I argue for this in my *Social Action*, ch. 8.

transported to a land of freedom and material well-being, when in fact they are going to an impoverished 'homeland'. Assume further that when some groups of blacks disbelieve these claims, they are forcibly made to board the transport vehicles; indeed, deadly force is used on a number of occasions. However, enforcement is used only as a supplement to fraud. Now suppose the civilians who planned this policy of removal to 'homelands' by fraud did not envisage or believe that deadly force would be, or was being, used; and nor did the civilians who organized and timetabled the transport. So in post-apartheid South Africa these civilians claim that whereas they have a share in the collective moral responsibility for violating the rights of the blacks, including their property rights, they are in no way responsible for the use of deadly force that took place from time to time to further this collective end. In short, they acknowledge their guilt in relation to perpetrating non-life-threatening rights violations, but deny that they were guilty of enforcing these violations (and deny, therefore, any guilt in relation to life-threatening rights violations). Their claim seems reasonable.

The upshot of this discussion is that there may well be civilian groups who have a share in the collective moral responsibility for the non-life-threatening rights violations without necessarily being in any strong sense morally responsible for the enforcement of these rights violations. Such civilians would not have a moral right to immunity in war, as would be the case if they were innocent civilians—i.e., civilians who did not perform actions that either consisted of rights violations (or the enforcement thereof) or that assisted rights-violators *qua* rights-violators (or enforcers thereof).

Notwithstanding their lack of a *right* to immunity, these civilians might be expected to enjoy a degree of immunity not possessed by combatants. For the argument in favour of using deadly force against these civilians has less moral weight than it has in the case of others—especially combatants—who are not only collectively responsible for the non-life-threatening rights violations, but also for the enforcement thereof. Accordingly, other things being equal, such civilians might be expected to enjoy civilian immunity in *some* wars—e.g., ones in which it was not necessary to target both combatants and civilian rights-violators who were not enforcers.

In this section I have not considered a whole raft of familiar arguments relevant to the issue of civilian immunity. Let me simply note that there may be other grounds, such as consequentialist or contractarian grounds, for restricting the use of deadly force against civilians.[23] For example, conventions may have been set in place to prohibit the use of deadly force against civilian administrative personnel, and the abandonment of these conventions may bring about a situation which is morally worse, all things considered, than respecting them. Or the policy of violence may lead to counter-violence and a general escalation in violence which is less morally acceptable than the state of affairs in which legitimate targets were left unharmed. Nevertheless, there may be situations in which directing violence at combatants and their leaders alone is not sufficient to terminate the rights violations, and in which widening the set of targets so as to include civilian non-life-threatening rights violators is necessary to terminate the rights violations, and in which such widening is not overridden by consequentialist or contractarian considerations. In such situations these categories of civilians may become legitimate targets, given that they lack a right to immunity.

Civilian Immunity and Culpable Omissions

Thus far we have mainly been concerned with civilians who are individually and collectively morally responsible for human rights violations implicitly understood as violations of negative rights—e.g., a war of conquest or an active and sustained policy of forcible removal (ethnic or racial cleansing). We have not been concerned, at least explicitly, with positive rights and duties to assist as such. So our focus has not been on culpable omissions. That said, I have already acknowledged that the category of non-life-threatening rights violations includes violations of some positive rights. In this final section I will discuss the collective moral responsibility of certain categories of culpable non-attackers.

Earlier on in this chapter I argued that deadly force can in principle be used to enforce some positive rights, as well as to enforce negative rights. These positive rights include rights to goods other than life; they include rights that can be unrealized, even when the right to life is realized.

---

[23] G. I. Mavrodes, 'Conventions and the Morality of War', *Philosophy and Public Affairs*, 4 (1974/5), 117–31.

Moreover, as is the case with negative rights, third parties—at least in principle—have rights, and indeed duties, to use deadly force to ensure that some positive rights are respected.

This point has clear implications for certain civilian members of governments who intentionally refrain from respecting the positive rights, including subsistence rights, of their citizens. For governments have a clear institutional responsibility to provide for the minimum material well-being of their citizens; or at least, this is so if the governments in question have the capacity to do so. Accordingly, the moral responsibility based on need—and the fact that those in government could assist, if they chose to—is buttressed by this institutional responsibility that they have voluntarily taken on. Consider Saddam Hussein's refusal to distribute much-needed food and medicine to his own citizens, albeit in the context of UN-sponsored sanctions.[24] Citizens in such states may well be entitled to use deadly force against the government officials in question, notwithstanding the fact that these officials are neither combatants nor the leaders of combatants. Perhaps such use of deadly force, including assassination, is to be regarded as terrorism, on the grounds that the victims of terrorism are not themselves attackers.[25] If so, then terrorism can be morally justified in some circumstances. However, the civilian victims in this kind of scenario are not innocent; their intentional acts of omission constitute violations of the positive rights of their citizens.

Some of these rights or duties to use deadly force to enforce positive rights might be exercised against certain categories of people with diminished responsibility. Consider a variation on our earlier HIV AIDS example. Suppose that one of the employees of the company is not actually responsible for the company policy not to provide cheap drugs for AIDS sufferers, but is, nevertheless, the person who is refusing to provide the sufferer in question with the drug.[26] Assume also that the AIDS sufferer is not in a position to credibly threaten the company owner-managers

---

[24] Sandra Mackey, *The Reckoning: Iraq and the Legacy of Saddam Hussein* (London: Norton, 2002), 363. There was moral complexity here in that, given Saddam was refusing to dispense food and medicines under the oil for food programme—citing sanctions as his reason—then almost certainly sanctions should not have been continued to be applied. But this does not relieve Saddam of culpability.

[25] This depends on the definition of a terrorist.

[26] Assume also that he does not have an adequate reason for refusing to provide the drug: e.g., if he provides the drug, he will be fired and unable to get another job, with the consequence that his young children will be brought up in abject poverty.

who are responsible for the policy. Although the employee seems to have diminished responsibility for failing to respect the AIDS sufferer's right to the life-preserving drug, nevertheless, the AIDS sufferer might still be held to be entitled to shoot the employee dead, if that was the only means by which he could preserve his own life.

By analogy, government employees, such as administrators who intentionally refrain from assisting those in need because instructed to do so by their government, might well be legitimate targets of 'terrorists'. Consider our example of blacks in apartheid South Africa who were forcibly removed into desolate 'homelands', such as Qua Qua, and, once there, found that they could not provide themselves with a basic level of subsistence; malnutrition and disease were rampant. Now suppose South African politicians declare such homelands to be independent states—as in fact happened—and thereby try to absolve themselves and their administrators of their pre-existing institutional responsibility for the minimum material needs of the 'citizens' of these alleged new states. Since the 'states' were not legitimate—and were not in fact internationally recognized as legitimate—these politicians and other officials did not succeed in absolving themselves of their institutional responsibility. Accordingly, the South African government officials who refrained from assisting the relocated people were conceivably legitimate targets, on the assumption that killing these officials was necessary in order to ensure that the subsistence rights of these people would be realized. This might be so, even if the officials in question were not the same officials who planned and implemented the policy of forcible removals. Perhaps by this time the latter officials have retired, and have been replaced by a new cohort of politicians and administrators. If so, these new or succeeding officials would simply have inherited the institutional responsibility to provide for the minimal material needs of the 'citizens' of these alleged new states. (They would also have an institutional responsibility to redress the past injustice of dispossession that was consequent upon the policy of forcible removal; but that is another matter.)

Let us focus on the collective responsibility of the members of a group or community who intentionally refrain from assisting their needy fellows. Here we need some theoretical account of collective responsibility for omissions.

I offer the following account of culpable collective responsibility for omissions; it provides only a rough approximation[27] of a *sufficient* condition for such culpability. Members of some group are collectively responsible for failing to intervene to halt or prevent some serious wrongdoing or wrongful state of affairs if

(1) the wrongdoing took place, or is taking place;

(2) the members of the group intentionally refrained from intervening;

(3) each or most of the members intervening, having as an end the prevention of the wrongdoing, probably would have prevented, or have a reasonable chance of halting, the wrongdoing;

(4) each of the members of the group would have intentionally refrained from intervening—and intervening having as an end the prevention or termination of the wrongdoing—even if the others, or most of the others, had intervened with that end in mind;

(5) each of the members of the group had an institutional responsibility—jointly with the others—to intervene.

Note that on this account, if an agent would have intervened, but done so only because the others did—i.e., not because he had as an end the prevention or termination of the wrong—then the agent would still be morally responsible, jointly with the others, for failing to intervene (given conditions (1)–(3)).

Now there are additional theoretical complications that arise when the intervention in question has to be performed by representatives of a group or community, rather than by the members of the group or community themselves, or by third parties who are mere bystanders. Thus, in representative democracies, the government has to enact policies to intervene; the citizens cannot themselves intervene as a community. Moreover, some organization—authorized by the government—has to implement these policies, has to actually do the intervening. However, it needs to be said that the large voting populations in contemporary democracies cannot be assimilated to organizational structures, such as an army, or to small-scale directly participatory bodies, such as the cabinet in a Westminster-type system of government. Therefore, notions of collective responsibility that might apply to such organizations, or to such small

---

[27] e.g., I have not bothered to spell out the conditions for moral responsibility, such as self-mastery.

structured groups, do not apply to large populations. Accordingly, the failure of a democratic government to do its duty and engage in humanitarian intervention does not generate a moral justification for the wholesale targeting of the civilian voting population by (say) terrorists, much less the targeting of a civilian population living in an authoritarian state that fails to do its duty in this regard.

Nevertheless, in the light of the above definition, it might well be the case that civilian members of governments and their administrations—such as Iraqi politicians and administrators who failed to meet their responsibilities to distribute food and medicine to their own citizens, and South African politicians and administrators who failed to adequately assist destitute blacks in the 'homelands'—are collectively morally responsible for omissions of a kind that might justify the use of deadly force on the part of their citizens to ensure that the rights to assistance in question are realized. In short, members of civilian groups who culpably refrain from assisting those who have a human right to assistance from them might thereby forfeit their right to immunity in the context of a conventional war or armed struggle.

6

Collateral Immunity in War and Terrorism

C. A. J. (TONY) COADY

The world will not help us; we must help ourselves. We must kill as many of the Hamas and Islamic Jihad leaders as possible, as quickly possible, while minimizing collateral damage, but not letting that damage stop us.

Jerusalem Post, 11 September 2003

I recognized beforehand that someone might be ... bringing their kid to work ... However, if I had known there was an entire day-centre, it might have given me pause to switch targets. That's a large amount of collateral damage.

Timothy McVeigh

The phrase 'collateral damage' is one of those euphemistic phrases that help to sanitize the horrible reality of war and other employments of political violence. It has taken its place along with 'surgical strike', 'revisiting the area' (i.e., renewed bombing), and 'neutralizing assets' as part of the linguistic camouflage that contemporary war-fighters use to disguise the human and moral costs of what they do. Perhaps the most astonishing military euphemism is that recently coined to describe a bomb that missed its ostensible target and hit a residential area: 'seduction off the target'![1]

---

[1] This occurred in a report by John Davison, published in the British newspaper *The Independent*, on 10 April 1999. Davison was reporting a NATO admission (correcting an earlier denial) that their bombing in the Kosovo capital, Priština, had killed civilians and badly damaged homes in the context of the NATO bombing of Serbia. The admission was made by Air Commodore David Wilby, who said that the attack was aimed at the main telephone exchange in Priština, which he claimed to be a legitimate target because it was being used for communications between Serbian forces in Kosovo and

This delightful touch not only helps the speaker disclaim responsibility, but manages to shift the blame on to the victims who have somehow managed to 'seduce' the bomb into killing them.

This extreme case illustrates something that is nonetheless present less idiotically in other military euphemisms. So it is that many uses of the term 'collateral damage' suggest both an excuse and a belittling. The excuse: these deaths and maimings are not really what we want to happen. The belittling: these sufferings and killings are a very small part of a big picture. The *Jerusalem Post* editorial that serves as the first epigraph to this chapter appeals to both with its talk of minimizing the damage and its resolute plea for desperate measures of self-help in an emergency. In what follows I want to examine the legitimacy of the excuse and the significance of the belittling.

Targets and Terrorism

The excuse is essentially connected with the idea that there are legitimate and illegitimate targets in war or in other instances of political violence, and, in particular, that non-combatants (or 'innocents' in a slightly technical sense of the term) have some form of immunity from direct attack. This is a key element in traditional just war theory, and has become increasingly embodied in international law. It is an important ingredient in the popular understanding of terrorism and the moral condemnation of it that usually follows. Indeed, the idea of attacking the innocent has been crucial to various definitions of terrorism in the scholarly literature, including my own writings. I have argued for what I call a tactical definition of terrorism, as opposed to a political status definition, and in consequence have viewed terrorism as a tactic that can be used by governments and their agencies as well as by non-government groups. This thus provides an important link between terrorism and inter-state or revolutionary war, even if terrorism doesn't always take place in the context of all-out conventional warfare. My definition is 'the organized use of violence to attack non-combatants

Belgrade. The full quote from Wilby is: 'One bomb appeared to be seduced off the target at the final moment. Close inspection of imagery indicates that it landed some 200 to 300 metres away in what seems to be a small residential area' (*The Independent*, 10 April 1999, 2).

("innocents" in a special sense) for political purposes'. This is a pared-down version of a more complex account that addresses such things as the inclusion in the definition of the threat of such violence and of the property of non-combatants. There is the further question of the precise intermediate purposes for which the violence is deployed and the place in the definition of such purposes. My preference is to exclude any reference to such purposes, even the very plausible purpose of inducing fear, since I would rather leave the determination of these matters to empirical investigation. If it were discovered that the agents of attacks upon non-combatants were interested in gaining their ultimate political ends by inspiring anger rather than fear (in order, for example, to provoke over-reactions that would gain their group further supporters), then I doubt that we would want to refuse their deeds the title 'terrorism' simply because they did not aim at producing fear. But for our present purposes this definitional debate does not matter greatly. Somewhat broader tactical definitions will still link terrorism to the just war principle of discrimination that disallows attacks upon non-combatants as immoral. It is perhaps worth repeating what I have said in a number of places: namely, that my account does not make terrorism immoral by definition. You have to take the further step of accepting the just war principle of discrimination (in particular, the immunity of non-combatants) to reach the moral conclusion. There is also the further issue of whether that principle should be treated as exceptionless. Nonetheless, given the widespread acceptance of the discrimination principle (at least notionally), the tactical definition helps explain why there is such widespread condemnation of terrorism—at least, the terrorism of sub-state agents. I have argued elsewhere that the tactical definition has two other consequences that are not readily accepted. The first is that states can engage in terrorism both against each other and against sub-state groups or individuals, and the second is that not all resorts to violence by sub-state agents need be terrorist.[2]

A final cautionary point. I do not use the terms 'combatant' and 'non-combatant' as equivalent to 'soldier' (or 'member of the armed forces') and 'civilian'. This can be a source of considerable confusion. Jeff McMahan, for instance, has cogently criticized the idea that non-combatants, understood

---

[2] For further elaboration of my approach to the definitional issues, see my 'Terrorism and Innocence', *Journal of Ethics*, 8 (2004), 37–58, and 'Defining Terrorism', in Igor Primoratz (ed.), *Terrorism: The Philosophical Issues* (Basingstoke and New York: Palgrave Macmillan, 2004).

as civilians, are immune from direct attack, and takes himself to be criticizing the 'traditional' just war theory.[3] It is perhaps debatable whether the tradition is as unambiguous on this as McMahan believes, but in any case his argument mostly proceeds by showing that there are civilians who are as responsible, or more responsible, for the wrongdoing that legitimates violent response as the front line soldiers, many of whom may have been coerced to fight or be non-culpably ignorant of the injustice of their cause. I can accept this conclusion with equanimity, since my use of 'non-combatant' does not produce the thesis that McMahan criticizes. What is true, as he admits, is that, pragmatically, there will often be great difficulties in determining which enemy civilians are (in my sense) combatants. Moreover, there may be considerable utility in adhering to a ban on attacking civilians when that has gained a wide degree of acceptance and leads to some containment of the worst effects of war. Nonetheless, especially in the context of a discussion of terrorism, we need to be aware that there can be perpetrators of great wrongs who are not in uniform or bearing arms themselves, though they use and provide direct, significant support to the enterprise of those who do. Insurgents who attack and kill 'civilian contractors' whose contracting promotes the evil that the insurgency is aimed at preventing are not thereby terrorists. They may, of course, be wrongdoers, nevertheless, if the cause they pursue is unjust and the evil they fight against is non-existent or insufficient to justify resort to arms.

Some acknowledgement of the immunity is clearly present in both of the comments that serve as epigraphs to this chapter. There are of course those who reject the significance of the distinction between combatants and non-combatants and who argue that, once you decide to employ political violence in what you see as a just cause, you do what you need to do in order to win. This is essentially a cost–benefit, utilitarian or consequentialist approach (though a particularly narrow one, since the good outcomes factored in to the calculations tend to favour only the benefits to one side in the conflict and also tend to have a relatively short-term focus).[4] Thus

---

[3] Jeff, McMahan, 'The Ethics of Killing in War', *Ethics*, 114 (2003), 693–733.

[4] Consequentialism is a very elastic doctrine, and there are forms of it that can attribute moral significance to a combatant/non-combatant distinction. It can, for instance, be argued that granting non-combatant immunity makes for better outcomes in war (less suffering all round, etc.), or that such respect for the innocent is part of what the best moral code for human beings would be (in terms of

a great deal of the Allied city bombing in World War II was justified, at least in private counsels and sometimes in the public arena, as a deliberate attack upon civilian populations with the purpose of destroying popular and political morale so that the war would end more quickly in an Allied victory. As Hendrik Hertzberg put it recently, 'the damage inflicted upon London and Dresden, Rotterdam and Tokyo, Leningrad and Hiroshima was anything but collateral. It was the whole point.'[5]

So some of the argument in defence of the bombing simply ignored military tradition and just war theory, in a single-minded pursuit of victory. It was a simplistic utilitarian argument to the effect that the costs were worth it for the benefit of victory. This thinking has hardly gone away. It was chillingly echoed by the then US Ambassador to the UN, Madeleine Albright, when she was interviewed by the US television programme, *Sixty Minutes*, on 12 May 1996, about the effects of the US-inspired UN sanctions in Iraq. The programme segment, called 'Punishing Saddam', covered a visit to Iraq by presenter Leslie Stahl and her crew. It showed dying children in damaged hospitals, open sewage, and ambulance graveyards, and featured interviews with doctors and international aid workers, as well as Madeleine Albright. The video of the segment has been shown repeatedly throughout the world, though seldom in the USA. Here is Albright's key comment:

Stahl (brow deeply furrowed): We have heard that half a million children have died. Why, that's more children than died at ... Hiroshima. And, and ... is the price worth it?
Albright (calmly): I think this is a very difficult decision. But the price, we think the price is worth it.

Yet, if the World War II justification for the city bombing was often of this kind, it sometimes paid implicit, if back-handed, tribute to non-combatant immunity by arguing that the civilians attacked were not really innocent. The idea was that modern war had made all civilians combatants, so imposing a sort of 'collective guilt' on all of them. This seems to me deeply misguided. It is sufficiently refuted as a wholesale doctrine by the fact that it counts babies and small children who have the misfortune to be born in enemy territory as combatants. Hence the bombing of a day

---

outcomes of adherence). Consequentialists might, I suppose, also find some use in this connection for the doctrine of double effect (discussed below), but typically they reject it.

⁵ Hendrik Hertzberg, 'Collateral Damage (Iraq)', *New Yorker*, 7 April 2003, 33.

care centre has no different moral status from the bombing of an attacking army. But I shall say no more about this position, though I have discussed it elsewhere, since my interest is in those who think that there *are* enemy non-combatants whose immunity should be respected in some way.[6] The primary interest of the talk of collateral damage arises only for those who accept the significance of the combatant/non-combatant distinction and the immunity it brings.

Two Types of Collateral Damage

The idea of collateral damage encompasses two quite different things. One is that of damage to property and life that is caused accidentally. The other is that of destruction or injury or death that is not accidental, but is nonetheless unintended. This latter category has puzzled many people, including philosophers, because it requires the idea that an agent can know that his action will have a particular consequence, but can still go ahead with the action not intending that consequence. (The verb 'know' should be interpreted flexibly here to include the strong, reasonably grounded belief that the consequence will follow.) Some philosophers, such as Jeremy Bentham, and some legal systems hold that the agent must be held to intend the known consequences of his or her action. Even here, it is noteworthy that Bentham acknowledges some need for a distinction by talking of 'oblique intention', whereas those he opposes want to talk of 'foreseen but unintended consequences'.[7] There is an extensive literature on this topic that we cannot explore here, but it is clearly connected with such issues as the validity of the doctrine of 'double effect', the scope and significance of 'negative responsibility', and the relative importance of the character of an act and an agent compared to good or bad outcomes. In certain cases, at least, it seems that there is both point and moral relevance to the idea that certain outcomes can be foreseen but not intended. I may know with practical certainty that if I refuse a gangster's invitation to murder a colleague, the gangster will murder two other people who stand

---

[6] For the discussion and defence of the importance of the non-combatant/combatant distinction, see my 'The Morality of Terrorism', *Philosophy*, 60 (1985), 47–70, and 'Terrorism and Innocence'.

[7] Jeremy Bentham, *An Introduction to the Principles of Morals and Legislation*, ed. J. H. Burns and H. L. A. Hart (London and New York: Methuen, 1982), ch. 8, §6.

in his way; but it would surely be very strange to describe me as intending, by my refusal, the deaths of the other two. Here there is the will of another involved in the outcome, and perhaps that is enough to vitiate the idea that it is even 'a consequence' of my action of refusal. But this is at least disputable, and, in any case, there are other examples that do not involve the mediation of another's will. For example, suppose I am walking along a footpath and am aware of another pedestrian walking behind me. A runaway truck comes into view and is careering at me with the driver dead in the cabin. In the instant I have left, I leap aside in the full knowledge that the person behind me will be hit and probably killed. Surely it is clear that I did not intend by my self-preserving action to inflict injury and death on that person, even though I could reasonably foresee that outcome?[8] Or consider my plight as a surgeon in a war zone who must choose who amongst the wounded to aid with scarce life-saving drugs. In choosing to save Brown and Smith with the foreseeable consequence that Black, Jones, and Grey will die, it surely makes sense to describe me as intending to save Brown and Smith with the foreseen but unintended consequence that the latter three die, rather than as intending to save Brown and Smith but intending to kill Black, Jones, and Grey.

For my purposes, we need not assume that this defence of the category is unequivocally successful. The point of the discussion above is principally to explain the initial appeal of the category and thereby to make comparative sense of the way in which it might be explicitly employed, or implicitly relied upon, in discussions of the morality of 'collateral damage'. As we shall see, there are ways in which this initial plausibility can be stretched and even eroded in those discussions.

Let us call the form of collateral damage that requires the idea of foreseen but unintended damage 'incidental damage', to contrast with the other form of 'accidental damage'. First let us consider the moral problems associated with accidental damage. Demonstrating that some effect of one's actions is 'accidental' does not automatically excuse or eliminate the need to justify it. It shows that the effect was not intended: it was not aimed at under any description available to the agent at the time. As far as your

---

[8] If it is urged as a defect in the example that the person behind will be killed whether I jump aside or not, we could amend the example so that my staying put will save the other's life. Instead of a truck, it is a maniac with a spear whose spear throw will kill only me if I don't move and only the other person if I do.

intentional control is concerned, the effect was the product of chance. As J. L. Austin pointed out long ago, there is a distinction between 'mistake' and 'accident'. Like all distinctions, this has blurred edges, and Austin doesn't bother to give an account of it, but it is, roughly speaking, the distinction between going astray because of something wrong with one's thought processes or perceptions and getting it wrong because of some mishap in the 'outside world'.[9] But, for ease of exposition, I will collapse this distinction and treat mistaken damage under the same heading as genuinely accidental damage. In both cases, for different sorts of reasons, the agent does not know that the damaging effect will occur, at least under the relevant description. If the American authorities are to be believed, the bombing of the Chinese Embassy in Belgrade during the NATO attack upon Serbia was a mistake—they meant to hit that building, but didn't mean to hit the Chinese Embassy because they didn't think it was the Chinese Embassy. On my last trip to China, I could find no Chinese who believed the American claim of mistake, and my European colleagues sneered at my naiveté in accepting it. (By contrast, I was surprised that they were all convinced that the CIA would have reliable maps of Belgrade.) But, if the mistake story were true, it would provide the beginnings of an acceptable excuse for the deaths and damage that ensued. Similarly, with the bomb that went off target in Kosovo. Unless the residents of the Priština suburb exercised some magical powers to bring about their own destruction ('seduced off target'), then the NATO explanation aims to provide the excuse of accidental deaths and damage. In the embassy case the question that needs to be answered to render the attackers blameless is whether the mistake was the result of negligence; in the Kosovo case, whether the accident was due to recklessness. Although a primary interest in moral assessment is a concern for intentional actions, that concern does not exhaust the scope of moral assessment. People who do not intend the deaths of others but who do not take reasonable steps to guard against accident or mistake are morally culpable, even if the culpability will often be of a different order to that borne by those who set out to kill and maim. Incidental deaths, injuries, and damage are to be avoided if they can be. If the American military could have known, by taking reasonable steps

---

[9] See J. L. Austin, 'A Plea for Excuses', in *Philosophical Papers* (Oxford: Oxford University Press, 1961), 133 n. 1.

to discover it, that the building they planned to attack was the Chinese Embassy, then they are guilty of the deaths and damage. If the NATO bomber command, or some relevant figures in the chain of command, could have known that they were using defective weapons, then the same applies to them. In both cases, if they couldn't have known at the time, then the episodes may provide grounds for more care in the future about targeting and weapon reliability.

The general point behind the morality of accidental damage is that actions that accidentally or mistakenly kill people whom you are not entitled to kill have done a great harm to those people (and a real but lesser wrong when it is not a matter of killing but of damaging their property). This harm becomes a wrong when the accident or mistake could reasonably have been avoided. Hence we have a place for the moral and legal categories of negligence, recklessness, and due care. It is incumbent upon people not to put themselves in positions such that accident and mistake are liable to eventuate in the death or injury of others or damage to their property. This point can be obscured, especially in war, by the otherwise perfectly legitimate concentration upon preventing intentional killing of the innocent. Murder is a dreadful thing, but we cannot congratulate ourselves on avoiding it if we are casual about manslaughter and negligent homicide.

Of course, it would be too much to insist that war may proceed only when all possibilities of accident or mistake have been eliminated. Any large-scale undertaking will involve unavoidable accidents and mistakes, or accidents and mistakes that could have been avoided only at too great a cost to the enterprise. If we assume that there are some just wars, then some such accidents or mistakes will be a regrettable accompaniment to their successful prosecution. Even here, however, the just war requirement of proportionality may be in play. If in the course of a war it becomes clear that the weapon systems are heavily prone to accident or mistake, then the verdict may have to be that the harm done may well outweigh the good that the war is expected to achieve. But at this point the awareness so created moves us into the category of incidental, rather than accidental, damage.

I should say that the points made above do not incline me to include the morally reprehensible infliction of collateral damage (accidental or incidental) within the definition of terrorism. Here I depart from my friend and colleague, David Rodin. Rodin has argued for a sense of the term 'terrorism' that includes such infliction within its scope.[10] Our difference is to some degree simply terminological, inasmuch as we are agreed on the moral case against such damage. Indeed, I was at one stage inclined to take the same path as Rodin, at least to the extent of calling such infliction 'neo-terrorism'. It is tempting to venture down that path just because the negligent and reckless infliction of harm on the innocent displays a similar spirit to that involved in intentional infliction. Similar, yes, but not the same. The reckless and negligent do not have *enough* respect for the safety of non-combatants, but they are not positively aiming at their destruction. It seems to me important to mark this difference, and the term 'terrorism' is at hand to do it, with sufficient backing in the popular understanding of the word. This is not to deny that in some circumstances the reckless and negligent may present a greater threat to the well-being of non-combatants, and hence be responsible for a greater crime in those circumstances. I don't think that these remarks are enough to settle the matter of appropriate language, though they have, I hope, some persuasive force. In general, I tend to favour narrower definitions of contentious political terms because I think that what wide definitions gain by emphasizing similarities between what seem initially diverse things, they lose by obscuring important differences. The very breadth of such definitions also tends to lessen the utility of the relevant concepts in political debate. Elsewhere, I have argued this case in connection with wide definitions of 'violence', such as that involved in the idea of 'structural violence', and I think something similar can be argued here.[11]

Incidental Damage and 'Double Effect'

This brings us to the category of incidental damage. This is where agents proceed with an attack, intending to damage a legitimate target but reasonably believing that their attack will kill innocent bystanders or

---

[10] David Rodin, 'Terrorism without Intention', *Ethics*, 114 (2004). Rodin does not distinguish between accidental and incidental collateral damage, and seems to use the terms 'reckless' and 'negligent' in ways that could apply in both categories. I have been using the terms principally to apply to the accidental, but incidental damage that violates the restrictions of the doctrine of double effect, especially proportionality, might well qualify as reckless.

[11] C. A. J. Coady, 'The Idea of Violence', *Journal of Applied Philosophy*, 3 (1986), 3–19.

neighbours (and/or damage their property). Here the attackers tend to justify their bringing about of deaths and damage to the bystanders by resort to the doctrine of double effect (DDE) or some related maxim. The DDE holds that the foreseen but unintended consequences of an action are morally acceptable when certain conditions are fulfilled. It does not hold that incidental damage is acceptable merely because it is incidental to intent. The usual conditions are:

1. The action at issue must not itself be morally bad; nor should any intended effect of it be morally bad.
2. The anticipated bad effect must be genuinely unintended, and not merely secondarily intended (e.g., intended as a means to a further end).
3. The harm involved in the unintended outcome is not disproportionate to the benefit aimed at in the act.[12]

There is another condition (or, as I would prefer, pre-condition) that I will discuss later. For now I want to say a little about these three conditions. The first simply specifies that the moral utility of the DDE arises only when what is intended by the agent (the action that has the unintended but foreseen bad consequence) is a benefit that is either morally neutral or morally good. The second condition is aimed at precluding what Elizabeth Anscombe once called 'double think about double effect'.[13] As we saw earlier, people faced with the difficult choices about what tactics to use in their war efforts will often adopt a simple utilitarian or consequentialist stance about the means they will employ. But where they don't adopt such a stance, there is a strong temptation to stretch the DDE in order to gain maximum tactical advantage in the deployment of violence. So, it may be argued that the real intention in attacking a day care centre is to win the war, not to kill the children and their carers. Admittedly, this is an extreme in sophistry, since it blatantly ignores the fact that having an ultimate purpose for some action does not exclude the having of an intermediate purpose that requires fulfilment in order to achieve the ultimate objective. Generally speaking, someone who intends an end also intends the means

---

[12] These conditions are expressed differently by different authors. This list is my distillation of the sense of those treatments I have read.

[13] G. E. M. Anscombe, 'War and Murder', in Richard A. Wasserstrom (ed.), *War and Morality* (Belmont, Calif.: Wadsworth Publishing Co., 1970), 50.

chosen to that end. But there are philosophical manœuvres that seek to complicate this.

Consider one propounded by David Lewis in connection with arguments about nuclear deterrence. A political leader, call her Jones, who has suffered from a nuclear attack on one of her cities, considers launching a nuclear attack on an enemy city as a response, in order to dissuade the enemy commander-in-chief from further attacks. Lewis argues that she need not intend the massive civilian deaths and casualties, that 'result' from her action. How so? Well, according to Lewis, Jones does not intend the deaths and casualties, since she needs only to affect the reasoning of the enemy commander and so needs only the flight path of the missile and the flash of light as the city explodes to figure as premises in the reasoning that the commander will engage in. The commander will reason from the detected flight and subsequent fireball to the conclusion that the city has been destroyed and be persuaded to desist from further attacks. He does not need the later, more direct information about deaths and devastation to come to his conclusion. So Jones intends the flight and flash, but the massacre is an unintended though foreseen consequence.

Quite apart from the fact that such 'persuasion' has a somewhat tenuous hold on probability of success, this argument of Lewis's shows the way in which double-think about double effect can lead even so humane and intelligent a man as David Lewis into what is surely sophistry. Of course, Lewis himself does not endorse the DDE, for he has a largely consequentialist approach to the problem of collateral damage. He is merely arguing that an attack to obliterate a city, if that is the only way to prevent massive nuclear devastation, does in fact comply with the DDE. (Lewis in fact opposes such attacks because they are more disproportionate than his preferred option of finite counterforce.) To this extent, his argument is a sort of *reductio*: if the DDE will let you get away with this, we might as well forget about it.[14] But the problem surely resides in Lewis's treatment of Jones's intention, rather than in the defects of the DDE. A philosophical account of intention is fraught with complexities; but whatever account we give, it must respect plain thinking about what someone does and what they mean to do. And the idea that Jones doesn't intend to devastate

[14] See David Lewis, 'Finite Counterforce', in Henry Shue (ed.), *Nuclear Deterrence and Moral Restraint* (Cambridge: Cambridge University Press, 1989), 112–13 n. 45.

the city when she carefully plans the missile's trajectory and explosive capacity to that very end, and wants that destruction and death to figure in the enemy commander's reasoning and response, is just dotty. It is simply irrelevant to this attribution that the enemy commander can reason from certain features of the action other than direct observation of the devastation to the fact of the devastation. Perhaps Lewis thinks that the fact that Jones might be happy were a 'miracle' to occur, such that the flight and flash occurred without the devastation, but the enemy commander was nonetheless persuaded, shows that Jones does not intend the devastation. But again this is simply confused. There are many things that we intend as means to some good end that we don't feel pleased about, but we intend them nonetheless. The 'miracle' device could be cheerfully and absurdly employed in every case to show that we don't intend them. In the case of the city's destruction, Jones can infer that the enemy commander will come to his conclusions on the basis of reports (or direct observation) of flight and flash; but she needs the deaths as well, since a later report that the flight and the flash were, say, cunning visual deceptions will mean that the commander's reasoning will not go through.

Further Complexities in the DDE

The DDE requires that we think in common-sense ways about what people intend and foresee. This means that there are various disentanglements of parts of action that we cannot really allow. Consider someone who has a great hatred of flies. To his horror, he finds a fly in his apartment, and the only swatting implement to hand is a big, heavy hammer. The fly is very hard to keep up with, but it eventually settles on the bald head of his best friend, where it is clearly visible against the bald surface. If he smashes the hammer down upon the fly and the head it rests on, fully aware that he will thereby kill or severely injure his friend, it would surely be absurd of him to plead that he did not intend his friend's death or injury. The remark 'I only intended to kill the fly; my friend's death was a foreseen but unintended side-effect of my action' just doesn't make sense. (Of course, if it did make sense, it would still be no excuse under the DDE, because of the proportionality requirement, but the more important point is that here we cannot take apart the smashing of the fly and the smashing of the head.)

Grossman gives a good, real-life military example of this double-thinking evasive mind-set. It concerns illegitimate attacks upon combatants rather than non-combatants, but the mode of thinking is similar. He records a conversation he heard amongst US troops who had just completed a training exercise about treatment of prisoners of war. Several of the soldiers held straightforwardly barbaric views, such as that prisoners of war should be marched through an area saturated with persistent nerve gas or just killed outright. Another suggested using them for minefield clearance. The chaplain intervened to cite the Geneva Conventions, and one of the soldiers reported that in training school they had told him that the Geneva Conventions forbade firing white phosphorus at troops, 'so you call it in on their equipment'.[15] Here is convenient double-think with a vengeance. The equipment happens to be attached to the people (or nearby), so attacking it achieves your real objective of attacking them, but you can disavow this with a verbal device.

I am not suggesting that the DDE is immune from defects, merely that these evasive devices will not work. I think, for instance, that the notion of 'means' that the doctrine employs needs more attention, and that the DDE is much more plausible where the foreseen effect is risk to non-combatants rather than certain death; but this is not the place to engage further in the very extensive debate about the doctrine.[16] It is worth remarking, however, that unless the DDE, or some other principle that serves a similar purpose, is allowed, then the possibility of waging a modern war that respects the immunity of non-combatants is vastly reduced. This is because there will be many situations in which non-combatant deaths and injuries can be foreseen as a result of attacking important military objectives, and without something like the DDE these attacks will be ruled out by the immunity of non-combatants. This consequence has been taken by at least one critic as a powerful argument for pacifism.[17]

I have so far said nothing directly to elucidate the third condition of the DDE to do with proportionality, though its importance will

[15] Lieutenant-Colonel Dave Grossman, *On Killing: The Psychological Costs of Learning to Kill in War and Society* (Boston: Little, Brown and Co., 1995), 203.

[16] See P. A. Woodward (ed.), *The Doctrine of Double Effect: Philosophers Debate a Controversial Moral Principle* (Notre Dame, Ind.: University of Notre Dame Press, 2001), and Alison McIntyre, 'Doing Away with Double Effect', *Ethics*, 111 (2001), 219–55.

[17] See Robert L. Holmes, *On War and Morality* (Princeton: Princeton University Press, 1989), esp. 193–203.

have emerged in the above discussion. The notion of proportionality is employed extensively in just war theory, both in the context of the resort to war in the first place and in the context of the legitimacy of incidental collateral damage and the DDE. Yet its employment is often a curious combination of the natural and the theoretically opaque. It seems natural in that there is obvious intuitive sense to the requirement that we should rule out the use of violence that is disproportionate to the ends that supposedly legitimate it. Yet what is it to be disproportionate or proportionate? Certainly, there are few developed accounts of what such proportionality amounts to, and it is impossible to settle the problems that surround this notion here; but some brief comment on the complexities is necessary.[18]

It is tempting to think that there is a simple utilitarian or consequentialist construal of the concept available: the violence is proportional if it brings about more overall benefits than harms, disproportional if not. But this seems false to both the just war tradition and to our intuitions about particular cases. For any but the most dedicated utilitarian, it cannot be that the concept invokes the quest for answers to the question of whether this action here will more likely bring about the optimal state of the world, all things considered, than any of the available alternatives. But, if not, what can it be doing? We cannot solve this vexed question here, but some pointers may be developed. Any answer must lie in the direction of what might be called middle-range assessment. What we need to ask is broader than the question 'Will this offensive drive the enemy back and allow us to occupy the ground he now occupies?' But it is also narrower than the question: 'Will this offensive make the world safe for democracy?' Of course, the first question is absurdly local, and should be inadequate by strategic military canons as much as by moral standards; and the second is ridiculously lofty. Nonetheless, both have played their parts in disproportionate military campaigns, ranging from some of the battles of World War I through to the follies of Vietnam. The idea of proportionality calls upon us to assess the proclaimed necessities of military means to military ends against the tragic human certainties of death and injury to combatants and

[18] For the best recent discussion of proportionality as a tool of just war analysis, see Thomas Hurka, 'Proportionality and the Morality of War', *Philosophy and Public Affairs*, 33 (2005), 34–66. Hurka's subtle analysis still leaves, as he acknowledges, many questions unanswered.

non-combatants (on both sides) and the moral and political purposes of the conflict.

Assuming, for instance, that the First Gulf War was a morally legitimate undertaking for the purpose of decisively removing an aggressive force from Kuwait—about which assumption doubts may well be raised—we may nonetheless judge that the killing of so many routed Iraqi soldiers, as they fled the battlefield weaponless, was disproportionate.[19] To claim this is to judge those deaths to have been recognizably excessive for achieving that aim, but it is not of course thereby to assert that they would have been unnecessary for some other aim, such as the toppling of Saddam Hussein's government and the establishment of an independent Kurdish state. The problem with these further calculations is, first, that the war was not publicly justified and endorsed on such grounds in the first place, and very likely could not have been so justified morally, given the sort of valuations thereby involved; and second, that the prospects for establishing such outcomes by such methods (even were the outcomes, in all their complexity, morally desirable) are far too remote and uncertain to be worth the deaths of so many people. Nor is this simply a matter of epistemic uncertainty, important as that is. There are some good outcomes that may be highly probable but seem nonetheless irrelevant to the judgement about appropriate violence. In the context of the DDE, for instance, it may be that our killing of a large number of non-combatants in the course of bombing a military target is likely to be perceived as an atrocity committed by the enemy, and this could result in recruiting a powerful ally to our good cause. The many non-combatant deaths may be unintentional, but I would argue that this prospective good outcome, no matter how important, cannot make them proportional. Similarly, for the role of proportionality in the *jus ad bellum*: the fact that a war against some minor offender (over, say, a border incursion) would increase international economic activity in a way that would bring considerable benefits to the world cannot make resort to war proportional.[20] It would seem that proportionality cannot be invoked where the beneficial outcomes are merely possible or speculative (as against the certain or highly probable harms foreseen), or where the benefits are too unrelated to the justifying

---

[19] There is serious room for dispute about the numbers killed in this way, or indeed more generally in the war itself.

[20] This point is made by Hurka, 'Proportionality'.

conditions for the resort to war in the first place. Clearly more needs to be said about proportionality; but whatever is said, it seems certain that the determination of what is proportional will leave a great deal to concrete, circumstantial judgement rather than the application of some hard-and-fast rule.[21]

Instead of pursuing the critique of the DDE's viability further, I want to emphasize an aspect of the DDE that is easily overlooked. It is related in spirit to a direct qualification to the usual statements of the DDE that has been suggested by Michael Walzer. I shall look at Walzer shortly, but the aspect I want to stress is more a pre-condition for the application of the DDE. This pre-condition is that where there are other feasible ways of achieving the good end that do not involve the harmful side-effects or involve fewer or less grave such effects, the agent should choose them. And this holds even where the alternatives involve somewhat more costs to the agent. I call this a pre-condition because the spirit of the DDE remains restrictive, even where it has a permissive form. In the case of war, or political violence more generally, the protection of the innocent remains a primary value of the *jus in bello*, and hence dictates that incidental injury or killing of the innocent be entirely avoided where possible. Of course, the 'where possible' needs unpacking in the particular setting; it will include such things as the degree of risk to one's troops and to one's prospects of success, but a serious commitment to the protection of innocent people requires giving their safety a high priority. Michael Walzer treats something like it as part of the condition specifying that the bad effect be not really a means to the intended goal. Walzer's version goes as follows: 'aware of the evil involved, he seeks to minimize it, accepting costs to himself'.[22] This is in the same spirit, but it seems to ignore the possibility that means might be available, and should be sought (other things being equal), that avoid the incidental damage altogether. Perhaps Walzer means his talk of 'minimizing' to include the limit of

---

[21] There is a further problem with allowing the proportionality test of the DDE to those who are waging an unjust war. It is not at all clear that those whose cause is unjust can invoke the idea that their unintended but foreseen killing is proportional in any sense to their military and political objectives where these are unjust. This point is made by Hurka, 'Proportionality', 45, and a similar line is taken by Jeff McMahan in several places, notably in 'Innocence, Self-defence and Killing in War', *Journal of Political Philosophy*, 2 (1994), 193–221. There are many complexities raised by this point that I cannot address here.

[22] Michael Walzer, *Just and Unjust Wars: A Moral Argument with Historical Illustrations*, 3rd edn. (New York: Basic Books, 2000), 155.

zero evil, or perhaps he thinks the pre-condition too obvious to need attention.

The Moral Background to Restricting Collateral Damage

Certainly the moral point of the DDE should mandate such a pre-condition; but it is nonetheless worth explicit emphasis, since strategic resort to the DDE can obscure its deeper moral significance. The pre-condition is thus important in reinstating the value of avoiding the deaths of innocent people, a value that can be obscured by casual employment of the DDE. It can be obscured because, if the legitimate goal is important enough, the innocent casualties can be too lightly discounted by the idea of necessity or even proportionality. This comes out very clearly in the tone of the first epigraph from the *Jerusalem Post*. There is the breezy reference to minimizing collateral damage, but this is immediately followed by the assertion that such damage must never stand in the way of killing the leaders of Hamas and Islamic Jihad. This looks like trying to have your cake and eat it. It suggests that the talk of minimizing is simply a ritual gesture to morality or world opinion. There is no suggestion that the intentional killing may have to be abandoned altogether if the minimizing is not sufficient. There is no sense that alternative ways of killing the enemy should be sought that might have no incidental damage. Here, the understanding of what the DDE might license is remote from the spirit of such just war theorists as Vitoria, who says: 'It is never lawful to kill innocent people, even accidentally and unintentionally, except when it advances a just war *which cannot be won in any other way*.'[23] As I read Vitoria, he is saying that the killing of the innocent in war can be licit only when it is done either accidentally or unintentionally (i.e., foreseen but not intended); but even then, it is only licit where there is no alternative to it. Thus put, the pre-condition expresses an idea that is somewhat parallel to the last resort condition of the *jus ad bellum*.[24] Other ways of

---

[23] Francesco de Vitoria, *Political Writings*, ed. Anthony Pagden and Jeremy Lawrance (Cambridge and New York: Cambridge University Press, 1991), 316; my emphasis.
[24] I owe the suggestion of this parallel to Igor Primoratz. My thanks to him also for pointing out the reference to Vitoria.

achieving the military objective without the high risk of injury or death to non-combatants should be the first priority. And this applies not merely to the war at large, as the quote from Vitoria might seem to say, but to particular campaigns, battles, etc. within it.

The trouble with the DDE expressed without the pre-condition can be seen if we imagine a scenario in which clearly identified enemy troops (or terrorists) are moving in a crowd of people, a procession perhaps, and they can be shot while in the crowd with the foreseen result that some few of the innocent civilians will be injured or killed. As long as their deaths are unintended and the need to kill the terrorists is grave enough, the DDE (without the pre-condition) will allow the shooting. But suppose we know or have good reason to believe that the terrorists are going to part company with the crowd at the next intersection, where our troops will have a clear shot at them without the risk of any civilian deaths. The troops who ignore this option and shoot into the crowd have done a grave wrong, and the DDE would be defective if it could justify them. And even if the army authorities don't know precisely when else they can get a shot at enemy soldiers or terrorists, surely a genuine respect for non-combatants would counsel the seeking of alternatives to attacking them when they are surrounded by non-combatants and not engaged at that time in armed offensive. The Israeli army was clearly in horrible violation of this counsel when it used a 1 tonne bomb to blow up a block of flats in order to kill a solitary Hamas leader, Sheikh Salah Mustafa Shehada, with the result that fifteen non-combatants, eight of them children (one of whom was two months old), were killed in the bombing. Indeed, not only is this action in probable violation of the pre-condition, but it has distinct similarities to the hammer example used above. Like that example, it is hard to see how the action could be so disentangled as to claim with any plausibility that the bombers intended to kill *only* the Hamas leader; and, even were this plausible, the considerations of proportionality would also very likely defeat the excuse.

Is the pre-condition the same as Walzer's additional sub-condition? Walzer makes the intention that the agent minimize the harm to non-combatants, accepting costs to himself or herself, a part of his third condition of the DDE (in effect, my second condition). But the intention to minimize the evil of non-combatant deaths and injuries is itself a consequence of the pre-condition that requires avoidance, where possible, of even incidental non-combatant deaths, etc. If we are enjoined to avoid, wherever we can, getting into a situation where we cause collateral damage of the incidental kind, then it seems to follow that when we cannot avoid it, we should take positive steps to minimize the casualties.

There are other ways in which the idea of 'collateral damage' can be abused in either its accidental or incidental forms. Curiously enough, one is by loudly proclaiming a commitment to non-combatant immunity as a way of disguising one's contempt, or marginal respect, for it in practice. This form of insincerity is a particularly common political device as the case of torture also illustrates: those who authorize and instigate forms of torture and extreme interrogation are often loudest in their public denials of complicity. Another abuse is the expansion of the permissible scope of the category of collateral damage by expansion of the scope of legitimate military targets. This is the strategy of targeting 'dual-purpose' facilities, a practice that has become increasingly familiar in recent US military practice, though it has a more ancient lineage. The war against Serbia over Kosovo provides many examples, as also does the recent attack upon Iraq. The case of the Priština telephone exchange, mentioned earlier, provides one such example, since, even if the bomb had not been 'seduced', the destruction of a central telephone exchange is, in the modern age, a massive blow to civilian well-being, given all the services in a contemporary city that depend upon modern communications. There may indeed be many cases in which an institution or facility principally serving non-combatant purposes may also serve some subsidiary military purpose. I do not want to deny that sometimes a grave enough case may exist to treat that subsidiary purpose as sufficient to allow an attack. But the mere existence of a dual purpose is not itself enough to legitimate an attack and treat the damage to non-combatants as permissible 'incidental' injury. Enemy soldiers often use the same water supply as civilians, but this will hardly license the destruction of water supplies and the subsequent deaths from thirst and disease that will ensue. The casual attitude to the destruction of power supplies, oil reserves, bridges, communications networks, and media facilities also needs more careful scrutiny, lest it really display a disregard for the rights and protections that should be accorded non-combatants.

This point is connected with the fact that, whether we are dealing with war or terrorism, much discussion of collateral damage has, understandably, focused upon the *killing* of non-combatants. But there are many other harms, damages, and sufferings that can be inflicted that do not result in immediate death. The dual-purpose strategy tends to involve viewing the infrastructural features of an enemy population as connected with short-term military gains and short-term civilian discomforts; but the moral gaze needs to be broader than that, because, especially in modern societies, the infrastructures are increasingly crucial to well-being and even sometimes to life itself. Something like this point can be extended to the problems raised by direct or incidental damage to the natural and human environment of the enemy's country. Forests, rivers, architectural and artistic creations, and the like can be viewed both as valuable in themselves or as part of the significant life of the enemy's civilian population, or indeed as part of the broader human heritage (hence the outrage at the Taliban's destruction of ancient statues of another faith).

More broadly, whatever the problems with DDE, there are moral attitudes underlying the different approaches to collateral damage that are reflected in the application of the DDE that are themselves of clear significance in the prosecution of war. These fall into (at least) four camps:

1. Sadistic contempt for non-combatants' lives and well-being, leading to the intentional killing of them.
2. Instrumental disdain for them, leading again to the intentional killing of them.
3. Indifference to their lives and well-being, leading to a casual attitude to collateral damage.
4. Concern for their lives and well-being, leading to attempts to avoid or limit the collateral damage.

However we work out the formula that allows for some foreseen but unintentional killing of non-combatants, it is the moral superiority of (4) over (1), (2), and (3) that gives significance to the attempt. Decisions about proportionality that can justify some collateral damage to non-combatants will, I think, always involve an element of concrete judgement in situations of uncertain outcome and the pursuit of debatable goods. The difficulty in making these decisions, and the costs involved, are reasons for not resorting to war, revolution, or insurgency in the first place. But assuming that wars and other resorts to political violence can sometimes be justified, and that politicians and peoples will continue to make that judgement, no matter how mistakenly, we need to allow for the feasible prosecution of a just war, or one believed to be just, while giving a moral priority to protecting the lives of non-combatants. Disallowing intentional targeting of them is an important step forward. Producing a frame of mind that will limit collateral damage is a good next step.

PART II

7

Airpower and Non-combatant Immunity: The Road to Dresden

STEPHEN A. GARRETT

In late 1944, during the last months of World War II, British and American military planners proposed the following scheme, code-named Thunderclap, for bringing the war against Germany to a final conclusion. Thunderclap envisioned a joint assault by several thousand British and American bombers on the German capital of Berlin in which there would be round-the-clock bombing over a period of four days and nights. The expectation was that this type of cataclysmic assault would totally shatter the German people's will to continue the war. In order to accomplish this objective, the explicit military premiss behind Thunderclap was that much, if not most, of Berlin would be reduced to smoking rubble.

For a variety of reasons, Thunderclap was never fully implemented, yet the whole saga of strategic bombing in World War II—and particularly attacks on enemy cities—represents perhaps one of the most striking developments in the history of armed conflict. It is instructive to consider how all this came about, both in terms of the march of technology and even more in terms of the march of ideas as to how war could successfully—and legitimately—be waged. For purposes of this essay, the prime focus here will be on the British approach to strategic bombing during World War II.

The Past as Prologue

There are scattered historical examples prior to 1914 of the use of air power as a method of warfare, such as the use of Italian aircraft in the Italo–Turkish conflict over Libya in 1911–12, but it was not until World War I that the application of aerial attacks on an enemy's homeland was introduced as a regular part of the strategy of the warring powers. From 1916 onward, French aircraft launched strikes against several German cities in retaliation for enemy assaults on Paris and other French towns. The British undertook a series of raids on Zeppelin factories and other military targets in Germany in the area of the Saarland, Mannheim, and Stuttgart. It was the Germans, however, who led the way in demonstrating how aircraft could be used against the enemy's own territory.

From January 1915 to November 1916, Zeppelins were employed to attack targets in the north of England and the Midlands as well as the British capital. Beginning in May 1917, the so-called Gotha raids on London and other cities were initiated. These were genuine bombers, rather than airships, and their employment served to reinforce the earlier impression of a basic threshold having been crossed in the means of modern war. Overall there was a total of 208 airship and 435 airplane sorties undertaken against England by the German air force. About 300 tons of bombs were dropped, killing around 1,400 people and wounding another 3,400.[1]

Compared to the figures that were to be produced by the next great war, these may have been relatively modest results, but they established an ominous precedent. The notion that civilians could no longer feel sacrosanct from air strikes seemed to have acquired at least tentative acceptance. As one authority on the use of air power in World War I wrote, 'One principle seems to have been followed [which was] that military objectives could be bombed wherever found, regardless of their location, and, it seems, regardless of the injury to non-combatants and private property.'[2]

In the inter-war period a heated and generally rather abstract debate developed over what the experience of World War I had to say about the potential of strategic bombing. In the generic sense the strategic application of air power simply meant the use of aircraft for direct assaults on the enemy's homeland and his fundamental capacity to make war (as

---

[1] John Pimlott, 'The Theory and Practice of Strategic Bombing', in Colin McInnes and G. D. Sheffield (eds.), *Warfare in the Twentieth Century* (London: Unwin Hyman, 1988), 121.
[2] Quoted in Geoffrey Best, *Humanity in Warfare* (New York: Columbia University Press, 1980), 269.

distinguished, for example, from the use of aircraft in tactical support of ground forces). The discussion remained somewhat abstract, because there was, after all, a rather slim body of actual evidence on which to base conclusions. However, this did not prevent writers such as the famous Italian air power theorist General Giulio Douhet from advancing a whole new theory of the potential decisiveness of strategic bombing in a future war. His essential proposition was that a massive air attack by a fully developed strategic bomber force at the outbreak of hostilities would prove decisive to the outcome of any war.

A complete breakdown of the social structure cannot but take place in a country subjected to this kind of merciless pounding from the air. The time would soon come when, to put an end to horror and suffering, the people themselves, driven by the instinct of self-preservation, would rise up and demand an end to the war—this before their army and navy had time to mobilize at all![3]

Douhet impatiently dismissed any notion that such an attack might seem unduly harsh. Indeed, he argued that 'mercifully, the decision will be quick in this kind of war, since the decisive blows will be directed at civilians, that element of the countries at war least able to sustain them'. Thus a conflict fought in these terms might yet 'prove to be more humane than wars in the past in spite of all, because they may in the long run shed less blood'.[4]

Within British official circles the leading voice in the inter-war years arguing for the importance of a strategic bombing capability for Britain was undoubtedly that of Sir Hugh Trenchard, the first Chief of the Air Staff for the Royal Air Force. Trenchard's views were perhaps best summarized in a memorandum to the other service chiefs in May 1928.[5] He put his case directly: 'It is not necessary for an air force, in order to defeat the enemy nation, to defeat its armed forces first. Air power can dispense with that intermediate step ... and attack directly the centres of production, transportation and communication from which the enemy war effort is maintained.' Trenchard envisioned his bombing campaign as

---

[3] Giulio Douhet, *The Command of the Air*, trans. Dino Ferrari (New York: Coward–McCann, 1942), 57–8.

[4] Ibid. 54–5.

[5] The full text of the memorandum may be found in Noble Frankland and Charles Webster, *The Strategic Air Offensive against Germany 1939–1945* (London: Her Majesty's Stationery Office, 1961), iv. 74 (hereafter cited as *SAOG*).

actually having two fundamental purposes: to destroy the enemy's technical capacity for continuing the war effort, and to undermine his will for doing so. On the latter point, he put the 'moral' effects of bombing as more important than the physical effects by a factor of 20 to 1.

Trenchard did accept that it was 'contrary to the dictates of humanity [to engage in] the indiscriminate bombing of a city for the sole purpose of terrorizing the civilian population'. On the other hand, he regarded it as entirely legitimate to terrorize munitions workers into ceasing their work or stevedores to stop loading arms on to ships. 'Moral effect', he said, 'is created by the bombing in such circumstances but it is the inevitable result of a lawful operation of war—the bombing of a military objective.' Put in this way, many later critics of British bombing policy in World War II would have been forced to nod assent. The question was to be, however, how the concept of a military objective was subject to elaboration and expansion as the air offensive evolved.

Sir Hugh Trenchard's confident predictions about the effect of a modern strategic bombing campaign remained unproven, but even so, both the Government and the British people more generally tended to nurse rather apocalyptic images concerning the probable effect of air strikes during the first days of a new war with Germany. The widely held belief was the Germans would initiate hostilities with massive bombing of vulnerable British cities. Winston Churchill himself estimated that under a continuous air assault on London at least three or four million people would be driven out into the surrounding countryside. On the eve of war in 1939, the Government was prepared for about a quarter of a million casualties in the capital alone for the first three weeks of air attack, along with three million psychiatric cases, an equivalent number of refugees, and up to 50 per cent destruction of property.

The fears expressed were given a certain degree of impetus by the scattered examples of air strikes against cities which had taken place in the years after 1918. The Italians bombed the Ethiopian capital of Addis Ababa in 1936, the Japanese devastated Nanking in China in 1937, and there was the attack of the German Condor Legion on the undefended Basque town of Guernica in the same year, in which about 1,000 people were killed and 70 per cent of the buildings destroyed. To be sure, each of these attacks took place against relatively primitive or even non-existent air defences, but they seemed to cast a sinister shadow, nonetheless.

The Normative and Legal Background

When technical developments first introduced the possibility of using air power on a large scale to undertake direct attacks on an enemy's homeland in wartime, the international community was perforce confronted with a compelling question: would such attacks be in accordance with the traditional laws of warfare, and even more, would they be consonant with accepted standards of moral and humanitarian restraint by civilized nations concerning the tools of violence?

As early as 1899, the Hague Peace Conference had unanimously adopted a declaration to prohibit 'for a period of five years... the discharge of projectiles or explosives from balloons or by other new methods of a similar nature'.[6] Article 25 of the 1907 Hague Convention forbade 'any attack on undefended towns, villages, residential places or buildings by any means whatsoever'. This stipulation reflected a fairly elementary moral consideration, in that it was hardly necessary to attack an undefended town except for reasons of pure revenge or reprisal.

The introduction of genuine strategic bombing in World War I, and in particular, fairly indiscriminate attacks on urban areas, led to renewed pressures for defining more precisely the laws of war as they applied to aerial combat. To address this issue, a special Commission of Jurists met at The Hague from December 1922 to February 1923. The Commission consisted of legal experts from the United States, Great Britain, France, Italy, Japan, and the Netherlands, and they were assisted by various military and naval advisers in their deliberations. The Hague Draft Rules which emerged from this conference established for the first time a body of principles specifically related to the exercise of strategic air power.[7]

The jurists did not bother to conceal their feeling that the introduction of aerial attacks on cities was an abhorrent development in war. 'The conscience of mankind revolts against this form of making war outside the actual theatre of military operations, and the feeling is universal that limitations ought to be imposed.'[8] The Hague conferees eventually agreed

---

[6] Richard H. Wyman, 'The First Rules of Air Warfare', *Air University Review*, March–April 1984, 95.

[7] Lee Kennett, *A History of Strategic Bombing* (New York: Scribner's, 1982), 63–4.

[8] 'General Report of the Commission of Jurists at the Hague', *American Journal of International Law*, 17 (Oct. 1923), suppl. 249.

on a set of Rules of Aerial Warfare, comprising sixty-two articles, of which five related specifically to air attacks on cities. Article 22 stated that

aerial bombardment for the purpose of terrorizing the civilian population, of destroying or damaging private property not of a military character, or of injuring non-combatants, is prohibited.

The critical part of the Hague Draft Rules, however, could be found in Article 24, which contained, *inter alia*, the following provisions:

Aerial bombardment is legitimate only when directed at a military objective, that is to say, an object of which the destruction or injury would constitute a distinct military advantage to the belligerent.

The bombardment of cities, towns, villages, dwellings or buildings not in the immediate neighbourhood of the operation of land forces is prohibited. In cases where [legitimate military] objectives are so situated that they cannot be bombarded without the indiscriminate bombardment of the civilian population, the aircraft must abstain from bombardment.[9]

The Hague Draft Rules, when published, met with a good deal of hostility from various circles, especially in terms of what constituted a genuine military objective and the supposed impracticality of attempting to restrain technical developments in air power. For these reasons, among others, the participating governments at The Hague drew back from formal ratification of The Hague principles. As of 1939, they remained simply Draft Rules, and thus not technically binding on any of the belligerents. Even so, the deliberations at The Hague had set out a code of aerial warfare that represented a combined juridical and military judgement from representatives of the most important air powers of the day. They thus had considerable influence, even if not officially ratified, and as one leading authority put it, constituted 'an authoritative attempt to clarify and formulate rules of law governing the use of aircraft in war'.[10]

The other major international attempt during the inter-war years to deal with the issue of permissible conduct in air operations came at the Geneva Disarmament Conference in 1932. In this instance there was an emphasis

[9] 'The Hague Rules of 1923', *American Journal of International Law*, 17 (Oct. 1923), suppl. 250–1.
[10] L. Oppenheim, *International Law*, ed. H. Lauterpacht, 7th edn., ii (New York: Longmans, Green, 1952), 519.

on limiting the capabilities of the powers for city bombing, rather than on simply trying to hold them to legal standards of discrimination, even though the Conference did state that air attacks on civilian populations were in violation of the laws of war. Serious consideration was even given to the total abolition of long-range bombers, except for a residual force to be under the direct control of the League of Nations to enforce sanctions against aggression. This received surprising political support in Great Britain, save for the Air Ministry, which favoured retention of a bombing force for policing the Empire. A spokesman for the Royal Navy, however, supported a total ban on bombers, saying that 'only the Air Ministry want to retain these weapons for use against towns, a method of warfare which is revolting and un-English'.[11] Ironically, in view of later events, Winston Churchill was one of those who voiced support for the abolition of aircraft designed for strategic bombing. The coming to power of Hitler in Germany, however, undermined whatever chance there was at Geneva for a fundamental agreement on air power restrictions. He withdrew Germany from the Conference in October 1933, although the Nazi government did propose in March 1936 that a general prohibition be established against 'the dropping of bombs on open towns and other inhabited places'.[12]

What we are left with, then, seems clear enough. Prior to World War II there was no convention that was legally binding on Great Britain, forbidding her from indiscriminate air attacks on German cities (generally referred to as 'area bombing'). At the same time the whole direction and substance of international discussion on the parameters of strategic bombing suggested that such attacks were seen as indefensible. More to the point, the British government itself seemed clearly to accept that area bombing as such was an unacceptable strategy. The British announced that they would adhere to The Hague Draft Rules, even though they were not formally binding, as long as others did so. Prime Minister Neville Chamberlain went before the House of Commons in June 1938 and summarized the case against area bombing with admirable directness:

We can strongly condemn any declaration on the part of anybody, wherever it may be made, that it should be part of a deliberate policy to try to win a war

---

[11] Kennett, *History of Strategic Bombing*, 70.
[12] Hans Rumpf, *The Bombing of Germany* (New York: Holt, Rinehart & Winston, 1963), 17–18.

by the demoralization of the civilian population through the process of bombing from the air. This is absolutely contrary to international law, and I would add that, in my opinion, it is a mistaken policy from the point of view of those who adopt it, but I do not believe that the deliberate attacks upon a civilian population will ever win a war for those who make them.[13]

What is interesting about Chamberlain's stance on air power is his commingling of both a legal/moral argument and a practical one. In the time-honoured phrase, area bombing, from Chamberlain's point of view, was more than a crime, it was also a mistake. The Prime Minister reiterated his position on the matter even after war had broken out. 'Whatever be the lengths to which others may go, his Majesty's government will never resort to the deliberate attack on women and children, and other civilians for purposes of mere terrorism.'[14]

The Coming of the Strategic Air Offensive

For some months after the initiation of hostilities between Britain and Germany on 3 September 1939, the controls on British air power tactics that Chamberlain had established as policy remained substantially in force. From early September to about the middle of May 1940, the Royal Air Force's Bomber Command divided its time between dropping leaflets over the German Reich and occasional attacks on naval and other 'precise' military targets, and showed a distinct concern to avoid any unnecessary harm to enemy civilians. For example, in November 1939, the War Cabinet secretly considered a plan for bombing targets in the Ruhr in response to a German invasion of Belgium, but there was great reluctance to do so because of the expected effect on the civilian population.[15]

The factors in this self-restraint were actually somewhat varied, and went beyond simply honouring the Prime Minister's pre-war declaration. For one thing, Bomber Command hardly had the resources at this point to undertake a major strategic bombing effort against Germany. There was

[13] Great Britain, 5 *Parliamentary Debates* (Commons), 337 (21 June 1938), 936.
[14] Great Britain, 5 *Parliamentary Debates* (Commons), 351 (14 Sept. 1939), 750.
[15] John Colville, *The Fringes of Power* (New York: W.W. Norton & Company, 1985), 52–3.

also concern about the reaction of world opinion, and especially that in the United States, to a major aerial assault on Germany that would put civilians at risk. On 1 September 1939, President Roosevelt had addressed an appeal to all the belligerent powers calling for a restriction of aerial warfare to specifically military targets. The French and the British announced their acceptance of this standard on the following day, and the Germans added their assent as well on 18 September.[16] The Nazi motivation in doing so was clear enough: their concern that in an unrestrained contest of strategic bombing, Germany might well be at a disadvantage. As Hitler himself said, 'the guiding principle must be not to provoke the initiation of aerial warfare by any action on the part of Germany' (a somewhat striking statement in view of the pre-war fears in Great Britain about the German threat to British cities).[17]

What may be regarded as a period of innocence for Bomber Command during the first eight months of the war came to a close on 15 May 1940, when in a directive signed by Winston Churchill, who had replaced Neville Chamberlain as Prime Minister a few days earlier, the RAF was now authorized to attack a greater variety of targets east of the Rhine. The spur to this decision was evidently a reduced concern about the possibilities of German retaliation on British cities as well as the fact that at least some strategic bombing of the enemy seemed at this point to be one of the few ways in which the British could carry the war to the enemy, a consideration that acquired particular currency after the evacuation at Dunkirk.

For approximately the next two years, Bomber Command undertook a steadily widening series of strikes against the German homeland. At the official level the stated emphasis was on what were called precision or selective attacks against carefully defined military and industrial objectives (the German oil industry, communications, and aircraft plants, for example). There were further references to the necessity of sparing civilians as much as possible. An instruction from the War Cabinet to the Air Ministry in early June 1940, for example, stressed that air attacks 'must be made with reasonable care to avoid undue loss of civil life in the vicinity of the target'.[18] At the same time, 'area bombing', or generalized assaults on urban targets,

[16] George Quester, *Deterrence before Hiroshima* (New York: John Wiley & Sons, 1966), 106.
[17] Hugh Trevor-Roper, (ed.), *Hitler's War Directives* (London: Sidgwick & Jackson, 1964), 6-7.
[18] Max Hastings, *Bomber Command* (New York: Simon & Schuster, 1987), 84-6.

was, like Banquo's ghost, never very far from the proceedings. As early as October 1940, the Air Staff issued a new directive that oil targets should be attacked on clear nights, but that whole cities could at least be considered as alternative targets in less favourable weather. In December 1940, what is generally considered the first open British effort at area bombing came with an attack on the city of Mannheim, a raid specifically described as a retaliation for the earlier German assault on Coventry.

Perhaps the principal voice calling for a less restrained approach to Bomber Command's activities was that of the Prime Minister himself. As far back as July 1940, he had written to Lord Beaverbrook, Minister for Aircraft Production, that there was only one thing that would bring Hitler down, and that was 'an absolutely devastating exterminating attack by very heavy bombers from this country upon the Nazi homeland'.[19] Several months later, Churchill expanded on this theme in a statement to the War Cabinet which suggested that, 'whilst we should adhere to the rule that our objectives should be military targets, at the same time the civilian population around the target areas must be made to feel the weight of war'.[20] Churchill's Chief of the Air Staff, Sir Charles Portal, also was increasingly persuaded of the merits of area bombing. Portal suggested that twenty to thirty towns and cities should be selected as potential targets for Bomber Command, with the primary aim being the deliverance of very heavy material destruction and a demonstration to the enemy of the expanding power and severity of air bombardment from Britain. As one individual privy to the discussion on bombing policy at this point put it, 'the moral scruples of the Cabinet on this subject have been overcome'.[21]

The Government's wavering between an ostensible programme of precision bombing and an increasing tendency toward area bombing was resolved finally in a policy statement of 14 February 1942. The bomber offensive, according to Directive No. 22 issued to Bomber Command, was now to be 'focused on the morale of the enemy civil population and in particular of the industrial workers'. In case there was any doubt at Bomber Command headquarters about what was now intended, the Chief of the Air Staff sent a follow-on communication the next day: 'Ref the new

[19] R. V. Jones, *Most Secret War* (London: Hamish Hamilton, 1978), 183.
[20] Charles Messenger, *'Bomber' Harris* (New York: St Martin's Press, 1984), 40.
[21] Colville, *Fringes of Power*, 311.

bombing directive: I suppose it is clear that the aiming points are to be the built-up areas, not, for instance, the dockyards or aircraft factories. ... This must be made quite clear if it is not already understood.'[22] Sir Arthur Harris, who was to become head of Bomber Command on 23 February, indicated that he at least had no misunderstanding on this point.

The decision by the British to adopt a straightforward strategy of area or indiscriminate bombing of Germany after 1942 (in other words, the systematic devastation of German cities) was obviously a landmark in the evolution of warfare, and more particularly the concept of total war. Over the next three years, about three-quarters of the bombs dropped on Germany by Great Britain were against area targets. How to account for the adoption of such a momentous course of action?

A rather curious mix of emotional, political, technical, and theoretical considerations seems to have been involved. For some there was clearly the feeling that the Germans had, after all, initiated city attacks, first with the bombing of Warsaw, then the assault on Rotterdam in May 1940 (which was said to have caused 30,000 fatalities), and finally with the Blitz on Britain itself. Extending in its most intense form from the autumn of 1940 to the spring of 1941, the Blitz eventually resulted in some 50,000 tons of bombs being dropped on British cities, which led to about 40,000 civilian deaths. Given this record of events, it was not hard to argue that, after all, the Germans had sowed the wind and now were to reap the whirlwind. The Prime Minister himself sometimes seemed to suggest that even though he personally had little desire as such for revenge, the British people did expect retaliation in kind. In a flight of hyperbole, he commented that the people now demanded that all Germans should be massacred or castrated. He told the House of Commons that 'on every side is the cry, "We can take it", but with it is also the cry, "Give it them back"'.[23] In effect, Churchill's argument seemed to be that in order to sustain the nation's morale, it was necessary to do unto others as they were doing to Britain.

It is hard to gauge how significant a factor the calls for pure retribution were in the 14 February directive to Bomber Command. As it happens, however, there was a key operational factor confronting the Government

<hr/>

[22] *SAOG*, i. 323–4.
[23] J. M. Spaight, *Bombing Vindicated* (London: Geoffrey Bles, 1944), 45.

in early 1942 that may be seen as pushing the RAF toward a strategy of area bombing quite on its own. It became apparent early in the war that the lack of sufficient fighter support and the growing effectiveness of German air defences presented the RAF with the prospect of prohibitive losses if it attempted to attack German targets in daylight. As a matter of policy, then, Bomber Command by the spring of 1940 had come to concentrate almost entirely on night-time bombing of the enemy.

Could such raids achieve sufficient accuracy to allow the targeting of precise military objectives? For a time, the analysts at Bomber Command attempted to maintain the fiction that such was possible, but the evidence as it accumulated seriously undermined their case, and was dealt a particular blow by the so-called Butt Report of August 1941. At the behest of Lord Cherwell, Churchill's principal scientific adviser, Mr D. M. Butt of the Cabinet Secretariat undertook a systematic study of the efforts of Bomber Command to date. His analysis revealed that in British air strikes against specific targets in the Ruhr, only one-tenth of the bombers even found their way to within five miles of the assigned target. For other areas, the figure was a still depressing one in three.[24] The inevitable conclusion seemed to be that if Great Britain were to continue its strategic bombing offensive against Germany, the only feasible targets were large urban areas, where the problems of inaccuracy would be much less compelling. Since few if any of the major figures in the Government were inclined simply to call a halt to the bombing offensive—particularly as it was the only major evidence at the time of Britain's determination to carry on the war effort—the turn to indiscriminate bombing followed almost as a matter of course.

Still, it would be somewhat misleading to suggest that those involved simply, and rather mindlessly, adopted area bombing without thought as to its practical military utility and only because it was the one thing Bomber Command could do. There were in fact attempts by those in authority to develop a broader strategic rationale for area bombing beyond simply the limitations that Bomber Command then confronted. Lord Cherwell was a particular contributor to this process, and his ideas reflected one of the standard themes of the pre-war air power theorists. In a famous minute to the Prime Minister on 30 March 1942, Cherwell concentrated on the

---

[24] *SAOG*, i. 178.

impact on German morale of a major British area bombing campaign. Based on his analysis of the German bombing of British cities, he argued that 'having one's house demolished is most damaging to morale. People seem to mind it more than having their friends or even relatives killed.' He went on from there to estimate that with adequate resources and by concentrating on the fifty-eight major German population centres, Bomber Command could by 1943 render a third of the German people homeless. 'There seems little doubt that this would break the spirit of the people.' The concept of the shattering of the German people's morale, and thus of Germany's will or ability to continue the war, was enshrined henceforth as one of the guiding premises of British bombing policy. As the official history of Bomber Command puts it, 'Because of the position which he occupied and the time at which he submitted his minute, Lord Cherwell's intervention was of great importance. It did much to ensure the concept of strategic bombing in its hour of crisis.'[25]

There were, to be sure, other rationales brought forward to justify the bombing of German cities aside from its putative effect on morale. One of these was that it would help to divert German resources from the Russian campaign and the Middle East, in order to provide for the air defence of the Reich. Moreover, since German industry was naturally concentrated in and around the major German cities, even so-called indiscriminate attacks on these places was bound to damage or destroy some of the relevant factories. Such attacks would also lead to a shattering of the whole fabric of German civil life, which in turn would create a basic dislocation in war production and the German home front's ability to support the Reich military machine. Sir Arthur Harris was particularly ardent in advancing these propositions, and he even went so far as to suggest that if the British government gave its full support to the bomber offensive, Germany could essentially be defeated by air power alone.[26]

The Area Bombing of Germany: The First Phase

Harris did not wait long after assuming leadership of Bomber Command before beginning his long campaign to demonstrate that the theory of area

[25] Ibid. 331–6.
[26] Arthur Harris, *Bomber Offensive* (London: Collins, 1947), 74–5, 113.

bombing could be translated into a productive reality. The Baltic port city of Lübeck provided a convenient early test case. An old medieval town constructed largely of wood ('built more like a fire-lighter than a human habitation', as Harris observed), Lübeck was attacked on the night of 28 March by 234 RAF bombers. Some 200 acres, or about half the city, was levelled, the German estimate being that more than 15,000 people had their homes destroyed as a consequence of the raid. Another old Hanseatic city, Rostock, was given similar treatment later in April. More than 100,000 civilians were forced to evacuate the city as a result of this attack.

Despite these early successes, Harris was acutely aware that the credibility of Bomber Command as a major, perhaps *the* major, focus of the British war effort was hardly accepted by everyone in authority. In a rather striking admission of the situation in which he now found himself, Harris recalled that he 'had to regard the operations of the next few months as a commercial travellers' samples which I could show to the War Cabinet'. He decided that there was a need for a truly spectacular operation that hopefully would lay to rest the doubts of his critics, and in particular ensure support for Bomber Command from the Prime Minister. It was thus that the plan for Millennium was conceived, the first thousand-bomber raid of the war. The target chosen was Cologne, and the results were impressive indeed. Approximately 600 acres of the city were devastated on the night of 30 May 1942, and as the final wave of bombers approached, the city was burning with such ferocity that the light from the flames could be seen from 150 miles away. More than 45,000 people were rendered homeless, and the roads out of Cologne were clogged with a massive exodus of refugees. When Harris reported the results of Millennium to Churchill, he was gratified by the Prime Minister's reaction. 'I knew at once that he was satisfied then. ... He wanted above all to get on with the war and no one understood better than he the vast strategic consequences of this operation.'[27] Thus the continuation of a full-fledged area bombing offensive, together with the necessary commitment of resources, had apparently been accepted by the one person whose opinion was decisive.

---

[27] Harris, *Bomber Offensive*, 112–13.

The British area bombing offensive against Germany over the next two years involved a host of different operations, but the assaults on Hamburg and Berlin deserve special attention. Hamburg was on the receiving end of thirty-three major air attacks (code-named Operation Gomorrah) from July to November 1943. The night raids on 24, 27, and 29 July represented the apex of the assault on Hamburg. In each instance, well over 700 bombers from the RAF rained a combination of incendiary and explosive bombs on the central city area of Hamburg. Approximately 74 per cent of the most densely populated section of the city was destroyed. About 50,000 people were killed in these attacks, and around one million refugees fled to safer outlying areas.[28] Perhaps the most noted aspect of the Hamburg raids was the phenomenon of the fire-storm, which produced hurricane-type winds of 150 miles an hour and sucked people, trees, even whole buildings, into the centre of the flames. The Police President of Hamburg summarized the fate of his city this way:

Its horror is revealed in the howling and raging of the firestorms, the hellish noise of exploding bombs and the death cries of martyred human beings as well as in the big silence after the raids. Speech is impotent to portray the measure of the horror, which shook the people for ten days and nights and the traces of which were written indelibly on the face of the city and its inhabitants.[29]

The devastation of Hamburg was henceforward referred to by the Germans simply as *die Katastrophe*.

The so-called Battle of Berlin began on the night of 18 November and continued for four months until the end of the following March. During this period some thirty-five raids of more than 500 bombers each were launched against the German capital as well as other cities. Sixteen of the missions were directed at Berlin itself, which represented the greatest single focusing of Bomber Command's efforts since the beginning of the war.[30] Arthur Harris had begun the Battle of Berlin with high hopes. In a typically self-confident communication to the Prime Minister, he had asserted that

[28] The standard treatment of the attack on Hamburg remains Martin Middlebrook's *The Battle of Hamburg* (London: Allen Lane, 1980).

[29] Martin Caidin, *The Night Hamburg Died* (New York: Ballantine Books, 1960), 9. Caidin reports without comment that the British employed phosphorus bombs in considerable quantities over Hamburg because of their 'demonstrated ability to depress the morale of the Germans'.

[30] H. R. Allen, *The Legacy of Lord Trenchard* (London: Cassell, 1972), 149–51.

'we can wreck Berlin from end to end if the U.S. Army Air Forces will come in on it. It will cost between us 400 and 500 aircraft. It will cost Germany the war.'[31] As it happened, there was only marginal American participation in this enterprise, and the results of Bomber Command's own efforts proved to be a great disappointment. For various reasons, far less devastation was inflicted on Berlin than in the raids against Hamburg (only about one-third of the acreage destroyed, as compared to the earlier attacks). Moreover, these results had to be balanced against the increasing losses which Bomber Command was now suffering in its campaign against Berlin and other major cities. The potency of the German night-fighter force, as well as their anti-aircraft defences, was reflected in an average loss rate for British bombers on the order of about 5.0 per cent. Sometimes it was even more severe: in an attack on Nuremberg in March 1944, some ninety-four bombers were lost, and another seventy-one damaged out of a total force of 795 employed.[32]

This level of attrition could not be long sustained, and in view of the rather problematic effect which area bombing seemed to be having on the German ability to maintain her war effort, something of a crisis of confidence developed at Bomber Command and amongst others in authority about the future of the air offensive. As it happened, however, the doubts that had now arisen became submerged in the planning for D-Day, the Allied invasion of Europe. In what, under the circumstances, may be regarded as a blessing in disguise for Bomber Command, Harris was now ordered to divert virtually all his aircraft from the bombing of Germany to more direct support for the coming landings in Normandy. Over the next several months Bomber Command devoted the brunt of its operations to attacks on the German rail system in France and the Low Countries in order to disrupt German transport of reinforcements and material to the front after D-Day. They did so with admirable success, and the evidence in fact suggests that the combined British and American assault on these targets played a critical role in the successful Allied invasion. By late May, traffic on the railway network in France had declined to 55 per cent of the January figure, and by D-Day itself had fallen to only 30 per cent of the earlier figure.[33]

---

[31] *SAOG*, ii. 47–8.
[32] Noble Frankland, *The Bombing Offensive Against Germany* (London: Faber & Faber, 1965), 74.
[33] John Keegan, *The Second World War* (New York: Viking, 1989), 416.

The Area Bombing of Germany: The Second Phase

By September 1944, Allied forces had not only firmly established themselves in France, but were making rapid progress against the increasingly shattered German defences. At this point the debate resumed over strategy for Bomber Command in its attacks on Germany itself. There was a clear consensus on the part of the Allied Combined Chiefs of Staff as well as most other informed observers that Bomber Command would do best at this point to concentrate on German oil facilities as well as the enemy's communications network. The prospects that Harris's forces could now carry out this sort of precision bombing campaign, moreover, seemed almost beyond dispute. Earlier limited strikes by the British and Americans against petroleum targets in Germany had proved a great success. By September the *Luftwaffe*'s fuel supply had been reduced to 10,000 tons of octane, whereas a monthly minimum of around 160,000 tons was needed. Bomber Command's ability to hit oil targets, as well as its demonstrated efficiency in attacking the German transportation system prior to D-Day, suggested that it was indeed now capable of a general precision-bombing campaign.

That this was within its reach was indicated even more by the severe deterioration in German air defences by this stage of the war. From September onward, in fact, the Allies came to enjoy what the British official history termed 'virtual operational omnipotence' in the air, both at night and even during the day. The latter point was a key one: daylight bombing, with relatively modest losses, promised a degree of accuracy in hitting targets that was crucial to any precision-bombing campaign. In pondering all this, however, Arthur Harris saw no need to abandon his long-held belief in the essential correctness of the area bombing strategy. As he put it, 'I strongly objected to stopping the [area] offensive for which we had worked for five years.' He dismissed the earlier success of Allied bombers in attacking oil targets by saying that 'what the Allied strategists did was to bet on an outsider and it happened to win the race'.[34] He remained sceptical of what he called 'panacea targets': that is, supposed choke points in German war industry the destruction of which could be decisive.

---

[34] Harris, *Bomber Offensive*, 220–3.

In the months that followed, the Chief of the Air Staff, Sir Charles Portal, repeatedly urged Harris to join with the Americans in a precision-bombing campaign against Germany. Harris strongly implied that he would resign rather than accept any significant limitations on his renewal of the area offensive, and he stubbornly continued to stress his own priorities. In the last three months of 1944, the British dropped more bombs on Germany than in the whole of 1943, and some 53 per cent of this was delivered on cities, compared to 14 per cent directed at oil facilities and about 15 per cent on transportation targets. Earlier, Harris had established a list of sixty German cities that he intended to destroy, the accomplishment of which, he believed, would effectively end the war. By December, Harris's list of cities ripe for destruction had been pretty well translated into reality. Bomber Command had devastated or seriously damaged 80 per cent of all German urban areas with more than 100,000 population. This exercise in destruction continued even into the spring of 1945, with almost 40 per cent of British bombing being directed at city targets.[35]

The most famous (or notorious) of these attacks was undoubtedly the raid on Dresden on the night of 13 February. One of the special rationales for this operation involved the Russians. The attack would help to relieve German pressure on the Eastern front and convince Stalin that, despite some recent Allied difficulties, in particular the Battle of the Bulge, his Western partners were still doing their fair share in defeating the Nazis. Dresden was attacked by two waves of approximately 800 Lancasters (the Americans delivered their own strikes on the following two days), and as a result burned for a week. Estimates of casualties vary widely, from a minimal guess of about 35,000 to a more drastic figure of more than 200,000. In order to prevent the spread of disease, the authorities cordoned off the centre of the city and constructed 25-foot-long grills where thousands of the victims were cremated.[36]

The British official history describes the Dresden raid as 'the crowning achievement in the long, arduous and relentless development of a principle of bombing [the area offensive]'.[37] At this point, Prime Minister Churchill evidently decided that Bomber Command's 'crowning achievement' should be left to speak for itself, and in perhaps the most controversial reference

[35] Basil Liddell Hart, *History of the Second World War* (New York: G. P. Putnam's Sons, 1970), 609.
[36] David Irving, *The Destruction of Dresden* (New York: Holt, Rinehart & Winston, 1963).
[37] *SAOG*, iii. 109.

to the area offensive that he offered during the War, he wrote to the Chief of the Air Staff thus:

It seems to me that the moment has come when the question of bombing of German cities simply for the sake of increasing the terror, *though under other pretexts,* should be reviewed. Otherwise we shall come into control of an utterly ruined land. ... The destruction of Dresden remains a serious query against the conduct of Allied bombing.

The Foreign Secretary has spoken to me on this subject, and I feel the need for more precise concentration upon military objectives such as oil and communications behind the immediate battle-zone, *rather than on mere acts of terror and wanton destruction, however impressive.*[38]

Sir Charles Portal was greatly offended by Churchill's reference to 'terror' as a previous goal of British strategy, and in response the Prime Minister delivered a revised minute that dropped such sensitive references and instead concentrated on the pragmatic benefits to be obtained from a redirection of the area offensive. Whatever qualms were now being felt, however, did not prevent area attacks on German targets being continued virtually to the last days of World War II. Thus Würzberg was devastated on 16 March, 1945; two days later the city of Witten was two-thirds destroyed; and a month later there was a further raid on the Berlin suburb of Potsdam by 500 Lancasters, resulting in about 5,000 civilian fatalities.[39] In a sense, all this could be considered as simply reflexive actions of the vast machine of destruction which Bomber Command had become by this point. At long last, however, the RAF Air Staff issued a directive on 16 April that officially ended Bomber Command's strategic air offensive against Germany. Harris accepted this directive on the practical grounds that there were essentially no more area targets to be attacked in Germany.

Conclusion

In all, British Bomber Command launched some 390,000 sorties against Germany in the entire course of the war, with area attacks accounting

---

[38] Ibid. 112; my emphasis.
[39] Martin Middlebrook and Chris Everitt, *The Bomber Command War Diaries* (London: Viking, 1985), 683, 695.

for about 70 per cent of the total effort. Some 8,900 British aircraft were destroyed in the conflict, and approximately one million tons of bombs were dropped on the enemy. It is estimated that more than 500,000 German civilians lost their lives to Allied bombing. Perhaps another million received serious injury. Around three million homes were destroyed.[40]

There is a long-held theory that democracies are slow to anger, but once aroused, notably violent and ruthless in their waging of war. The underlying logic is that democratic regimes depend on popular support for prosecution of a war effort—unlike, perhaps, more authoritarian regimes—and thus they attempt to arouse the more primitive instincts of their people for the righteous smiting of the heathen. Once such emotions are set loose, it is hard to control them, and thus the predilection, ironically, for democratic nations to wage war without restraint. British military historian Basil Liddell Hart seems to have subscribed to this theory. He suggested that normally Britain was on a higher plane of decency and humanity than most other nations, but that 'our methods of war... tend to be more inhuman than those of battle-minded Continental countries'. More specifically, he argued that British military tactics in World War II tended 'to be less human than that of the Germans... their inhumanity being manifested rather in the political consolidation of military results'.[41]

There are many who will be made uneasy—or angry—by this disquisition on the comparative 'humanity' of German versus British military operations in World War II. After all, Liddell Hart had been at one time a strong *supporter* of the strategic air offensive, and the German armed forces were certainly guilty on occasion of quite horrendous violations of the laws of war. Nevertheless, it is a fact that the Germans never came close to matching the British area bombing offensive of Germany in their own air attacks on Britain, although it can easily be argued that this was more because of operational limitations than concerns about limits in war. Even so, this may miss the point: the point is that Britain was fighting for a particular vision of the future of humanity. That vision was intimately related to the value system that had been so laboriously constructed in

[40] Robin Cross, *The Bombers* (New York: Macmillan Publishing Company, 1987), 160; Hilary St. George Saunders, *Royal Air Force 1939–1945*, iii (London: Her Majesty's Stationery Office, 1954), 392.
[41] Brian Bond, *Liddell Hart* (London: Cassell, 1979), 155.

Britain itself over several hundred years: in particular, respect for the dignity and integrity of the individual and the value of a single human life. The troubling question remains whether in defeating the larger threat Britain did not in some ways diminish the very cause for which she was fighting. In writing about the American Civil War, Bruce Catton caught the essential dilemma facing free societies at war. He observed that in the search for victory democracies may be driven to 'perform acts that alter the very soil in which society's roots are nourished'.[42]

---

[42] Bruce Catton, *The Civil War* (New York: American Heritage Press, 1971), 185.

8

Civilian Immunity in the Precision-Guidance Age

HUGH WHITE

The Allied strategic bombing of Germany and Japan in World War II still provides the key test cases for thinking about civilian immunity in war. For good reason: sixty years on, they are still the most sustained and most lethal campaigns ever waged on civilian populations by Western democratic states. They have been extensively studied, so we have a wealth of data and interpretation to draw on. And because we mostly agree about the justice—in the sense of *jus ad bellum*—of the Allies' commitment to the wider war in which these campaigns took place, they offer a kind of laboratory situation in which questions of *jus in bello* can be isolated and explored with greater clarity.

However, some things have changed since World War II. In particular, technology has changed the way in which aerial bombing (or 'strike') campaigns are waged. This in turn is changing the kinds of decisions that military commanders and political leaders are called upon to make, in ways that affect the ethical dimension of those decisions. They are also changing the kinds of wars that Western countries are choosing to fight. These trends have become evident as Western governments have deployed forces on operations in many different locations and for many different reasons since the end of the Cold War in 1990. Those campaigns include Kuwait and Iraq in 1991, Kosovo in 1999, Afghanistan in 2001, and Iraq in 2003. This chapter aims to explore how the trends flowing from new technologies are affecting the conception and application of the principle of civilian immunity in war.

The first section looks briefly at how new weapon technologies have changed the nature of strike operations, and the second touches on how this is changing the kinds of wars that Western societies decide to fight. The third section looks at the evolution of the principle of civilian immunity, based on Michael Walzer's classic account in *Just and Unjust Wars*. The fourth section explores how Western militaries today approach the task of avoiding civilian casualities in strike operations. The fifth section explores how old questions concerning civilian immunity have emerged in new forms, and suggests some interesting questions that need further work.

From Dresden to Baghdad

The key difference between the strike operations of World War II or Vietnam and modern strike operations such as those in Iraq in 2003 is the development and proliferation of precision-guided munitions—PGMs. Although guided weapons began to be developed many decades ago, they have transformed the nature of strike operations only over the past twenty years, as the use of precision guidance has accelerated sharply. The numbers tell the story. In the Gulf War of 1990–1, around 10 per cent of air-delivered munitions used were precision-guided. In the Kosovo campaign of 1998, the proportion reached 35 per cent. In the invasion of Iraq in March and April 2003, it was around 90 per cent. It is worth noting that the increasing preponderance of PGMs in modern strike campaigns does not reflect any spectacular recent breakthrough in technology, but rather the steadily accelerating spread of relatively old technologies as their price falls. The key factor in the high proportion of PGMs in Iraq in 2003 was the introduction of simple guidance kits which turn ordinary iron bombs into PGMs by using the 1970s technology of the Global Positioning System satellite network. They are cheap and highly effective, working well in some conditions that can defeat other more expensive guidance systems.

The spread of PGMs has changed the way in which strike operations are conducted in profound ways. Because they can be delivered so much more precisely, fewer weapons need be used to achieve the same effect. Weapons carry less explosive, their effects can be more carefully tailored, and their impact can be better predicted. It is now possible to control what a weapon hits, and what happens when it hits, with a confidence incomparably greater than was possible sixty or even forty years ago. These developments have made a big difference to the ways in which force can be applied. Early students of air power—both opponents and proponents—expected that aircraft could deliver bombs with a precision comparable to the accuracy of aimed artillery fire. Of course, that proved an illusion: in World War II, 'precision bombing' became a bitter oxymoron, and the Allies moved to area bombing more or less by default. Now the early promise of air power is close to realization. PGMs, and the more sophisticated weapons design that precision guidance allows, offer a high probability that weapons can be placed on a target, and a higher level of confidence that the weapon's effects can be limited to those targets.

The other key technological development that is reshaping strike operations is the development of surveillance and reconnaissance technologies that significantly improve the ability of Western militaries to find and identify targets. Again these technologies are not necessarily very new. The US JSTARS system, for example, which uses powerful airborne radar to locate targets on the ground over wide areas, was one of the stars of the Iraq invasion in 2003, but it was already in service in the First Gulf War in 1991. Unmanned aerial reconnaissance vehicles using similar technologies have also been around for some time. But as they have become more commonplace, and have been better integrated into conservative military doctrine, they are revolutionizing the old military tasks of reconnaissance and target identification. It is the combination of this improved capacity to find targets with an improved capacity to hit them that has transformed the nature of air strike operations.

Of course, these technologies are not foolproof. Failures do happen both in the identification of targets and the delivery of weapons. Much attention has properly been paid to recent noteworthy examples, such as the bombing of the Chinese Embassy in Belgrade in 1999. These failures cannot be dismissed as simply aberrant exceptions. The probability of a certain level of both equipment failure and human error is both operationally and ethically significant, especially in the area of target identification, and we shall explore the implications for decision-makers of this fallibility in what follows. But the probability of a small but significant level of failure should not blind us to the bigger and more significant trend. Failures notwithstanding, PGMs and their associated technologies are changing—perhaps revolutionizing—the delivery of force from the air. And that is not just true for the United States. While these technologies are most widely available to US Armed Forces, they are also well within the technical and financial resources of most advanced militaries, many of which already have them in service or are in the process of acquiring them.

New Wars of Choice

The spread of cheap and reliable guided weapons is not just changing the way in which strike operations are conducted. It is also changing the ways in which wars are fought—and through that, changing the kind of wars we are fighting. The growing ability of Western militaries to find and attack specific targets effectively from the air is making it much easier to achieve some kinds of military and strategic objectives with less risk and less cost than would have been possible before. This first became evident in Kuwait in 1991. The sustained air campaign over the first weeks of Operation Desert Storm did much to degrade Iraq's forces in Kuwait, which were then expelled from Kuwait in a swift ground campaign with very few Coalition casualties. Kosovo in 1999 and Afghanistan in 2001 were even more compelling demonstrations of how much could now be achieved from the air without the risks and costs of major ground campaigns. These demonstrations were amplified in the invasion of Iraq in 2003. Though the dominant image of that campaign was the advance on Baghdad of American ground forces, the evidence suggests that the bulk of the effective attrition of Iraqi forces was achieved by the air campaign.

All this has real strategic implications. Precision-guidance technologies mean that Western countries now have options to achieve military objectives at far less risk and cost to themselves. This has been a major factor in encouraging them to resort to armed force more often, for less reason. It seems likely that none of the four campaigns I have mentioned so far—Kuwait in 1991, Kosovo in 1999, Afghanistan in 2001, and Iraq in 2003—would have been mounted if precision air power had not promised such substantial reduction of risk and cost of military operation compared to the costs involved in the Vietnam War. Partly as a result, Western societies are resorting to armed force in circumstances that they would not have contemplated only fifteen or twenty years ago—including against non-state and non-conventional military adversaries.

Of course, these campaigns have illustrated the limitations of precision-guided air power, and indeed of armed force more generally, in achieving longer-term strategic and political objectives. It is not my intention here to explore, and certainly not to advocate, the wider strategic prudence or ethical legitimacy of these campaigns. Each of them to some degree, and some to a high degree, raise questions both of policy judgement and of *jus ad bellum*. My focus is narrower—on the ways in which questions of civilian immunity have arisen in relation to these campaigns. I think this is worthwhile for three reasons. First, it provides an opportunity to explore such traditional issues of *jus in bello* in the new circumstances created by new technologies—and, as I shall argue, those new circumstances do indeed affect important aspects of these issues. Second, it allows us to explore these issues in the context of the new types of conflict to which Western countries are now committing their armed forces. And third, they have real importance for the application of this field of study to practical ethical issues. The questions raised by these recent conflicts are very real ones for national governments today. I write from an Australian perspective. Australian aircraft were involved with those of the UK and the USA in precision strike operations over Iraq in March and April 2003, and issues of civilian immunity presented real political, ethical, and legal issues to the Australian Defence Force and the Australian Government. They will occur again.

A Long Way from 'Bomber' Harris

I want to start by observing that quite stringent principles of civilian immunity have become deeply entrenched in policies and practices of Western governments and militaries, and in the expectations of public opinion. We have come a long way from the days of 'Bomber' Harris. Planning for nuclear war remains a striking exception, to which I will return, but with that exception there is now a clear and apparently robust consensus that it is no longer acceptable to target civilian populations in war, either deliberately or incidentally, as an expected but unsought consequence of operations designed to achieve other ends. This is not completely new: similar norms were becoming accepted by Western societies in the decades before 1914, but they were discarded in the struggles that followed, leading to the bombing campaigns of the 1940s.

When we look at the way in which military operations are planned and conducted by Western armed forces today, and at the way they are discussed and evaluated by governments and opinion leaders, we see at work a set of standards that broadly correspond to the criteria set out by Walzer in his argument about double effect in chapter 9 of *Just and Unjust Wars*.[1] In essence, Walzer's position is that actions deliberately intended to cause civilian casualties are always unacceptable,[2] but that actions which cause unintended civilian casualties are acceptable when

- the actions are legitimate acts of war in other respects;
- the civilian casualties are proportionate to the legitimate military objectives sought;
- 'the intention of the actor is good, that is, he aims narrowly at the acceptable effect; the evil effect [civilian casualties] is not one of his ends, nor is it a means to his end, and aware of the evil involved, he seeks to minimise it, accepting costs to himself.'[3]

If anything, this formulation looks too weak to capture the practice, or at least the avowed principles, of today's Western militaries and governments. Under current practice in US, NATO, and Australian forces, commanders are required not simply to 'seek to minimise' civilian casualties, but to design military operations at the tactical and operational level specifically to reduce to the absolute minimum the possibility of civilian casualties, and to accept a risk of civilian casualties only when that is demonstrably unavoidable in the achievement of key campaign objectives.

Of course, as mentioned above, planning for the use of nuclear weapons remains a significant exception to this standard. There is a stark difference between the scrupulous standards now espoused for avoiding civilian casualties in the use of conventional munitions and the unavoidable fact that use of today's nuclear arsenals would usually involve civilian casualties on a scale that would dwarf the worst of the bombing campaigns of World War II. Does this undermine the claim that tougher norms have now been

[1] Michael, Walzer, *Just and Unjust Wars: A Moral Argument with Historical Illustrations* (London: Allen Lane, 1977), 151 ff.

[2] In a later chapter, Walzer qualifies this claim, arguing that deliberate killing of civilians may be justified in cases of 'supreme emergency'. See ibid. ch. 16.

[3] Ibid. 155.

re-established? I think not: massive and indiscriminate effects are inherent in nuclear weapons—at least, those in today's inventories. But those weapons are a product of another time and place. For most nuclear powers, including the five nuclear weapons states under the Nuclear Non-Proliferation Treaty, the use of nuclear weapons remains almost unthinkable precisely because they would cause such indiscriminate damage. Thinking in Washington about developing new classes of nuclear weapons that might be more discriminating, and therefore more usable against targets like deep bunkers, might change all that. But it is noteworthy that the key reason why smaller weapons are being considered is precisely to make them more usable by limiting unintended effects. So the persistence of nuclear arsenals is not a counter-argument to the broader view that standards of civilian protection from the effects of military action among Western countries have become much higher in recent years.

How did today's more rigorous norms of civilian immunity emerge? Perhaps surprisingly, they do not appear to have been a reaction to the horrors of World War II bombing campaigns, but rather have to do with the widespread Western reconsideration of the use of force after Vietnam. Both in the Korean War and in Vietnam, operations were undertaken with markedly lower regard for the safety of civilians than would be tolerated under today's norms. Walzer's book was of course largely written under the shadow of Vietnam, and he provides some compelling examples of operations, especially infantry operations, in Korea[4] and in Vietnam,[5] that reflect norms of conduct quite remote from those that are now espoused and, in general, enforced. Walzer's examples show how far we have come since 1975. There is simply no question of American or Australian forces adopting as an accepted practice the kind of deliberate or reckless targeting of civilians described in these episodes.

Why the change? We should not overlook the role that Walzer's own work played in the changes of attitude to the use of force. His work clarified and codified new attitudes to the use of force that emerged in reaction to the experience of Vietnam, and specifically sharpened the focus on the plight of civilians caught up in war. The fate of civilians had become a central concern after World War II, especially in the nuclear age in which

---

[4] Walzer, *Just and Unjust Wars*, 154–5.   [5] Ibid. 188–9.

civilian casualties were likely to outnumber by far combatant casualties in any future major war. But it was the vivid images of Vietnam, the extensive coverage given to events like the My Lai massacre, and the serious doubts about the legitimacy of the war as a whole that added force to ethical questions about the way in which the war had been fought. After that, the limits to circumstances in which civilian casualties are deemed acceptable were very substantially tightened, both in the ethical literature and in the law and practice of armed forces.

How durable has this change been? Tighter norms of civilian immunity evolved over a period of nearly two decades from the early 1970s through to the late 1980s. Those were years in which armed force was used very rarely by Western governments, which made it easy to place tighter limits on how force would be used. It might have been expected that with the swift increase in the number and range of military operations undertaken by Western armed forces since about 1990, the pressure of operational experience would serve to push the boundaries back somewhat. This has not happened—at least not until recently. One key reason is that the often small operations that Western militaries have been involved in over the past decade have generally been seen to be less critical to direct and immediate national interests than the major conflicts of the last century. Maintaining public support for these operations—especially in the television age—has required that they be fought in ways that raise as few moral qualms as possible. This imperative is amplified when the war is supposedly being fought for the interests of the people on the battleground themselves.

However, there remains the possibility that under the pressure of more major wars, in which national security interests are seen to be more directly at stake, public and governmental perceptions of the limits on action causing civilian casualties would be relaxed. There has clearly been some potential for this to happen in what has been called the 'War on Terror'. The new norms have been deeply institutionalized in the values, doctrine, equipment, and legal framework of modern Western armed services, as well as in public values and expectations. But there is at least a risk that the pressure on Coalition forces fighting the insurgency in Iraq may be leading to less discriminating use of fire than the post-Vietnam norms would require. And the lack of public interest in this possibility suggests that public expectations of the conduct of their forces have been relaxed somewhat by the demands of the post-9/11 world. We should not be complacent about the progress made since Vietnam in the evolution of higher standards for the protection of civilians in military operations.

This is especially true for ground forces. As military operations move from the now relatively controlled environment of precision-guided air power to the still chaotic milieu of the minor infantry engagement, the standards of civilian immunity start to slip. There is a big difference between a strike pilot, safely out of range of enemy air defence systems, deciding not to deliver his weapon against a target because he cannot get a clear visual confirmation that it is not a civilian installation, and a frightened infantryman under attack in a back lane in Iraq, firing his weapon at anything that moves. For the infantryman, there has been no technological revolution; war has changed little in recent decades. The dilemmas faced by individual American GIs in Iraq today are hardly different from those faced by Frank Roberts in the account cited by Walzer[6] of cellar-to-cellar fighting in a village in France in World War I, and the choices faced by junior infantry commanders in Iraq are hardly different from those faced by their predecessors in Korea.[7] As war in Iraq reverts to less manageable small-scale infantry operations against irregular forces, in which the West's technological assets offer less advantage—the kinds of operations which Western governments have hitherto been so careful to avoid since Vietnam—a host of hard old moral dilemmas will reappear. These deserve, and will no doubt receive, careful examination. But my purpose here is to look at how the newer technologies that underpin precision-guided air power have affected the approach of Western militaries to the protection of civilians from the effects of their operations.

The Process of Choice in Iraq

It might be helpful to begin by sketching the process that is employed by Western militaries to choose what targets may or may not be attacked, and how the risks of civilian casualties are managed. In doing so I will draw

---

[6] Walzer, *Just and Unjust Wars*, 152.   [7] Ibid. 154.

on Australian experience of strike operations in Iraq as part of the US-led Coalition in 2003.[8]

It is worth starting by noting that the air strike campaign in Iraq in March and April 2003 did not, on the evidence so far available, cause large numbers of civilian casualties. There were no major tragedies comparable to the bombing of a civil air raid shelter in Baghdad in 1991, and relatively few reported incidents of civilian casualties from air strikes, even compared with those claimed in the Kosovo campaign of 1999. Of course, the evidence to date remains highly fragmentary, and there may be much yet to learn. But it seems reasonable to reach at least an interim conclusion that the Coalition forces succeeded in avoiding civilian casualties from air strikes to a surprising degree, especially considering the scale of the air campaign. An outline of the process suggests that in achieving this result the Coalition did in fact conform to principles similar to those set out by Walzer and paraphrased earlier in this chapter.

The post-Vietnam norms have been enshrined in the law of armed conflict through a requirement for 'reasonable precautions' to ensure that only military objectives are targeted, and to minimize the effects of actions on civilians. How were those 'reasonable precautions' taken? One important early contributor was the careful preparation of the target list. A comprehensive plan for air strikes against Iraq had been drawn up over the months, and even years, before the invasion. Target lists were compiled, the kinds of weapons that might be used against them were analysed, the risks of civilian casualties were assessed, and measures to minimize those risks were developed. Before being authorized for strike, targets on the list had first to be validated as military targets within the rules of engagement. This process gives rise to some important questions that we will consider further below. Second, targets were classified according to the risk that an attack on them would pose of collateral damage to civilians, property, or the environment. This process involved both assessment of how close to possible civilian locations the target was and, secondly, judgements about how effectively the risk of civilian casualties could be reduced in the way in which the attack was delivered. The USA has developed a very sophisticated modelling program—called *Bugsplat*—that allows planners

---

[8] The following account is drawn from personal interviews with officials and officers involved, conducted in late 2003.

to model the effects of different kinds of weapons and predict with some accuracy what the risks to civilians would be from different types of attack. The model allows planners to explore variations in angle of approach, weapons type, time of attack, and other variables, to see what approach offers the lowest chance of unintended casualties.

This process provides a better, more rigorous basis than has ever been available before for minimizing the risk of civilian casualties from strike operations, and providing a robust understanding of the residual risks. Nonetheless, judgements still need to be made about the level of residual risk that should be accepted in deciding whether or not to attack a target. During the invasion of Iraq, these judgements were made through a four-tiered hierarchy of decision-makers. The higher the likelihood of civilian casualties, the higher up the command chain the decision to attack a target was taken. Clear-cut criteria, related primarily to the physical proximity of civilians to the target, were applied to determine what level of approval was required. The most risky decisions were made at the highest of the four tiers, which for US forces in Iraq required reference back to Washington, where they were taken at high political levels. The decision-makers at each level were required to balance the risk of civilian casualties—or other forms of collateral damage—with the military or strategic benefits of attacking the target, and to assess the proportionality of risks to benefits.

This whole process of course took some time. Where time-sensitive targets were identified, a speeded-up version of the process was undertaken, but it retained the same essential elements. Either in its full or its abbreviated form, the key feature of the process was the way it impelled a structured and auditable assessment for each target of the risk of civilian casualties, of measures to reduce those risks, of the countervailing operational considerations in favour of attacking the target, and assignment of clear responsibility for the final decision to attack at a level commensurate with the seriousness of the risks involved.

But the process did not preclude the need for tough decisions, including ones in which a clear risk—indeed, a high likelihood—of civilian casualties was accepted in order to strike what were seen to be high-value targets. For example around 8 April 2003 a decision was made at a very high level to strike a restaurant in Baghdad because it was thought that there was a good chance of killing Saddam Hussein, although the attack also ran a high risk of inflicting civilian casualties. This decision involved perennial choices and judgements involving the reliability of intelligence—in this case mistaken—and proportionality.

However, the circumstances in which these decisions are taken are very different today from what they would have been in 1945 or 1965. Decision-makers now have much more extensive knowledge than their predecessors of the targets, of the effects of an attack, and of the risks of civilian casualties flowing from the attack. This more perfect knowledge of the likely consequences of different courses of action sharpens the moral dilemmas in some ways: civilian casualties may remain unintended, but it will be much rarer for them to be unexpected or accidental. Decisions which result in civilian casualties will be less often the consequence of ignorance, and more often the consequence of a detailed knowledge of probabilities which makes the decision to sacrifice civilian lives a more deliberate and better informed one than it might have been in the past.

Old Issues in New Forms

In particular, in an era of precision air power, military and government leaders will have to address old questions and dilemmas about civilian immunity in new forms. In this section we look at the implications of this new era in five areas.

Human shields

As Western forces have become more careful to prevent civilian casualties, their adversaries have greater incentives to use the presence of civilians to shield military targets from attack. This is of course an old idea, but it assumes increased significance in the precision-guidance age. In future it will be pretty certain that any country that is not in the front rank of air defence capability will have very little defence against an enemy capable of mounting a precision-guidance strike campaign, and will be susceptible to the destruction of any target the enemy chooses. Concealment will be the first line of defence. But for assets that cannot be concealed, deploying human shields is perhaps the only way to prevent valuable targets being destroyed. If successful, this tactic could have real strategic significance. Precision air strikes have become so central to the way in which Western countries wage low-cost war that a tactic which deprived a Western adversary of this option might well deter them from attacking at all.

We perhaps saw this tactic in action in the Kosovo War in 1999, when the Serbian authorities allegedly placed civilians on bridges to deter Allied attacks. Before the invasion of Iraq in 2003, it was widely expected that Saddam would withdraw most of his forces into Baghdad, where they would be so tightly mixed with civilians that attacks on them could only be made at the cost of massive civilian casualties. In the event, this did not happen, but some civilians did post themselves as human shields at potential targets during the campaign. If the war as a whole is legitimate—as many would think the Kosovo action was, for example—how does the use of civilians as human shields in this way affect civilians' immunity from attack?

One key question is whether the people serving as human shields willingly place themselves in danger, or have been coerced. There are a number of recent examples of voluntary human shields. Some of those who allegedly served as human shields during the Kosovo campaign may have done so willingly. Some Iraqis may have done so in 2003, and certainly significant numbers of foreigners opposed to the US-led invasion travelled to Iraq specifically to place themselves at what they expected to be high-value targets. Their aim, of course, was to prevent a war they believed lacked legitimacy in terms of *jus ad bellum*. But if they are wrong, and the war is legitimate, do those who intentionally place themselves in the way of attacks on what would otherwise be legitimate military targets lose their immunity as civilians? One could argue that voluntary human shields become *de facto* combatants and thus lose their civilian status, if, for example, their action is intended to contribute to the war effort of one side by limiting the military options of the other side. But this is not always the case: the foreign human shields in Iraq in 2003 were arguably not intending to support Iraq's war effort, but simply to prevent the war happening at all. And more generally, the passivity of a person acting as a human shield seems to argue against them being considered a combatant. They pose no threat to anyone: they are not engaged in fighting, or in providing the means to those who fight. To draw them into the class of combatants seems a significant extension of a concept which it is better to keep as narrow as possible. My conclusion is that, provided human shields do nothing to support the war effort beyond passively placing themselves at potential targets, they retain civilian immunity.

But that is not the end of the matter, because their civilian status does not mean that voluntary human shields cannot under any circumstances be deliberately targeted. It does mean that a stringent test of proportionality must be applied in any decision to do so. And in taking such decisions, it would seem legitimate to take account of the choices made by voluntary human shields. They are deliberately using their civilian status to place constraints on legitimate military operations in ways which might cost the lives of soldiers on the other side, and perhaps—as might have been the case in Kosovo—prolong other evils as well. It seems appropriate that they should not have the same degree of immunity as civilians who are simply going about their normal business and making no effort to affect the course of the fighting one way or another. So while a stringent test of proportionate benefit would still need to be passed to justify an attack causing casualties among voluntary human shields, it would be an easier test than if the civilians at risk had not deliberately placed themselves in peril to deter military operations.

In the case of coerced human shields, the issues are rather different. They are more like those addressed by Walzer in discussing the treatment of civilian populations of cities under siege.[9] No one would doubt that civilians forced against their will into positions in which they face risks in war are entitled to full civilian immunity. The question is how we allocate responsibility for any casualties they suffer as a result: to those who place them at risk or to those who inflict the injury? Walzer suggests that where civilians are forcibly moved from their normal location to serve as shields—the example he cites is from the Franco–Prussian War—then responsibility for any casualties rests with those who have coerced them into the situation of danger, not with those who actually inflict the casualties.[10] In such a case, he concludes, the attackers are not required to refrain from otherwise acceptable actions which might do these civilians harm; all responsibility lies with those who coerce the civilians to remain in a place of danger. This seems too permissive. The presence of coerced civilians at a legitimate military target should, one would think, place some constraints on an attacker over and above those he would face were they not there.

---

[9] Walzer, *Just and Unjust Wars*, 160 ff.   [10] Ibid. 174 n.

It should at least raise questions of proportionality in justifying an attack. On the other hand, it seems right that this should not impose an absolute prohibition: where the operational or strategic stakes are high enough, an argument could still be made that an attack which cost the lives of coerced human shields might still be justifiable. It is clearly wrong for one side to force civilians to become human shields, but it is also wrong for the other side to regard those civilians as having lost their civilian immunity as a result of the wrongs done to them by those who have placed them in danger.

Avoiding own-force casualties and the rights of combatants

The question of proportionality remains central to the choices made today about the degree of risk of civilian casualties that can be accepted in the conduct of military operations. One aspect of this question has special prominence in the age of precision guidance, and that is the extent to which it is legitimate to place civilians at risk in order to reduce risks to one's own comrades-in-arms. Western nations are more casualty-averse than they used to be—overall, a healthy development—and there is a certain reluctance today to value the life of a soldier much below the life of a civilian. Perhaps unexpectedly, this reluctance has if anything been amplified by the move to all-volunteer forces, where soldiers are likely today to be seen by public opinion as selfless professionals committed to a life of service. It has certainly been amplified by the recent experience of relatively low-cost wars in which precision air power has provided largely casualty-free victories. To modern governments and publics, the taking of casualties tends to be seen as a proof of policy failure.

Walzer takes a tough line on this issue. He suggests that commanders have to 'risk soldiers before they kill civilians', and accept risks to the lives of their soldiers if reducing those risks would endanger civilians.[11] This tough line rings true to me, but within limits. In the precision-guidance, low-casualty age, our thinking about the status of soldiers may be evolving in ways which come into play when we are faced with straight choices between risks to civilians and risks to soldiers. Traditionally, we have argued that by choosing to be soldiers and accepting the concomitant rights of that status, soldiers take on obligations as well. Those include the

---

[11] Walzer, *Just and Unjust Wars*, 155–7.

obligation to accept risks themselves, rather than transfer them to civilians. However, other considerations are increasingly coming into play. National leaders have a self-interested political imperative to avoid casualties. But in my experience they often also have a genuine sense of obligation as a government towards the soldiers they employ not to put them at risk unnecessarily. Modern governments—and public—tend to feel a strong responsibility to their own military personnel, and many ministers and voters would feel repugnance at the idea that the lives of their soldiers would be held of less value than the lives of strangers. They might agree that civilians deserve protection as innocents. But they would also argue that they owe their own soldiers special consideration as employees for whom they are responsible.

A similar set of considerations is at work at the tactical, personal level. In the culture and ideology of today's Western military forces, it would be asking a lot to require a platoon commander to place less value on the lives of those under his command, for whom he feels responsible, than on the lives of civilian strangers. Again, I think this argues for the application of the principle of proportionality. Walzer's tough line on this issue seems to imply that avoiding harm to civilians should always take precedence over protecting one's own soldiers. That suggests that a combatant forfeits all rights to have his or her welfare weighed in the balance of consequences. I think it is more reasonable to require commanders to lean heavily towards protection of civilians, but to allow that when the risks are sharply disproportionate, it is legitimate to incur small added risks to civilians where this would reduce big risks to combatants.

Standards of evidence

Intelligence is the weak point of precision-guidance air power. Modern air forces can put a bomb accurately on any designated point, but they cannot be certain what it is they are hitting when they do so. As the lessons of Iraq so vividly show, modern intelligence capabilities are much less omniscient than popular fiction—and some leaders—would have us believe. In the precision-guidance age, intelligence and reconnaissance failures leading to mistaken identification of targets are the most probable cause of unintended civilian casualties from air strikes. Two examples come immediately to mind. The first was the bombing of a bunker in Baghdad in 1991, in which a facility identified by US intelligence as an Iraqi military command post was destroyed by PGMs. But on the day of the attack it held some hundreds of Iraqi civilians using it as an air-raid shelter. Another example was the accidental missile strike on the Chinese Embassy in Belgrade in 1999; again, the strike hit the intended location, but the intended target was not at that location.

In the first of these cases, the evidence suggests that there was legitimate reason for the intelligence agencies to believe that the target was a military command post, though it may have been that more and better analysis would have prevented the error. In the second case, the error was more flagrant: it was a significant failure of procedure. Both cases suggest that there is an obligation on commanders to ensure that they know what they are hitting. When our capacity to hit targets has increased so much, the obligation to know what we are hitting comes more clearly into focus. There seems to be no doubt that commanders should be held culpable for civilian casualties which occur as a result of targeting decisions which have been made without sufficient care to ensure that they are based on accurate information about the target. Of course, it cannot be morally wrong simply to make an error, but it can be morally wrong to make a critical decision without exercising due diligence to ensure that the decision is based on a fair assessment of all the relevant information and that reasonable steps have been taken to avoid error. Precision guidance seems to impose a fairly strict requirement for due diligence on commanders responsible for ordering air strikes.

Choosing targets (i): who is a civilian?

Many of the military operations launched by Western governments since 1990—which we might call the dawn of the precision guidance age—have been directed not against the formal uniformed forces of adversary states, but against a wide range of other people. Precision-guidance raises temptations to use force in new ways, which pose important questions about who deserves to enjoy the protection of civilian immunity. For example, during the Kosovo strike campaign of 1999, close associates of the Serbian leadership were targeted by NATO precision strikes. Some have argued that this was wrong because they were not combatants. This seems to me to be relatively uncomplicated, where the targeted people are clearly part of the command chain that directs a military effort. Such people have been accepted as combatants for a long time. But the Kosovo campaign raised some harder cases. It is much less certain that attacks can be justified against people who have no direct role in the command or prosecution of military operations, no matter how distasteful the regime which they support.

In the Kosovo campaign, for example, strikes were planned and mounted against paramilitary and police forces in Kosovo, and even in Serbia itself. These attacks were presumably seen in the context of humanitarian intervention: they were aimed at helping to stop the repression in Kosovo by attacking the personnel responsible for it. This is understandable, but it raises some disquieting questions, because to approve such actions would seem to extend significantly the range of those who can legitimately be targeted by military action. Police and paramilitary forces responsible solely for internal security, and not engaged in operations against attacking forces, can hardly be considered combatants in the normal sense of the term. A combatant loses his immunity from attack by an opposing force because he has declared his intention to join in or support attacks on that opponent. But it is not clear that, for example, Serbian police officers in Kosovo in 1999 would fall within these categories. These officers may have been guilty of terrible crimes. But they were not necessarily combatants engaged in operations against NATO forces. Military attacks on them could therefore be justified only if that was the only available means of stopping an immediate and serious breach of human rights. That might, for example, have justified attacks on Serbian police units on operations in Kosovo. But it could not have justified attacks on police barracks in Serbia. Where there is no such immediate necessity, attacks on non-military personnel start to look like the use of military force to mete out summary justice. That cannot be right, no matter how grave the crimes suspected. The correct approach in such situations is judicial, not military. Those suspected of crimes should be arrested, tried, and, if found guilty, punished, not subjected to military attack.

Choosing targets (ii): imposing hardship

Precision-guided air power provides new opportunities to impose hardship on civilian populations without substantial risks of direct injury or death. For example in 1999, during the Kosovo campaign, attacks were made on the Serbian electricity grid with non-lethal weapons which severely disrupted power supplies in Belgrade and elsewhere. Few civilians were killed or injured in these attacks, but they caused distress and hardship to millions. Some criticized the strikes for this reason. But they were probably among the key factors in Milošević's capitulation to NATO demands, and thus may have saved many lives. The traditional doctrine of civilian immunity seems at a loss in coming to grips with this type of operation. Clearly much depends on the degree of hardship imposed: in some circumstances hardship can be lethal, and in such cases the established doctrines apply directly. But often the systematic disruption of normal services in an industrial society will simply be massively disruptive, as was the case in Serbia. Are such operations against civilian populations proscribed? Do military commanders have a responsibility to respect not just the lives and property, but also the comfort, of civilians? My guess is that principles of proportionality apply here too. Commanders should not recklessly cause serious disruption to the lives of civilians, but where they can fairly judge that disruption will avoid worse evils, it may be that civilians become fair targets for disruptive campaigns.

Conclusion

The history of war is shaped by the dynamic interaction between technology and politics that determines the means and the ends of this strangest and most morally complex of human activities. Since 1990 we have entered an era in which precision-guidance technology provides to advanced militaries a new and unprecedented capacity to apply force from the air discriminatingly and at low cost and risk to that attacker. This has changed both the kinds of wars that advanced countries are prepared to fight and the ways they are fought. It has reinforced a trend towards tighter norms of civil immunity in the conduct of air campaigns, though the same may not be true of land warfare. And in the conduct of air campaigns, precision guidance has opened up a new range of questions, or new aspects of old questions, that need to be carefully considered. No one can be confident that we yet understand the ethical implications of the precision-guidance age.

9

Civilian Immunity in the 'New Wars'

PAUL GILBERT

I

'New wars' is the term that has come to be used[1] for the sort of conflict experienced around the world in recent years, where organized low-level violence is typically countered by the regular forces of states with results that expose civilians to death and injury from either side. The wars that followed the break-up of the Soviet Union and Yugoslavia exemplify such conflicts, continuing most notably, as I write, in the disputed territory of Chechnya. The Russian government's response to this insurgency is, so it claims, part of the global 'war on terror', and the various conflicts which form a part of these hostilities are, I suggest, also for the most part 'new wars'. How, though, should we more precisely characterize them?

New wars can best be thought of by contrasting them with old wars, and we can pick them out in terms of their typical conditions and modes of conduct. The old wars of the nineteenth and earlier twentieth centuries are usually wars between states or alliances of states aimed at promoting the interests of states *qua* states: namely, the security and prosperity of their present and presumptive citizens. In the case of internal conflicts, these aims are the same, but opposing groups of citizens seek control of the state or the division of the state in order to fulfil them. Old wars typically originate in disagreements—for example, about territorial rights—and erupt as a result of the tension these cause leading to perceived threats

---

[1] Following Mary Kaldor, *New and Old Wars* (Cambridge: Polity, 1999).

and reactions to them. In the absence of peaceful methods for resolving disagreement, each side is prepared to use military force to oblige the other to concede.

The way in which old wars are conducted reflects this pattern. Claimed territory is seized, or territory not claimed is occupied in order to put an opponent into a worse position than it would be in if it did not concede to the occupier's demands. Thus old wars are usually fought for control of territory. But this is not the only way that pressure may be put upon an opponent. Air raids inflicting material damage may have the same results, and so may those that inflict loss and injury upon the civilians for whom the state attacked bears responsibility. Its citizens may demand concessions to forestall further suffering. Notice, however, that even when citizens are directly targeted, contrary to the laws of war, in the old wars of which we speak, they are targeted only as one of a number of possible tactics for securing the aims of war: their death is not itself such an aim.

New wars contrast with old in both their conditions and their conduct. New wars are not essentially between states, or even between states and sub-state groups, or between different sub-state groups for the control of states, entire or divided. What marks them out is that they are fought, on one side at least and generally on both, as a continuation of the politics of identity. The goals of the politics of identity may indeed include the control of states or the obtaining of statehood; they may include the acquisition of territory from other states by established states, or even the cession of territory. But these are not goals sought in the interests of citizens *qua* citizens, that is to say, of members, actual or potential, of states; and hence they are not sought by states *qua* states, or by sub-state groups as *soi disant* representatives of states. They are goals sought in the presumed interests of members of the identity group as members, and are incidental to that.

The essential goals of identity politics concern the way in which a particular collective identity is recognized, so that what is presumed to be the central interest of a member of an identity group is that his or her identity should be recognized and the requirements of such an identity be fulfilled. The politics of identity is a politics not only because the sort of recognition demanded necessitates the deployment of collective power, perhaps even violence, as in new wars. It is a politics more especially because the kinds of identity with which we are concerned, since these are the kinds which drive new wars, are the identities in which their bearers are supposed to enter the political realm. It is, for example, as members of a certain nation, and thus as possessing this national identity, that they are thought of as participating in political activity, according to the politics of identity. That is why the sort of recognition that is crucial is political recognition—for example, the recognition of a nation as having a right to statehood.

The politics of identity is thus, in an important way, *prior* to the politics of inter-state relations and, indeed, prior to the political relations between members of states *qua* citizens. Or rather, it sees itself as prior to the politics of these relations. For it sees the entities that enter these relations as needing to be legitimated by, for example, nationhood as what needs to underpin states, and membership of a nation as what justifies citizenship of states. On this basis, the politics of identity will construe many wars between states as in reality wars between nations and so forth. More generally, then, we should view the new wars which spring from the politics of identity as wars between peoples or on behalf of peoples, where 'peoples' may be taken to connote groups of individuals for whom a collective identity of the appropriate kind is claimed. What groups constitute such peoples will depend upon the collective identifications that are made—ethnic, cultural, religious, and so on. Yet what occasions wars between peoples, such that the individuals involved are not, as in Rousseau's account of war, 'enemies only by accident',[2] but enemies because of who they are? What are the conditions of the new wars which are a continuation of the politics of identity?

Rather than disagreement, it is, I suggest, *discord* that is the typical cause of new wars. In the basic case this is discord between peoples who view themselves as having distinct identities, and which is experienced either when one party or both hates or despises the other, or when one party or both believes that the other does not accord it the recognition it deserves. Discord thus involves a mismatch between each party's perception of itself and the other's perception of it. It is, however, no simple matter of a disagreement as to whether claims should be met, but rather a feature of the state of relations between identity groups which may arise from or give rise to such a disagreement, yet is not equivalent to it. Discord is the state

---

[2] Jean-Jacques Rousseau, *The Social Contract*, many editions, bk. 1, ch. 4.

of a relationship between groups whose attitudes to each other are not as the others feel that they should be. The general claim to recognition, which can take many forms, is a reaction to being despised, demeaned, disrespected, and so on. But when these attitudes against a group continue to prevail, and the recognition they claim is not granted, there exists, in Thomas Hobbes's phrase 'one of the principal causes of quarrel ... a signe of undervalue ... in their Nation'.[3] This, it seems to me, is the characteristic condition of new wars.

The conduct of new wars, like that of old wars, mirrors their conditions. When discord between peoples erupts in violence, it is precisely other people who become the objects of attack, not for any instrumental reasons, but because they are despised, hated, and so on. New wars commonly originate or arise in communal or sectarian violence between small numbers of people from opposed identity groups. The violence involved is expressive rather than necessarily purposive. It expresses contempt or resentment dependent upon the 'signe of undervalue' that is to be inflicted or which has been borne. In these circumstances, recruitment to the irregular forces typical of new war operations is easy, and minor local incidents can, given appropriate political leadership, escalate into war proper. The aim of military operations in such a new war may, as in the old, be the acquisition of territory. But now it will characteristically be either to establish a state, as part of the drive to have an identity politically recognized, or to humiliate an opponent by taking his land. It is the goals of identity politics which determine what the military objectives shall be.

This is nowhere more apparent than where ethnic cleansing is one of the aims of the war. Here attacks upon the civilians of a different identity group reflect a complex set of attitudes that typify identity politics. For jealousy at another's share in the possession of territory can erupt in violence against them even when it represents no real threat to interests. This is because identity, especially national identity, is frequently constructed in terms of a shared attachment to a land. 'To observe the character of a particular people', St Augustine remarked, 'we must examine the objects of its love,'[4] and these may well be particular features of a land. But that others should also be attached to it threatens this shared attachment, and hence the

---

[3] Thomas Hobbes, *Leviathan*, many editions, ch. 13.
[4] Augustine, *The City of God*, many editions, XIX, 24.

identity built upon it. In an obvious way, the marks that another group leaves upon the land mirror a different kind of relation to it and one that may seem alien and inappropriate—as exemplified in the different relations to a place of indigenous peoples and of settlers. In these circumstances, the identity itself demands domination of the landscape, and this may require ethnically cleansing it. Attacks upon civilians to accomplish this are then integral to the preservation of an identity.

II

These brief observations upon the nature of new wars and the exposure of civilians to death and injury within them paint a bleak picture. What they suggest is that the principle of civilian immunity can have no purchase in them. For, while it is frequently violated in old wars, its applicability in them should, for reasons I shall discuss in the next section, not be doubted. Yet is my contrast too stark? After all, there are many respectable proponents of a 'politics of recognition' in which the goals of identity groups are defended as right and just. If they are wrongfully obstructed, might they not give a just cause for war, and might not such a war be fought justly, with respect for civilian immunity? And, on the other hand, might not the established states, against which the low level violence of irregular forces is typically directed in new wars, themselves avoid breaches of the immunity principle? Indeed, is not the typical new war one in which states protect civilians while insurgents target them, justifying the alternative description of many of the phenomena with which we are dealing as a 'war on terror' so far as state action is concerned?

This is not the place to scrutinize the politics of recognition and whether identity claims could provide a just cause for war. We are, after all, concerned with an aspect of *jus in bello*, not *jus ad bellum* (though there are connections between them which the next section will touch upon). What we need to do, however, is to set out the conditions under which civilian immunity will be respected and ask if they are likely to be fulfilled in military action that seeks to realize the goals of identity politics, on the one hand, or that which seeks to frustrate them when they are deemed inadmissible, on the other.

There are, broadly speaking, two ways in which one can regard the principle of civilian immunity. One way is to regard it as a general moral principle to the effect that unless someone is threatening one with harm, then one has no right to harm them. In particular, only a threat to one's life would justify killing them, as an act of self-defence. But civilians typically present no threat. Therefore, they should be immune from attack. The difficulty with this general moral principle is, of course, in its application, rather than in its substance. It invites endless discussion of the part that civilians play in the activities of a group, represented by a state or otherwise, which does threaten harm, and of the extent to which they can therefore become the object of attack. Where, for example, the group's activities involve settling on land claimed by others in a way that threatens their livelihoods, attempting forcibly to drive them off by means that put settlers' lives in jeopardy should they remain may seem to be justified. But if carried out by military or paramilitary forces, it would have to be seen as a breach of civilian immunity unless the settlers were themselves such a force.

The alternative strategy is to regard the principle of civilian immunity not as a general moral principle but as a principle governing the proper performance of a certain role: viz., that of a soldier (or member of the other armed forces). Principles regulating roles may themselves be moral principles, if, among other things, the role itself is such that its proper performance can be viewed as morally good, and thus contributory to a good life. But such principles are grasped, not by deriving them from more general principles, but by understanding what is involved in performing the role and undertaking to fulfil its requirements in circumstances where these are binding upon holders of the role. In order to carry out the role correctly, the role-holder must see when he or she is to act in his or her role and match his or her behaviour to its demands. Unless someone does in general act in this way, he or she cannot be regarded as acting in the relevant role—cannot, for example, be regarded as acting as a soldier.

There is, in fact, good reason to view the principle of civilian immunity in this light. As James Turner Johnson writes, it 'originated principally in the intentionality and customs of military professionals'[5]—that is to say,

[5] James Turner Johnson, 'Historical Tradition and Moral Judgement: The Case of Just War Tradition', *Journal of Religion*, 64 (1984), 306.

in the development of a public role whose holders could see themselves as fulfilling a social function and pride themselves on their performance. What makes this possible is precisely the drawing of a distinction between soldiers and the civilians on whose behalf they fight. For if it is accepted that the role of soldiers is to act with lethal force on behalf of those who do not so act, then it is natural to expect that those who assume the role may tacitly agree that neither side shall attack those on behalf of whom they fight. Adopting this convention has more than one point. First, it reflects a mutual recognition of the status of those for whom both sides are fighting. More than that, it creates this special status. For if just anyone is likely to be targeted by armed forces, then they will take up arms to defend themselves with lethal force if necessary. In that case, the distinction between soldiers and civilians disappears. The role of soldiers as those having exclusive access to the use of lethal force in conflict between groups requires general respect for the distinction.

Second, the convention honours what soldiers on the opposing side are doing in fighting for others by acknowledging the special status which those fought for have on their side, as well as on one's own. This is not just a matter of expediency, though no doubt it is partly that; for if one's task is to protect civilians on one's own side, then attacking those on the other will invite reprisals. Rather, it is to see those who do not bear arms—traditionally women, children, and the aged who, prior to modern weaponry usually could not fight—as proper objects of protection and concern on the other side if they are such on one's own, so that attacking them is dishonourable. Third, this limitation on who may be attacked, among others, makes possible the virtues associated with a soldier's role—courage, chivalry, and so forth—which without such restraints would be impossible. For if one were permitted to kill whomsoever one wished out of hatred or contempt, one could take no satisfaction in performing a military role whose standards are only to be achieved through combat with those who perform the same role on the opposite side, and whom one must respect as performing this role, whatever one's feelings are towards the group they represent.

If we take something like this view of civilian immunity, then it is easy to see that many of the presuppositions of respect for the principle are lacking in new wars. We may consider the manner of conduct of new wars first to appreciate this. On one side, at least, military forces are usually irregulars rather than professional forces. It is therefore unlikely that they will be fulfilling the role of soldier as something from which they can gain personal satisfaction and pride. Indeed, they may not see themselves as acting on behalf of civilian members of their group at all, but rather as acting simply as members of the group who happen to be particularly well equipped to advance its identity-based goals. They may, in that case, fail to recognize any sharp distinction between civilian status and combatant role. This failure is often mirrored in guerrilla or terrorist tactics which enable them either to switch seamlessly between military and civilian personae or to carry out military operations in the guise of civilians.

Needless to say, such tactics make it hard for their opponents to observe the distinction themselves, since effective action against insurgents may place civilians under suspicion or expose them to attack, direct or indirect, even when it is believed that it is insurgents who are targeted. In these circumstances, it is easy even for professional soldiers to give too little thought to the protection of civilians. Counter-terrorism tactics too may breach the principle of immunity or come very close to breaking it. The clearing of civilians to isolate insurgents or the destruction of their property may harm them, for example. Worse still, large-scale air strikes or bombardments to avoid exposing ground troops to sniper fire or bombs may well expose civilians to suffering disproportionate to the military objectives that are achieved. Such problems are not, of course, peculiar to new wars, though they are characteristic of them. In old wars too, whether in internal conflicts—for example, revolutionary ones—or in occupied territories, guerrilla warfare and terrorism expose civilians to danger, and state forces often fail to protect them. But, as we shall shortly see, the distinctive conditions of new wars exacerbate these perils.

The conduct of new wars by irregulars is not conducive to adherence to the role requirements of soldiering in general. For it should not be thought that these requirements are easily met or that internalizing the standards they reflect comes naturally. What is needed, and what is provided in professional soldiering, is military discipline. A chain of command from senior officers and experienced NCOs to junior ranks and raw recruits helps to ensure that the restraints on the use of force embodied in principles of civilian immunity, proportionality, respect for prisoners, and so on are complied with. For, in fear or anger, troops not subject to clear commands and sanctions will be liable to act in breach of the rules of war and vent their feelings upon their opponents, whether combatants or civilians. Yet in new wars the irregular forces of insurgents are seldom under such control, and certainly lack the training which subjects their behaviour to military law. The militias of established states may be in a similar position. Even their regular forces may, as we shall now see, be unable to maintain the discipline that in old wars they can preserve.

The reasons for this stem, of course, from the discord which, as I have suggested, is characteristic of new wars. Here, even combat itself is not a contest between troops who respect each other as soldiers and fight in such a way as to maintain this respect, but between opponents motivated by antagonistic attitudes to each other, anxious only to come off best and put down their enemies. Even in old wars the eruption of such sentiments fuelled by animosity between identity groups can overcome the normal restraints upon soldierly conduct. But in new ones they are the norm, and they commonly override the compunction of professionals as well as dictating the behaviour of the unscrupulous. This is evident, I suggest, from the fact that state responses to insurgency in new wars frequently fail to minimize civilian casualties, as the principle of immunity strictly requires, as much as from direct attacks upon civilians by anti-state forces. That huge numbers of civilians on the opposing side can be killed and wounded as a result of attacks upon relatively small numbers of insurgents is made possible only in consequence of attitudes towards them that make light of or justify their suffering. The sentiments engendered by identity politics instantiate such attitudes, and they are likely to be felt by members of a state against which insurgents act as much as by the insurgents, since it is in opposition to them as having their identity that the insurgents act.

All in all, therefore, I have to conclude that the circumstances under which civilian immunity will be respected are unlikely to prevail in new wars, neither with regard to its typical mode of conduct nor in its conditions. The reasons concern the way in which the role of soldier, whose requirements include respect for civilian immunity, is either not properly undertaken in new wars or is undermined, even among professional soldiers. Even the war on terror, then, can involve violations of civilian immunity when it evinces discord between identity groups.

III

The relationship between soldiers and their own civilian populations in the old wars which are conducive to respect for the principle of civilian immunity is best exemplified in wars of self-defence. Indeed, the classic justification for an old war is that it is fought in self-defence. Those who are taken to be defended, whether in terms of life, livelihood, or liberty, are members of the civilian population. It is in this way that soldiers fight on their behalf and, as I suggested in the last section, regard them as rightfully immune from attacks by opposing troops. Were they to be attacked, it could not be because these opposing troops took themselves to be also fighting in self-defence, as in many old wars both sides will so regard their actions. For, assuming civilians pose no threat, attacks on them cannot form any part of a self-defence strategy.

New wars originate, I claimed, in demands for the political recognition of some identity, though this recognition is sometimes maintained to be necessary to defend an oppressed people, and perhaps sometimes it is. But military action in support of recognition demands will usually be viewed as offensive by those against whom it is directed, and they will take themselves to be waging a defensive war against it. A defensive war, however, should always be a last resort, proportionate to the threat and likely to be effective in countering it. If it is unclear, as surely it is in respect of many recent operations, that large-scale military responses satisfy these criteria, then we need to look again at what is the character of such responses in new wars. Resort to war before diplomatic means or criminal justice measures have been exhausted, force that is disproportionate in its scale and political consequences to the low-level violence to which it responds, and action that can only defer rather than prevent further outbreaks—these things suggest that intentions other than peace and security are at work.

In new wars it is discord, I suggested, that provides such motives, and when discord between groups that define themselves in terms of their identities is involved, it will lead each to concentrate upon and to valorize their points of distinctness. This is nowhere more so than when these involve real or supposed differences in values. We should not think here only of groups that define themselves in terms of values, as, for example, religious groups may do. Other groups that define their identities in terms of language or other cultural features are still likely to find or to imagine differences between the values of their group—'the objects of its love'—and those of another with which it finds itself in conflict. For it is typically differences in values which lead peoples to hate or despise others and thus, in the others' eyes, to 'undervalue' them—sowing the seeds of discord or exacerbating existing disharmony.

Differences of values, however, are seldom simply acknowledged as such, or even recognized as causes of disharmony which some appropriate political divorce might resolve. Another's different values are typically the object of condemnation, as much as of contempt. And if his values stand condemned, his claim for political space in which to pursue them can scarcely be recognized. Opposing it now takes on the character of a moral mission, just as the original movement for political recognition may do. The ruthlessness of many new wars derives from their having this character; and here there are several cases to consider. In one type, the war can be viewed as seeking to convert opponents to one's own values. This is typically the case with Western state action against Islamists, for example, since it is to export Western liberal democratic values that the war is partly fought. Initially, at least, treatment that alienates civilians will be avoided, since the aim, after all, is to win them round. But their rejection of the value system offered may lead to punitive ill-treatment, if it is thought of as morally culpable. And that is precisely the way in which radical Islamists, for instance, treat Westerners—not only as infidels whose moral values are to be rejected by expressive acts of violence, but also as the source of corruption for Muslims, deserving of punishment.

We can see that when new wars involve such moralistic motivations, the position of civilians is different from that which they occupy in old wars. Their categorization as 'innocent' in old wars draws upon the etymology of the word as 'harmless', by contrast with the harm that combatants can do to each other in virtue of their role and equipment. It does not essentially concern the moral status of civilians as innocent of wrongs of which soldiers are guilty. But where what supposedly needs to be fought is a system of values, civilians who espouse them may be as guilty as combatants. Here, still older ideas of war as punishment resurface in new wars, and in these ideas it is not only combatants who may be targeted but those who perpetrate the wrongs the war aims to punish. Combined with more modern notions of collective responsibility, such ideas can make the killing of civilians seem nothing but a fitting retribution for crimes that spring from their abhorrent values. And collective responsibility does not here need imputing in virtue of alleged consent to the actions of a state, as is the case with revolutionary attacks on the civilian targets in capitalist states, for example. Rather, the logic of identity politics is that, since it is identity groups which are pitted against one another, mere membership of the group incurs the penalties that the group as a whole is deemed to warrant.

It is, I suggest, not only in direct attacks upon civilian targets by terrorists that this moralistic punitive attitude to civilians is evident. People do not consciously have to frame the reasons for their actions in such terms to be influenced by these attitudes. To think badly of someone, and thus as not undeserving of the misfortunes that befall him, can lead one to do less to mitigate them than if one thought differently. It is a pattern evident across a whole range of behaviour. It surfaces too, I believe, in the degree to which protection and concern for civilians will be offered when insurgents are targeted by state forces in new wars. For though civilian casualties should not be disproportionate to the military objectives thereby achieved, and in this respect civilian immunity should be respected, there are no clear norms of what level of loss counts as proportionate here. What is clear is that the identity of the civilians involved should be irrelevant to deciding the issue. Yet it is, I propose, inconceivable that in new wars the same level of loss would be imposed upon a civilian population sharing one's own identity as upon an alien one, even though it was required to achieve the same objective, of routing a band of guerrillas sheltering in a city, say. Civilians are allowed to suffer because of their identity, an identity whose moral deficiencies are evidenced above all by the behaviour of the terrorists who purport to fight on their behalf.

New wars, then, involve attitudes to civilian members of an opposed identity group that are liable to undermine respect for their immunity. Two sorts of factor work against it, therefore: these attitudes and the fragility of soldiers' roles which we investigated in the preceding section. The question to which we should now turn is whether there are ways in which deliberate atrocities against civilians or large-scale losses to them resulting from counter-terrorist actions can be prevented, on the assumption that new wars will continue as manifestations of the politics of identity.

IV

In considering how civilians might best be protected in new wars, there are, typically, two cases to consider. One is where the armed forces of some unrecognized identity group conduct a campaign involving attacks upon civilian members of another group. The other is where the forces of a state acting against insurgents—for example, those seeking secession for an identity group—inflict death and injury upon the civilian population they represent. The strategies for dealing with both kinds of case raise issues which it would be well beyond the scope of the present chapter to consider. It is, worthwhile, however, to touch upon some of them in order to indicate how difficult it is to escape the threat to civilians that new wars present.

First, then, let us look at responses to anti-state civilian rights violations. Here the agency responsible for dealing with the situation is primarily the state that is attacked. It is its citizens whose lives and livelihoods are threatened and whom it has a duty to protect. One obvious response is military action against the attackers, or perhaps the intensification of action that is already ongoing if war at some level is already under way. But the problem with this approach is that it has the potential for initiating or exacerbating a conflict of identities, as those attacked accept that it is in virtue of their own identity that they are victims and rally to defend each other *qua* fellow members of the identity group. Then the dangers, which we have noted, of the state campaign itself having the hallmarks of new war attitudes and methods present themselves. In that case the overall level of loss and injury to civilians on both sides may be greater than if no armed response had been forthcoming.

Another possible response, especially if terrorist attacks remain small scale, is a criminal justice one. Here, however, there are the opposite dangers to those that arise from a military response. A criminal justice approach will treat all acts of identity group fighters as criminal, whether directed against troops or against non-combatants. That will provide them with no motive for exempting the latter. And, more generally, if they are treated as criminals rather than as soldiers themselves, then they will have absolutely no incentive fully to adopt the role of soldiers, which, I argued, implies respecting civilian immunity. While in new wars with identity goals, the prospect of this is, I have argued, poor, it should not be discounted entirely, and indeed, every effort to encourage it should be made. Criminalization utterly obstructs it.

A further disadvantage of criminalization is that it stands in the way of conciliation. 'No negotiating with terrorists' is a familiar refrain of politicians. But it may be quite unrealistic. To refuse to treat with groups who believe that their identity goals are just may fuel frustration and lead to more, and increasingly atrocious, attacks. Nor should it be thought that to adopt a response of negotiation and possible concessions in the face of attacks upon civilians is somehow to reward attacks that should in justice attract not reward, but punishment. A state with a responsibility to its citizens needs to put their welfare before such abstract considerations—considerations which need to be sharply distinguished from the practical ones of whether a conciliatory response might encourage further attacks for further goals. For the abstract considerations lack force precisely because they are raised outside any concrete context of administering rewards and punishments. There is now, it might be objected, precisely such a context in the shape of the International Criminal Court, which could properly deal with the kind of case we are considering. This is not the place to discuss it, except to remark that, if peace is the best protection for civilians, then the ICC is an instrument of the criminal justice response just considered, and not necessarily best fitted to achieve it.

The real problem with the conciliatory response is, it seems to me, quite different. It is that the goals of different identity groups are inherently conflictual and unsusceptible to any satisfactory and stable resolution, unlike those of parties with different interests who can be satisfied with some compromise. If that is the case, then the only way to prevent identity conflicts erupting in violence which menaces civilians is to act so as to marginalize identity politics itself, which recognizing its representatives in negotiations, acceding to demands couched in identity terms and so forth, would militate against. What it would involve would be a serious concern with the injustice and deprivation that identity groups may well experience.

To deal with these fairly and generously may not eliminate identity politics, but it may reduce the support for identity groups and thus the potency of their operations. What stands in the way of such a strategy being effective, however, is any attempt to present it as the manifestation of a morally superior identity—Western democratic liberalism, for example. Nor is it necessary so to present it, for what counts as injustice or deprivation in the sort of case in question is something that can be agreed by groups professing a range of values.

I turn now to responses to state and pro-state attacks on civilians, or conduct which causes them excessive suffering or humiliation short of direct attacks. Here it is international agencies or strong neighbouring states who are turned to in new wars, to intervene to provide protection for civilians, though their record has been patchy, and the motives of those who intervene invariably mixed. The subject of humanitarian intervention is too large to embark on here, except to apply to it the points of the last paragraph. First, humanitarian intervention should not be undertaken in a way that advances the goals of an identity group sought in virtue of their identity, rather than to alleviate oppression, say. Yet this is how anti-state insurgents will attempt to use intervention to protect their civilian population. Second, intervention should not be presented as a manifestation of values which supporters of the state intervened in are taken to lack. Perhaps there will be cases where this occurs, and general humanity has been replaced by perverse norms needed to bolster a distinctive identity, though I suspect these are rare. But humanitarian intervention itself will become part of a war of identities unless it is represented, not as part of some cosmopolitan agenda, always questionable from any other ethical standpoint, but as a clearly *political* act against a regime that fails to fulfil the proper responsibilities of a state to its citizens.

Identity politics has an invidious power to metamorphose any political or military action into one of its forms. But once it is so transformed, the position of civilians is changed along with it. Their ancient passivity as objects of protection and concern gives way to an active identity as members of a group with political aspirations to be fulfilled on the presumption that its members enter politics willy-nilly in virtue of their identity. But it is exactly this presumption of inescapable complicity in the actions of the group that poses a threat to civilian immunity when those actions lead to war. Nor, so far as I can see, is there any way to restore it except to reinstate a politics that prescinds from identities and considers only roles and statuses. And that, I contend, cannot be combined with a politics of identity.

10

Women, War, and International Law

VÉRONIQUE ZANETTI

'I only remember that I was number twenty, that her hair was matted, that she was repulsive and covered with sperm, and that finally, I killed her.' With five bullets to the abdomen.

Rapist, cited in 'Universal Soldier'

She no longer could possibly be beautiful. Or even desirable. Only as the object of hatred could she still provoke an erection. Everything about her was defiled. She was deprived of everything she possessed: her bodily integrity, her honour, and finally her life. Such was the revolting fate she shared with thousands of other women, masked by the clash of arms and the silence of the media. For the sexual abuse of women remains a topic infrequently discussed. Perhaps out of shame and, in the best of cases, for fear of humiliating its victims a second time. Does this sense of unease explain the relative public indifference to a phenomenon that claimed thousands of victims in the twentieth century alone? One thing is certain: it is only in the last decade, due to the systematic use of rape as a weapon of ethnic cleansing in the war in Bosnia, that rape has finally come to be explicitly treated as a war crime under international law.

The current chapter traces the developments in international law which led to the definition of rape as a war crime. While I will concentrate on the question of sexual abuse, I will nevertheless suggest throughout that the particular vulnerability of women during times of war is not primarily due to their sex, but essentially devolves from the social role and status of women in their communities. When possible, I have preferred not to use the word 'rape' but the more general term 'sexual abuse', which pertains to numerous, and equally criminal, kinds of violence in relation to sex, such as sexual slavery, forced prostitution, forced pregnancy, forced sterilization, and other crimes.

I will first address some of the tragedies of the twentieth century, and how they have been treated under international law. This will be followed by a description of some of the characteristics of the status of women in traditional societies which cause them to be particularly susceptible to violence. Next I will show how the structure of what we now call 'new wars' heightens the vulnerability of women. I will examine the protection of women under international humanitarian law, as well as certain specific modifications to this protection enacted by the International Criminal Tribunal for the Former Yugoslavia (ICTY), the International Criminal Tribunal for Rwanda (ICTR), and the International Criminal Court (ICC). I will conclude by asking whether these developments in international legislation provide a sufficient response to today's armed conflicts, where civil populations are increasingly involved as instruments of military strategy.

Some Facts concerning Sexual Abuse in the Major Wars of the Twentieth Century, and their Treatment under International Law

In the context of armed conflict, the sexual abuse of women and girls, as well as the recourse to sexual violence as a weapon, has a long history.[1] An assessment of this sad situation reveals that the wars of the twentieth century have been particularly devastating. Historians estimate that during World War II alone, approximately 1.9 million women in Eastern Germany were raped by Russian soldiers.[2] In 1937, during the very first few months of the Japanese occupation, 20,000 women were raped, assaulted, or killed in Nanjing alone. An estimated 200,000 or more Koreans and women of other nationalities living on Japanese territory, cynically called 'comfort

---

[1] According to the legend, the rape of the Sabine women, at the origin of the war between the Sabines and Romans, was unleashed when Romulus sought to furnish women for his soldiers.

[2] Sabine Mandl, 'Krieg gegen die Frauen', in Elisabeth Gabriel (ed.), *Frauenrechte* (Vienna: Neuer Wissenschaftlicher Verlag, 2001), 107–16.

women', were forced into brothels as slaves for Japanese troops between 1931 and 1945.[3] Kidnapped, recruited by force or by deception, these women were stolen from their families, locked up in military brothels, given over to the violence and brutality of soldiers, and condemned to live in misery, suffering, and fear. At the end of the war, the vast majority were killed by the Japanese or by Allied bombing; the survivors were abandoned, left to fend for themselves, and often repudiated by their own families.

Despite the elevated number and severity of such violations, sexual abuse remained a grey area in international law up until just a decade ago. Not only was it not condemned with the same severity as other equivalent violations of rights, but it was long considered as a 'side-effect' of war or even, more cynically, as a bonus to soldiers, regardless of allegiance.[4] At the Nuremberg Trials, rape and sexual abuse did not figure among the war crimes which the Charter explicitly qualified as 'crimes against humanity'.[5] The same holds true for the Tokyo Trials.[6]

Not before the Bosnian War and the genocide in Rwanda, where sexual abuse was used as a strategic weapon to humiliate the enemy, sow terror, and accomplish ethnic cleansing, was rape finally included in the catalogue of 'grave breaches' of humanitarian law. Similarly, the few remaining survivors of Japanese military brothels were obliged to wait until the year 2000 before their voices were finally heard in civil court.[7] The legal and moral impact of this evolution will be examined below.

[3] See J. Pritchard and S. Zaide (eds.), *The Tokyo War Crimes Trial*, XX (New York: Garland Publishing, 1981), 49, 592, and Judith G. Gardam and Michelle J. Jarvis, *Women, Armed Conflict, and International Law* (Boston: Kluwer Law International, 2001).

[4] Christine Chinkin, 'Rape and Sexual Abuse of Women in International Law', *European Journal of International Law*, 5/3 (1994), online at <http://www.ejil.org/journal/vol5/No3/html>.

[5] See art. 6 (c) of the Charter: 'Crimes against humanity: namely, murder, extermination, enslavement, deportation, and other inhumane acts committed against any civilian population, before or during war, or persecutions on political, racial or religious grounds in execution of or in connection with any crime within the jurisdiction of the Tribunal, whether or not in violation of the domestic law of the country where perpetrated.'

[6] Gardam and Jarvis nevertheless point out a slight distinction in the second case, in that the inclusion of rape among the charges resulted in some convictions at the Tokyo Trials. Overall, however, 'the approach taken in the Tokyo Trials was to use evidence of rape and other sexual atrocities to support charges of crimes against humanity and aggression, rather than as crimes in their own right' (*Women, Armed Conflict, and International Law*, 207).

[7] See Christine Chinkin, 'Feminist Reflections on International Criminal Law', in A. Zimmermann (ed.), *International Criminal Law and the Current Development of Public International Law* (Berlin: Duncker and Humblot, 2003), 125.

The Heightened Vulnerability of Women

The sexual abuse of women during armed conflict acts like a distorting mirror, revealing fundamental lacks in the status of women in numerous traditional societies and individual value systems. Indeed, two common facts emerge: (a) wars exacerbate existing inequalities; and (b) criminal behaviour toward women reflects the fundamental lack of respect for women which the discrimination against them already conveys.

(a) Today, 80–90 per cent of the victims of war are civilians. Moreover, 80 per cent of refugees and displaced people, and hence those who are the most vulnerable, are women and children.[8] The death rate among women in refugee camps is three times higher than that of men.[9]

Because of their social role—and this is particularly true in traditional societies—women are more exposed than men in the enormous upheavals provoked by armed combat. It is women who are responsible for children and other dependants. Lacking protection themselves, women must ensure the survival of the family in the absence of men who have gone to war, been taken prisoner, have disappeared, or died. In their villages, just as in the course of flight or in refugee camps, women are responsible for lives other than their own, are obliged to share their often all too minimal resources, and suffer from hampered mobility. This handicap further aggravates a crucial social handicap derived from serious inequalities in their access to education, which renders women more dependent on their traditional role and more susceptible to certain dangers. Statistics show that women and children are actually more frequent victims of anti-personnel mines than men. Obliged to work in the fields, to search for water or wood, women and children must travel long distances over dangerous roads. 'During the 1990s it is estimated that small arms killed three million people and that eight out of every ten of these casualties were women and children.'[10]

As emphasized in a report by the International Committee of the Red Cross (ICRC) on women in war, as a general rule armed conflict only aggravates existent social inequalities toward women.[11] 'The low status of

---

[8] Sabine Mandl, 'Krieg gegen die Frauen'.   [9] Ibid. 109.
[10] Gardman and Jarvis, *Women, Armed Conflict, and International Law*, 23.
[11] Charlotte Lindsey, *Women Facing War: ICRC Study on the Impact of Armed Conflict on Women* (Geneva: International Committee of the Red Cross, 2001), 28 ff.

women in society is reflected in their treatment by the law, in property rights, rights of inheritance, laws related to marriage and divorce, and rights to acquire nationality or property or seek employment.'[12] Already victims of social discrimination during times of peace, women are put in an exceptionally precarious situation when they are widowed or when their husbands disappear, and they remain uneducated, unable to find work, and are without financial resources. The situation becomes even more catastrophic when they are rejected because they have been raped or have become pregnant with the child of their attacker or the 'enemy'. Victims of rape, in fact, are often exposed to a double tragedy: forced to carry a child engendered by violence, they are also rejected by their family and community.[13] Attempted abortion in the difficult material circumstances of war, without the necessary medical attention and even, perhaps, during the process of displacement or flight, can cost such a victim her life.

Finally, as women most often are prohibited from politics and have no access to positions of power, they are, moreover, deprived of the possibility to defend their own interests and specific needs, and thus of playing a role in changing their fate.

(b) Given this fundamental inequality and its cultural underpinnings, it is hardly surprising that when war fans hatred and unleashes behaviour formerly controlled by social norms, the lack of fundamental respect for women gives way to their abuse as mere objects.[14] 'Rape in war is not merely a matter of chance, of women victims being in the wrong place at the wrong time. Nor is it a question of sex. It is rather a question of power and control, structured by male soldiers' notions of their masculine

---

[12] Gardman and Jarvis, *Women, Armed Conflict, and International Law*, 8.

[13] In Bosnia-Herzegovina, husbands have in some cases gone so far as to kill their wives after learning that they had been raped. See Rosalind Dixon, 'Rape as a Crime in International Humanitarian Law: Where to from Here?', *European Journal of International Law*, 13/3 (2002), 705 n. 42.

[14] The sad irony is that in certain cases where women enjoy a high symbolic status, it is this, rather than their social inferiority, which renders them particularly vulnerable. This is emphasized in the study by the ICRC on women in war: 'the fact that many women in armed conflict situations are held up by the community as symbolic and the bearers of the community's honour heightens their vulnerability' (Lindsey, *Women Facing War*, 52). It is, furthermore, the fact that communities believe that the identity of women has a symbolic function that makes their systematic rape by an aggressor into a means of humiliation. Even though one dimension of this role undeniably values the dignity of women, it is nevertheless important to ask ourselves whether this valuation pertains to the individual, or is rather part of the overall image that the community has of itself.

privilege, by the strength of the military's lines of command and by class and ethnic inequalities among women.'[15]

New Forms of Warfare

The very clear rise in the number of civilian victims of armed conflict since World War II[16] is in large part due to the structure of what have come to be called 'new wars'.[17] This term is sometimes used to describe the newly legitimate use of force in wars fought for humanitarian purposes—in the former Yugoslavia, for example—or the doctrine of the 'new world order' proclaimed by Bush Senior—in the First Gulf War, for example. This is not the sense in which I use the term. 'New wars' are not *historically* new. (Münkler very convincingly compares the typology of violence in the Thirty Years War with that of the ethnic and religious wars which have decimated the populations of Afghanistan, Somalia, and the Balkans, and which continue to decimate those of South-East Asia and sub-Saharan Africa.[18]) The typology of violence common to such wars renders null and void the distinction between 'combatants' and 'non-combatants', and is 'new' only in that it seemingly characterizes the impact of globalization upon the development of organized violence throughout the world today. This organized violence is even more dangerous than traditional forms of warfare for women and girls exposed to armed conflict.

A brief description of how 'classic' and 'new' wars differ better reveals the reason why women and girls exposed to warfare today are more susceptible to violence.

- While traditional wars oppose military forces representing states, new wars are most often internal armed conflicts resulting from the disintegration of state structures. The economy of classic warfare is centralized; weapons and soldiers are financed by the state. By

---

[15] Chinkin, 'Rape and Sexual Abuse'.
[16] During World War II, about 50 per cent of the casualties were civilian; such casualties today are estimated at 80–90 per cent.
[17] In the following discussion I draw on Mary Kaldor, *New and Old Wars: Organized Violence in a Global Era* (Cambridge: Polity, 1999), and H. Münkler, *Die neuen Kriege* (Hamburg: Rowohlt, 2003).
[18] Münkler, *Die neuen Kriege*, 7 ff.

contrast, the financing of privately organized violence is decentralized. Characterized by the privatization of violence, new wars usually oppose forces of unequal strength which mix those of the state with paramilitary forces, warlords, or private individuals. Each of these parties benefits in its own way from pursuing warfare, and so has no interest in the cessation of conflict. Indeed, the dispersion of power and the generalized spread of corruption and favouritism lead to the development of a war economy which depends on the private exploitation of natural resources (gold or diamonds, for example), and trafficking in arms, drugs, or people. In such situations, trade and violence are interdependent.

- At the source of this profound difference in financing warfare, the imbalance between opposing forces also drastically alters the mode of combat. Because paramilitary groups or local militias are often under-paid or receive their salaries very irregularly, they depend on pillaging to survive, and this increases violence against civilians. Moreover, such wars have no front, where opposing troops confront each other in organized combat. Fighting is dispersed throughout the area, and this, too, is often directed against civilians. When they are inferior in number or in technological capacity, armed groups use civil pop-ulations as logistical support (marauding or pillaging) or as means to enact military strategy (human shields, ethnic cleansing, systematic rape).

- While opposing parties in traditional wars have every interest in limiting the length of combat in order to limit human and financial costs, new wars, by contrast, are characterized by lengthy conflict. (In Angola, the war will soon have been going on for thirty years; in Sudan for nearly twenty; and in Somalia for over fifteen.[19]) In such instances, we speak of 'low-intensity wars'. As the leaders of the various opposing forces benefit from the parallel economies which develop in the wake of such wars, armed conflict tends to be transformed into a way of life.

It is easy to foresee that if the consequences of the 'new wars' are extremely heavy for civilian populations, they are particularly so for women, whose

---

[19] Ibid. 22.

social role already places them in an especially precarious situation. Be it in their native villages, in the course of flight, or in refugee camps, women are everywhere exposed to the violence of armed groups and to sexual abuse in particular. 'Women are subjected to mistreatment by all participants in armed conflict: by "friendly" and "enemy" forces, by civilian and military personnel, including United Nations peacekeeping forces, who are entrusted with the task of protecting women.'[20] They often have no other choice but to trade sexual favours to members of the local militia in exchange for their own protection and that of others for whom they are responsible. 'They are frequently forced to offer sex in return for safe passage, essential food, shelter, refugee status, or documentation.'[21]

When rape is employed as an instrument of war, women are doubly victimized: as individuals and as symbols of their community. By raping women, enemy soldiers seek to humiliate the men of a community by showing them that they are not even strong enough to protect their own 'property'. In doing so, they stigmatize the women by making the girls 'impure' and, in a more general way, by transforming the women they have raped into 'foreign bodies' estranged from their community (a transformation which is all the more definitive if victims of rape become pregnant).[22]

If we take into account that new wars most frequently take place in impoverished countries with a high rate of unemployment and a population which is largely under age, it is easy to understand how simple it is for sexual aggression to explode under the pressure of armed struggle, be it initiated by external or internal conflict. In such situations, where local warlords and their hirelings have nothing to lose and everything to gain by brandishing Kalashnikovs, where young, uprooted, heavily drugged, and poorly paid adolescents are used as soldiers because they are cheaper than adults and totally without scruples, rape and murder become the norm. In such circumstances, rape is not a means of enacting military strategy; it does not result from a *systematic* practice. It is an emanation of sheer chaos.[23] As

---

[20] Gardman and Jarvis, *Women, Armed Conflict, and International Law*, 7.   [21] Ibid. 31.

[22] Testimonies exist in which enemy forces have purposely kept pregnant women in detention until abortion was no longer feasible.

[23] In his book on the war in Bosnia, Michael Ignatieff writes that the particular brutality of armed warfare in the 1990s has replaced the image of the soldier associated with honour and discipline by the image of the adolescent for whom a gun has an obvious phallic significance. 'When a war is fought by young irregular soldiers, sexual barbarity as a weapon becomes the norm' (*Die Zivilisierung des Krieges:*

shown below, this distinction has crucial consequences for the legal status of rape under international law.

The Protection of Women under International Law

The laws of war (*jus in bello*), which must be distinguished from the right to wage war (*jus ad bellum*), are regulated by customary law and conventions. Codification began in the second part of the nineteenth century with the Geneva Convention of 1864, which pertained to the protection of the wounded, the sick, and health professionals, and was continued by the two Hague Peace Conferences in 1899 and 1907. Following this legislation was the Geneva Convention of 1949, organized by the International Committee of the Red Cross, which gave birth to four Geneva Conventions followed by Protocol 1 and Protocol 2 Additional to the Geneva Conventions, in 1977. When we refer to international humanitarian law, we usually mean the four Geneva Conventions of 1949 and the two Additional Protocols of 1977. In addition to international humanitarian law, several other international documents adopted by the United Nations equally concern the laws of war, such as the Charters of the Nuremberg and Tokyo Trials, the Convention on Genocide, and the International Criminal Tribunals for the former Yugoslavia and for Rwanda.

What documents especially provide for the protection of women in the context of armed conflict? The Geneva Conventions as well as Additional Protocols I and II establish a code of behaviour between warring parties which limits the acts authorized in time of war and imposes the duty especially to protect several specific categories of persons, among which women are included. In addition to the equal protection accorded to the civilian population in general, international humanitarian law thus accords particular protection to women, which is especially provided for given their vulnerability during pregnancy and as mothers of dependent infants. (See, for example, articles 16, 17, 18, 20, 21, 23, 27, 89, and 91 of the Fourth Geneva Convention.) It may well be unfortunate that international humanitarian law thus first and foremost considers women in their role

Ethnische Konflikte, Menschenrechte, Medien (Hamburg: Europäische Verlagsanstalt, 2000), 161). See also Münkler, *Die neuen Kriege*, 39 ff.

as mothers; for while women's situation becomes all the more precarious if they are pregnant, nursing, or caring for dependent children during times of combat, this precariousness nevertheless does not derive from their biological role, as I have already indicated. Certain feminist interpretations of international law have justly denounced its limited, stereotypical image of women: notable, for example, are several articles of the Fourth Geneva Convention which categorize mothers with the sick, the wounded, and the infirm, and thus tend to mask the fact that armed conflict endangers women on levels other than that of sexuality.[24]

In addition to specific protections, the articles of the Conventions mention the kinds of behaviours forbidden by the laws of war. Although these include sexual violence, it is notable that rape does not figure explicitly in the catalogue of forbidden acts. Thus it is that Article 3, common to all four Geneva Conventions, stipulates that the following acts 'are and shall remain prohibited, at any time and in any place whatsoever:

a. violence to life and person, in particular murder of all kinds, mutilation, cruel treatment and torture;
b. taking of hostages;
c. outrages upon personal dignity, in particular humiliating and degrading treatment;
d. the passing of sentences and the carrying out of executions without previous judgment pronounced by a regularly constituted court, affording all the legal guarantees which are recognized as indispensable by civilized people.'

Although sexual abuse can certainly be included in 'humiliating and degrading treatment', it is nevertheless shocking that rape is not specifically mentioned as such.

In 1977, article 4 (2) of Additional Protocol II to the Geneva Conventions addressed this serious failure. Nevertheless, the measures within the article do not permit rape to be classified among the crimes which are liable to prosecution under international law. In fact, 'rape, forced prostitution, and any other form of indecent assault' figure among those acts 'prohibited at any time and in any place whatsoever', rather than among the acts specified

---

[24] This is the case for articles 16, 20, 21, and 27 of the Fourth Geneva Convention. See Gardam and Jarvis, *Women, Armed Conflict, and International Law*, 65 ff. Gardam and Jarvis conclude that 'the regime of special protection for women during armed conflict reveals a picture of women that is drawn exclusively on the basis of their perceived weakness, both physical and psychological, and their sexual and reproductive functions' (p. 95.)

as 'grave breaches' in article 147 of the Fourth Geneva Convention. Thus, not every violation of the laws of war is automatically punishable under international law.[25] Paragraph 5 of article 85 of the Protocol I establishes an equation between grave breaches and war crimes, thereby implying that *only* grave breaches are to be so considered.[26]

The distinction between 'prohibited acts' and 'grave breaches' is of considerable importance, for only grave breaches (as enumerated in article 147 of the Fourth Geneva Convention as well as in article 85 of Protocol I) oblige the signatories to take legal action against subjects so incriminated. Article 146 of the Fourth Convention stipulates that 'Each High Contracting party shall be under the obligation to search for persons alleged to have committed, or to have ordered to be committed, such grave breaches, and shall bring such persons, regardless of their nationality, before its own courts.' The penal system of the Conventions requires state parties to criminalize grave breaches and to prosecute or extradite the perpetrators of these acts. War crimes remain under universal jurisdiction, which means that all states have the right as well as the duty under international law to exercise criminal jurisdiction over the offenders.[27] Nevertheless, as shown above, rape—and sexual abuse in general—are not listed in the catalogue of breaches classified as 'grave' and thus considered to be war crimes.

It is further significant that the articles of the Fourth Geneva Convention and the two Additional Protocols denounce sexual abuse as an attack on a woman's honour, instead of an assault on her bodily safety and psychological health.[28] Moreover, review of the articles reveals that both the Fourth Geneva Convention and the Additional Protocols clearly emphasize *the particular protection* of women, rather than the *prohibition of atrocities* to which

---

[25] See Y. Dinstein, 'The Distinctions between War Crimes and Crimes against Peace', in Yoram Dinstein and Mala Tabory (eds.), *War Crimes in International Law* (The Hague and Boston: M. Nijhoff Publishers, 1996), 1–18. As Christian Tomuschat points out in the same volume ('Crimes against the Peace and Security of Mankind and the Recalcitrant Third State', 47), the International Law Commission (ILC) has been very restrictive in its definition of war crimes, requiring in article 22 that the violation be 'exceptionally serious'.

[26] Art. 85 (5): 'Without prejudice to the application of the Convention and of this Protocol, grave breaches of these instruments shall be regarded as war crimes.'

[27] Theodor Meron, 'International Criminalization of Internal Atrocities', *American Journal of International Law*, 89 (1995), 554 ff.

[28] See article 27 (2) of the Fourth Geneva Convention; article 76 (1) of Protocol I; Gardam and Jarvis, *Women, Armed Conflict, and International Law*, 11, 62; Chinkin, 'Feminist Reflections', 143.

they are particularly susceptible. Thus article 76 (1) of Protocol I states that
'women...shall be protected in particular against rape, forced prostitution
and any other form of indecent assault'.

On the one hand, emphasis is placed on the protection required by
the state; on the other, rape is not considered as a grave breach. These
two facts work together to greatly affect the status of sexual abuse under
international law and the justice meted out to the victims of violent sexual
acts. While it is indeed possible to reproach a state for failing sufficiently to
assure the safety of persons especially protected under the Conventions, it
is nevertheless impossible to prosecute such a state for negligence, unless
it can be proved that this was deliberate, and therefore constitutes a grave
breach.[29] As long as sexual abuse does not explicitly figure in the list of
grave breaches, neither the lack of protective measures to ensure women's
safety nor the perpetration of sexual abuse can be prosecuted as a crime
under the jurisdiction of international law.

The Geneva Conventions and the two Additional Protocols contain
yet another deeply regrettable lapse: the grave breaches provisions of the
four Conventions do not apply to the victims of non-international armed
conflicts. Prior to the adoption of Protocol II, relative to the protection of
victims in non-international armed conflicts, article 3 of the four Geneva
Conventions of 1949 was the only measure applicable in non-international
armed conflicts. However, neither article 3 nor the Protocol contains
provisions requiring states or other parties to a non-international armed
conflict to punish serious violations of international norms.[30] The basic
reason for this is the assumption that most violations of the laws of
war are also violations of general criminal law, which will be considered
as crimes by national criminal law. Consequently, the prosecution of

---

[29] Some writers criticize the distinction between grave breaches and other breaches as too strong,
because it invites the thought that other breaches which are nevertheless very serious are not equally
condemnable. 'The "grave breaches" listed in each of the four Conventions do not exhaust the range of
war criminality established by them. What are not "grave breaches" must be "suppressed". The French
text reads "faire cesser", a clumsy and imprecise phrase that is not helpful in the context of international
penal law or of justice to an accused. This leaves it open to each State Party to decide whether other
infractions of the Conventions shall be subject to the penal process, as crimes, or whether some or
all of them shall be dealt with by administrative or other dissuasive action by the State authorities'
(G. I. A. D. Draper, 'The Modern Pattern of War Criminality', in Dinstein and Tabory (eds.), War
Crimes in International Law, 164).
[30] See M. Bothe, 'War Crimes in Non-International Conflicts', in Dinstein and Tabory (eds.), War
Crimes in International Law, 294.

violations committed during non-international armed conflicts depends on the arbitrary nature of the extant legislation within the countries involved and the justifications they proffer for the recourse to violence.[31] We only begin to understand how deeply regrettable this restriction has actually been when we realize that non-international armed conflicts are often far crueller and more murderous than conflicts between states: indeed, internal warfare has accounted for approximately 80 per cent of the victims of all armed conflict since 1945.

The International Criminal Tribunals for the Former Yugoslavia and for Rwanda

The International Criminal Tribunals for the Former Yugoslavia and for Rwanda follow the pattern of the Nuremberg and Tokyo Trials. All were created by the United Nations Security Council following the commission of crimes against humanity during armed conflicts. After extensive media coverage exposed the systematic use of rape during the wars in the former Yugoslavia, the United Nations Commission on Human Rights appointed a Special Rapporteur, Tadeusz Mazowiecki, who denounced the use of rape as an instrument of war and as a method of ethnic cleansing 'intended to humiliate, shame, degrade and terrify the entire group'.[32] As a result, in 1992 the Security Council, acting under Chapter VII of the United Nations Charter, established through Resolutions 808 and 827 an International Criminal Tribunal for the prosecution of those responsible for serious violations of international humanitarian law committed on the territory of the former Yugoslavia since 1991. The violations fell into the categories of war crimes, genocide, and crimes against humanity. For the first time, rape (independent of the national or international nature of the conflict) was included among the list of crimes against humanity (article 5).[33]

[31] This indeed leaves open the great temptation for governments to justify the violent repression of opposition movements by asserting the need to maintain order.
[32] Report Pursuant to Commission Resolution 1992/S1/1 of 14 Aug. 1992, E/CN.4/1993/50 (10 Feb. 1993). Cited in Chinkin, 'Rape and Sexual Abuse'.
[33] The Nuremberg Charter made the first concrete formulation of 'crimes against humanity'. The list of crimes, however, does not include rape, as already mentioned. For Meron, 'the singling out

Two years later, following the massacres in Rwanda, the Security Council again created an International Criminal Tribunal to judge those responsible for crimes against humanity (Resolution 955, 1994). In this instance as well, rape was explicitly included in the list of crimes against humanity (article 3). It is important to note, however, that although sexual assault reached far higher proportions in Rwanda than in the former Yugoslavia, with a Human Rights Watch estimate of 250,000–500,000 rapes of women and girls, 'the Security Council made no reference to the sexual violence against women during its discussion of the conflict. Nor was sexual violence a focus of the investigations into the conflict instigated by the Security Council.'[34] Not until 1996 did a Special Report reveal the full amplitude of the sexual violence: 'rape was systematic and was used as a "weapon" by the perpetrators of the massacres ... According to consistent and reliable testimony, a great many women were raped; rape was the rule and its absence was the exception.'[35]

It is possible to make many conjectures about the origin of such discrimination in the legal system. It is important, nevertheless, to emphasize the enormous progress made by the official international condemnation of sexual abuse as a universally prosecutable crime. The impact of the International Criminal Tribunals for the Former Yugoslavia and for Rwanda cannot be measured only in terms of the punishment meted out to some of the principal culprits; their importance significantly includes their contribution to the evolution of international law. It is incontestable that the statutes of the ICTY and the ICTR have proved important instruments for advancing the codification of international law. Moreover, there is no doubt that the ICTY and the ICTR directly influenced the adoption of the Rome Statute of the International Criminal Court (ICC) at the 1998 Rome Diplomatic Conference. In this—to return to our current

---

of violations of humanitarian law as a major factor in the determination of a threat to the peace creates an important precedent, and the establishment of the tribunal as an enforcement measure under the binding authority of chapter VII, rather than through a treaty creating an international criminal court whose jurisdiction would be subject to the consent of the states concerned, may foreshadow more effective international responses to violations of humanitarian law' (Theodor Meron, 'War Crimes in Yugoslavia and the Development of International Law', *American Journal of International Law* 88 (1994). 79).

[34] Gardman and Jarvis, *Women, Armed Conflict, and International Law*, 152.

[35] Special Rapporteur of the Commission on Human Rights, *Report on the Situation of Human Rights in Rwanda*, UN Doc E/CN.4/1996/68 (26 Jan. 1996). Cited in Gardam and Jarvis, *Women, Armed Conflict, and International Law*, 153 n. 117.

subject—women have won an incontestable victory: from now on, it is possible not only to condemn sexual abuse in *ad hoc* tribunals with limited jurisdiction extending to specific conflicts; it can be universally prosecuted in a permanent International Criminal Court as a war crime (article 8 (2) (e) (vi)) and, more specifically, as a crime against humanity (article 7 (g)).

It is important to point out that the Rome Statute covers a much wider array of sexually abusive acts than do article 5 of the statutes of the ICTY and article 3 of the ICTR, which include only rape. Indeed, crimes against humanity now include the following: 'rape, sexual slavery, enforced prostitution, forced pregnancy, enforced sterilization, or any other form of sexual violence of comparable gravity'.

Assessment

The establishment of an International Criminal Court without doubt has provided the international community with a means of legal interference which strongly dissuades Heads of States or military leaders from engaging in criminal acts of war. Any individual guilty of a crime that falls within the competence of the Court is hence considered individually responsible for that crime, and is thus punishable under the law (article 25). Thus, while classical law dissociates individuals from states as legal entities, and thereby protects the immunity of officials by imputing their acts to the state, international criminal law, through the auspices of the International Criminal Court, henceforth has the means to treat the actions of officials as private acts. As article 27 (1) reads: 'The Statute shall apply equally to all persons without any distinction based on official capacity. In particular, official capacity as a Head of State or Government, a member of a Government or parliament, an elected representative or a Government official shall in no case exempt a person from criminal responsibility under this Statute, nor shall it, in and of itself, constitute a ground for reduction of sentence.'

Yet here we must return to a point made earlier regarding the evolution of the so-called new forms of war which, in comparison to the conventional organized violence of war, no longer respect the distinction between 'combatants' and 'non-combatants'.

The disappearance of this distinction is due to the fact that in current theatres of war, not only soldiers fight, but militias, paramilitary forces, and child soldiers, as well as mercenaries and private security corporations specializing in the logistics and techniques of war, who sell their services to states or warlords. The experts who lead and staff these private security corporations only very rarely actually engage in combat, preferring instead to advise and assist in the technical issues of war. Although they might carry guns and take part in the conflicts, mercenaries hired by private companies don't fall under military jurisdiction, and therefore are not subject to prosecution under current international law. From a moral point of view, this legalistic consequence of the recent collapse of the distinction between combatants and non-combatants is highly regrettable. Mercenaries paid by private companies for protecting persons or places of economic or strategic importance, even if they do not fight, must be considered as being actively engaged in the business of war. They carry the full moral responsibility for the consequences of their actions and for the damage caused by the techniques of war they introduce. Similarly, private persons or groups who raise funds through the black market economy (through trafficking in arms, drugs, or people, or raising funds for 'charitable' organizations) in my opinion carry a stronger responsibility for the waging of war than citizens who pay their taxes to their government in times of war.[36] By including non–combatant actors in the group of those individuals who should be held to a higher standard of responsibility for the funding and waging of war, we broaden the scope of those who are considered as being actively engaged in the business of war, thus expanding the definition of combatants and, consequently, the range of persons subject to the jurisdiction of the International Criminal Court.

Stigmatizing despotic leaders through indictment and prosecution undermines their influence. In addition to its power to dissuade, the Court also has a positive psychological effect on victims. Although the conviction of (at least some of) those who have committed criminal acts cannot restore lost loved ones or possessions to the victims of crime or their families, it does provide them with the recognition and support of the international community. Henceforth, they know they have not been doubly victimized:

---

[36] For a discussion of these aspects, see Ch. 1 in this volume.

first by an abuse of power or hatred, then by the indifference of other nations.

In another welcome evolution of international law, the conviction and punishment of crimes against humanity are no longer conditionally tied to their perpetration in the context of international armed conflict, or even to armed conflict at all, as far as the ICC is concerned. 'The tangled meshing of crimes against humanity and human rights militates against requiring a link with war for the former. The better opinion today, I submit, is that crimes against humanity exist independently of war.'[37] The first step in this extension was taken by the ICTR. (In the case of the ICTY, the conflict was treated as international armed conflict, because of recognition by foreign states of Slovenia, Croatia, and Bosnia-Herzegovina.) This development represents clear progress, given the brutality of national conflicts.

Although there have been positive new developments, we should not overestimate the effectiveness of international criminal law. Be they *ad hoc* or permanent, international tribunals have neither the time nor the resources to pursue every perpetrator of offences within their jurisdictions. If we consider their action only from the point of view of their ability to bring the guilty to justice, we have every good reason to despair of ever establishing the sort of justice truly worthy of the name: by late 2000, the ICTR, for example, had indicted only some fifty suspects.[38] To see its larger influence, we must therefore look at international criminal justice in another way. As stated above, it is important to see the effect it has had on the evolution of international law; but future assessments should equally take into consideration its use as a deterrent. Actions that have far too often been viewed as inevitable during armed conflict have now been criminalized, and states are obliged to condemn the guilty parties or extradite them for judgment before an international court: these facts should work to discourage nationalist leaders from using the language of racial hatred to shore up their power. Investigations of the wars in the former Yugoslavia and in Rwanda have clearly revealed that the massacres and systematic rape were not explosions of spontaneous racial hatred. In both cases, they were the product of a carefully pre-pared campaign which was forcefully imposed on the population. 'The

---

[37] Meron, 'War Crimes in Yugoslavia', 85.
[38] Steven R. Ratner and Jason S. Abrams, *Accountability for Human Rights Atrocities in International Law*, 2nd edn. (Oxford: Oxford University Press, 2001), 204.

organized and deliberate character of this policy emerged most clearly in Bosnia-Herzegovina, where half of the population had entered into mixed marriages.'[39] Likewise, in Rwanda, the radio–television station of Mille Collines organized the extermination of the Tutsi and Hutu moderates.

> They reviled the Tutsi as 'cockroaches' that had infested the country, and the ensuing rage was sustained by the careful political-military organization of Hutu extremists. The Hutu Interahamwe and other volunteer militia systematically infiltrated every town and village in Rwanda and compiled accurate lists of those slated for extermination. Only when the Rwandese people were saturated with racist hatred and fallacies, and extremists had positioned themselves in every corner of the country, did it become possible to execute the monstrous 'final solution' to the Tutsi 'problem' with such exceptional efficiency.[40]

These horrors bring to light the reasons why it is essential to condemn such acts, as well as the incitation to commit them, as crimes against all humanity.

The verdict of 'crime against humanity' or 'genocide' is nevertheless sometimes double-sided when applied to sexual abuse. In the Statutes of the International Criminal Court, these crimes are actually linked together by their *systematic* nature, and the fact that in the crime of genocide, actions are executed 'with intent to destroy, in whole or in part, a national, ethnical, racial, or religious group, as such' (article 6). As discussed above, the sexual abuse in the former Yugoslavia and in Rwanda conforms to this description. In both cases, it was carried out on a massive and systematic basis in order to produce babies of the rapists' own ethnic class, destroy the family life of the victims, and annihilate the identity of the community. However, it is not possible to say the same of the sexual violence perpetrated by local militias or child soldiers left to their own devices, instruments of pure violence who, rather than pursuing ideological goals, are seeking to escape the fate that misery has thrust upon them. Although an enormous number of victims fall prey to such violence, it is not 'systematic', and hence its perpetrators cannot be pursued in the system of international criminal justice.

---

[39] Payam Akhavan, 'Beyond Impunity: Can International Criminal Justice Prevent Future Atrocities?', *American Journal of International Law*, 95 (2001), 10.
[40] Ibid. 11.

Similarly, as Rosalind Dixon has emphasized, the verdict of genocide may, ironically, work against the cause of women: condemning acts of systematic rape as an attack on the identity and survival of a *community* rather than as a violation of women's *individual* rights can indirectly legitimize existent discrimination against women in the social order itself.[41] When the social identity and existence of the entire group is considered as the target of systematic rape, women are not only the first victims of aggression; those who survive are often doubly victimized, because they are condemned and rejected by their own society. Indeed, as already pointed out, women are particularly vulnerable—especially in traditional societies—not only because of their sex, but because of their social status and the fate they suffer after falling victim to sexual abuse.

In Bosnia, many women were not only raped by the 'enemy', but beaten and cast out by their fathers and husbands. They were not only forced to carry an unwanted child, but denied any right to establish a familial connection or bond with that child by a rigid (patrilineal or ethno-religious) concept of 'purity'. ... Defining these harms as harms against Bosnian men and the (ethno-religious) patriarchal 'order' they have created fundamentally obscures the double harm to women of primary and 'secondary' victimization.[42]

Although the use by the international criminal justice system of systematicity as a criterion for qualifying an act of violence as a war crime may have regrettable negative consequences, the criterion should be maintained. The qualification has to do with the very definition of violation of rights. Indeed, it is important to clarify that a violation of rights does not necessarily amount to the unjust deprivation of a freedom or of a fundamental right. When a person is the victim of aggression, whether the person be killed, raped, or beaten, he or she is the victim of an isolated criminal act. In this case, we cannot qualify the act as a violation, even if the attack on the integrity of the victim is identical to that carried out against victims of a massacre, collective rape, or torture. The difference is neither in the number nor the gravity of the wrong committed. It is in the underlying structure of the crime.[43]

---

[41] Dixon, 'Rape as a Crime in International Humanitarian Law', 705.   [42] Ibid. 704–5.

[43] See Thomas Pogge, 'How Should Human Rights be Conceived?', in B. Sharon Byrd *et al.* (eds.), *Annual Review of Law and Ethics/Jahrbuch für Recht und Ethik*, 3 (1995), 103–20.

An attack on fundamental rights becomes a violation when the official authorities of a country either actively order it or passively tolerate it. It is indeed an important difference if an individual knows whether a criminal attack is an isolated act or the result of an explicit strategy which is institutionally encouraged or tolerated. In the first case, an institution can be held responsible only up to a certain limit, which is recognized as tolerable. In the second, when the violence is institutionalized, it is the very idea of rights and justice which is violated under the cover of the allegedly legal actions of a sovereign state. It is morally scandalous for authorities who represent the law and on whom we depend to violate rights in this way. When this occurs, the quality of life of those ruled by such unjust institutions is seriously eroded, even if it turns out that, qualitatively speaking, most individuals were not exposed to more cruel and violent acts than are always to be expected, and which even a just state cannot entirely prevent. The violation of fundamental individual rights, when officially carried out, encouraged, or tolerated, represents an attack on the very essence of humanity—its dignity—by publicly denying the dignity of the people who are victim to official discrimination. When the use of power is perverted and made into an instrument of hate, domination, and racial discrimination, not only individual people but humanity as a whole suffers, and humanity itself is menaced and violated. As Johann Benjamin Erhard impressively puts it in his essay on the right to revolution, when the fundamental laws of a state hold the rights of man up to ridicule, the rights of an entire people are potentially scorned. In this case, he says, 'not me alone, but mankind in my own person simultaneously suffers from injustice'.[44] That is the reason why we rightly speak of 'crime against humanity'.

Behind the qualification of an act as being a systematic violation of fundamental rights is therefore the idea of the institutionalization of a crime, the idea of an officially sanctioned strategy. I thus retain the following characteristics as criteria that justify speaking of a violation of rights liable to be condemned by the International Criminal Court: (a) the official character of the violation, i.e., the fact that it is not the result of isolated individual acts but is instead led and supported

[44] Johann Benjamin Erhard, *Über das Recht des Volks zu einer Revolution und andere Schriften*, ed. Hellmut G. Haasis (Frankfurt am Main: Hanser, 1976), 50.

by a state institution; (b) its racist or ideological motivation; (c) its systematic nature, i.e., that it consists of repeated violations of such proportions that we are led to conclude that the discrimination taking place has been planned.

The trouble with the case of rapes that occur within contexts of intra-state conflicts typical of the new typology of violence we are dealing with is that, even when perpetrated on a massive scale, they might not be the result of a systematic strategy. The typological distinction between the four following types of rape might therefore be helpful.[45] We should distinguish between:

1. Truly *anomalous* rapes which happen in all wars. They are a matter for criminal justice dealt with by the national courts.
2. Rapes *tolerated* by the military and political leadership.
3. Rapes *expressly permitted*, being part and parcel of the right of pillage.
4. Rapes *deliberately and systematically* used as a means of warfare.

All except the first category involve a stand taken by the military and political authorities. Such acts can therefore be considered as being institutionalized, and should thus fall under the jurisdiction of the International Court of Justice. Only rapes of the third and fourth categories, however, should be qualified as crimes against humanity.

I would like to conclude by addressing one more crucial point. Although I have concentrated on sexual abuse and its treatment in international human-itarian law, it is important to underline the fact that women's heightened vulnerability to violence is essentially a socio-political phenomenon. If women are more exposed in armed conflicts than men, it is not only because they can potentially be threatened with sexual abuse everywhere they go and by everyone they meet; it is also because they do not enjoy the same rights as men.[46] Consequently, the international community should not limit its aims to the punishment of criminals. It should equally offer monetary compensation and aid to facilitate the rehabilitation of women. 'There might be an award to allow a woman to obtain adequate psycholog-ical and medical care, to relocate herself from a community in which she has and may be continuing to be victimized, to support herself, and to obtain

---

[45] Thanks to Igor Primoratz for this distinction.
[46] This aspect is particularly well covered in Gardam and Jarvis, *Women, Armed Conflict, and International Law*.

education and training in order to gain employment'.[47] By concentrating on the criminal dimension of sexual abuse, we risk ignoring yet another crucial dimension: we must go beyond the treatment of women as victims, and help them overcome their trauma and social handicaps once the war is over.

[47] Dixon, 'Rape as a Crime in International Humanitarian Law', 717.

11

War and the Protection of Property

JANNA THOMPSON

Immunity of Civilian Property

Cicero thought that pillage in moderation was acceptable providing it was done for the embellishment of the homeland and not out of personal greed.[1] Grotius thought it was all right to lay waste the land and property of the enemy in reprisal or to discourage opposition.[2] Most of our contemporaries disagree. Most statements of just war theory insist that civilian property, as well as civilians themselves, should be protected in war. International conventions also rule out destruction or seizure of civilian property. The Hague Convention of 1907 prohibits the destruction or appropriation of private property and some kinds of state property—including schools, hospitals, and religious and cultural institutions. The Geneva Convention on Civilians of 1949 says that 'any destruction of real or personal property belonging individually or collectively to private persons, or to the State, or other public authorities, or social or cooperative organisations, is prohibited, except where such destruction is rendered absolutely necessary by military operations'. The Hague Convention of 1954 specifically prohibits destruction or seizure of cultural property in war or occupation.

To attack property is often to harm or endanger civilians, and when this is so, prohibition of attacks on civilian property follows from a prohibition

---

[1] Jiri Toman, *The Protection of Cultural Property in the Event of Armed Conflict* (Dartmouth: UNESCO Publishing, 1996), 4.

[2] Hugo Grotius, *On the Law of War and Peace*, bk. 3, ch. 5.

on attacks on civilians. The bombing of a residential section of a town is bound to kill or injure many of the residents. An attack on a hospital endangers its inmates and also the lives and well-being of civilians who in the immediate future will need medical services. However, the property of civilians can be destroyed or seized without killing civilians or threatening their lives. Operation Defensive Shield, which the Israelis launched in 2002, involved the destruction of large numbers of Palestinian homes, but residents, given an advance warning, were mostly able to evacuate before their dwellings were bulldozed. Looting can destroy a civilian's means of life, but in moderation it need not do so. Taking away paintings or statues does not threaten lives. An independent justification is therefore needed for the modern conviction that offences against property are prohibited in war and occupation.

If civilian immunity means that civilians should be spared the effects of war—if they are entitled to carry on their lives and their businesses in war as they do in peace—then it would be a violation of this entitlement if their property were destroyed or seized. But combatants cannot be required to ensure that civilians do not suffer inconvenience. Most discussions of just war agree that a belligerent is entitled to strike at communication systems, bridges, electricity generators, and other things that count as military targets even when these also service the civilian community. In any case, it is doubtful that citizens can claim a right to be immune from all the effects of war—especially if they are citizens of a democratic country that has decided on war. Why, then, should the destruction or interference with civilian property be especially forbidden?

Right to Property and Right to Life

A lawful conqueror, says Locke, has 'absolute power over the lives of those who by an unjust war have forfeited them; but not over the lives or fortunes of those who engaged not in the war, nor over the possessions even of those who were actually engaged in it'.[3] A conqueror can justifiably confiscate or destroy an enemy's means of making war. But he is not justified in confiscating the estates of civilians or even belligerents. For this property

---

[3] John Locke, *The Second Treatise of Civil Government*, sect. 178.

rightly belongs not just to them but to their wives and children—and it would be wrong to deprive these heirs of what is rightly theirs. One of Locke's concerns is that wives and children not be made destitute by appropriations—a position that might not require an absolute prohibition on the taking or destruction of property. But his other concern is protection of property rights. We can attack belligerents, destroying them and their property when necessary for the sake of self-defence. But destruction or seizure that cannot be so justified violates their right to property, or the right of their heirs. If someone threatens to rob you, he says, you can justifiably defend yourself, but you are not justified in confiscating the property of the robber.[4] Nor would you be justified in attacking or seizing the property of either the robber's family or of members of his community.

Locke's account of why property is immune from attack or seizure depends on the idea that right of property is a fundamental human right and should be respected as such. One of the problems with this view is that many people either deny that there is such a right or think that it is not all that important. If property rights are merely customary or legal, or if right to property is less fundamental than right to welfare or other goods and objectives, then a prohibition which appeals to such a right is either unconvincing or far less stringent than Locke supposed. In fact, many people believe that right to life is far more important than right to property. But if this is accepted, then it seems that destruction or seizure of property can be justified in many cases where it is not strictly necessary for self-defence or to achieve a military objective.

Life, says McKeogh, is the most precious thing that an individual has. Loss of property is merely a pocketbook loss that can be compensated for or outweighed by a proportionate good.[5] Given the overriding importance of life, it is mistaken in his view to accord civilian property the same kind of immunity that civilians themselves are supposed to enjoy. It is never right, he insists, to trade off the lives of innocent civilians against some good or just end—even the end of saving more innocent lives. But destroying property would not be wrong as a means for avoiding the unjust taking of

---

[4] Ibid. sect. 182.
[5] Colm, McKeogh, *Innocent Civilians: The Morality of Killing in War* (Basingstoke: Palgrave, 2002), 165–6.

human lives.[6] He agrees with a suggestion made by Colonel Dunlap of the US Air Force that a strategy of attacks using 'smart weapons' on factories, banks, financial institutions, shops, and other sites not indispensable to civilian life could be a justifiable means of waging war if it is accompanied by a greater emphasis on protecting civilian lives. For example, an attack on property could be justified if it undermines morale and thus saves lives by shortening a war.

If life is so much more important than property, then saving the lives of combatants is also much more important than protecting property. Why should combatants be expected to take risks for mere 'pocketbook losses'? Taken to its logical conclusion, McKeogh's insistence on the overwhelming importance of life means that property is immune only from attacks that are not undertaken to save lives: from wanton destruction or from destruction motivated by revenge. This is considerably less immunity than it is given in most versions of just war theory or by international conventions.

Let us agree that it is better to save civilians than to save their property. Let us also agree that it *can* be better to save the lives of belligerents than to protect civilian property. Suppose, for example, that a commander has the choice between two battle strategies, both of which are likely to accomplish his military objective. One would require advancing tanks through the fields of villagers and thus ruining some of their crops. The other, though it avoids the damage, is likely to result in heavy casualties to his troops. It seems fairly obvious what strategy a responsible commander would and should choose—even though the destruction of civilian property is not absolutely necessary to achieve his military objective. However, a position which provides no immunity to property whenever lives can be saved is problematic, for several reasons. First of all, because not all losses of property are mere pocketbook losses. If the only objective is to save lives, then why not aim the smart weapons on churches or mosques, art galleries, museums, public monuments, and other emblems of national pride and accomplishment? Destruction of these things is likely to be more demoralizing than destruction of banks and insurance offices. Second, we do not always think that destruction of civilian property is preferable to risking lives. Israeli government officials defended the destruction of

<hr />

[6] McKeogh, *Innocent Civilians*, 171.

Palestinian homes in Operation Defensive Shield as a means of saving lives through prevention of future attacks or deterring would-be attackers. But even if they were right about the effects of the Operation, many people regard such attacks on civilian property as ethically objectionable.[7] Those who object, or those who think that at least some kinds of property should be immune, will want stronger prohibitions on attacking property than McKeogh allows.

The question remains why civilian and public property of certain kinds should be accorded so much respect. A satisfactory answer should help to explain when property is immune from attack and when it is not: when the objective of saving lives or accomplishing a military objective overrides its immunity and when it does not. There are three main reasons for protecting property in war that seem to me to carry weight. The first is pragmatic: the less destruction is done to property in a war, the easier it is for people to recover and establish peaceful relationships. The second reason has to do with the moral value of property or the relationships associated with property. The third focuses on property valued as heritage or for its aesthetic, scientific, or educational significance.

The Value of Property

The pragmatic reason for limiting the destruction of civilian property appeals to the common-sense idea that it is important for belligerents to be concerned with establishing peaceful relationships after hostilities have finished.[8] This concern is central to just war theory, with its emphasis on limiting war and making peace possible. If damage to civilian property during a war has been extensive, then survivors will be traumatized, needy, and lack the infrastructure that enables them to be productive, secure, and well governed. They are more likely to face serious economic and political crisis, states of affairs that are not conducive to peaceful relationships. It could be the case that many lives will be lost simply because of privation or civil unrest—thus undermining the justification for destruction. The victorious nation, if it is an occupying power or is involved in reconstruction, could

---

[7] For a critical report on Israeli actions, see United Nations General Assembly, *Report of the Secretary-General prepared pursuant to General Assembly Resolution ES-10/10* (July 2000).

[8] This reason for limiting destruction of property was suggested to me by Tony Coady.

face heavy expenses and serious political difficulties. This is especially likely if people of the defeated nation regard the destruction as unnecessary or unethical. The attitudes of people of the defeated nation will be affected not just by their economic losses but by the meaning that their property had for them. So let us look more closely at how values associated with property should affect the behaviour of belligerents in war.

Even if we reject Locke's view of property ownership as a fundamental natural right, we can still find good reasons for thinking that property is of value to individuals, and thus for insisting that it should be relatively immune from attack in war or appropriation by victors. Having property, says Lomasky, enables individuals to undertake projects that are central to their being able to live a good life.[9] Property, says Fabre, contributes to the autonomy of individuals by giving them freedom to pursue a good.[10] Others point out that property ownership increases security and well-being by giving individuals stable access to things and enabling them to plan for the future.[11] Those influenced by Hegel stress how property can come to be a material embodiment of a person as she shapes it and makes it serve her purposes. So if someone destroys or appropriates property without the consent of the owners, the consequent disruption of their lives, the frustration of their plans, and undermining of their projects give them good reason to complain of a violation of their rights.[12] The loss is in many cases not merely a loss to their pocketbooks and, depending on the nature of the thing in question, money may provide no adequate compensation.

To the extent that loss of property is the kind of harm described, it seems right to insist that civilian immunity should include immunity of civilian property. Civilians cannot expect to be spared all inconveniences associated with war, but they can reasonably demand that property central to their lives, their projects, and their plans for themselves and their families should be spared. Not all property does play a central role in people's lives. A person's five shares in a large corporation may play a small part in her plans

    [9] Loren Lomasky, *Persons, Rights, and the Moral Community* (Oxford: Oxford University Press, 1987).
    [10] Cecile Fabre, 'Justice, Fairness, and World Ownership', *Law and Philosophy*, 21 (2002), 249–73.
    [11] Christopher Ciocchetti, 'The Attraction of Historical Entitlements', *Journal of Value Inquiry*, 36 (2002), 59–71; Lawrence C. Becker, *Property Rights: Philosophic Foundations* (London: Routledge & Kegan Paul, 1977).
    [12] Jeremy Waldron, 'Superseding Historical Injustice', *Ethics*, 103 (1992), 17–18.

for the future, but are in no way central to her life. Possessions that are most likely to be of central importance to people's lives include their homes, some of their personal possessions—particularly those related to valued activities, friendships, family life, memories of the past—and in many cases their businesses. The fact that property can be more or less important to people perhaps explains why some cases of destruction or expropriation seem harder to justify than others. The crops of the villagers smashed by the tanks of an invading army can be compensated for and, in any case, replaced in the next season. Their loss seems fundamentally different from the loss of Palestinian farmers whose olive trees were uprooted, wells filled in, and buildings smashed because their farms stood in the way of Israeli operations. Such actions, like the destruction of family homes, are much more difficult to justify.

A strategy that destroys banks, insurance offices, or shops in order to shorten a war seems more acceptable than one that involves destroying homes (even when civilians themselves are spared). On the other hand, a shop can represent several lifetimes of family labour, and may play a central role in the plans and aspirations of its members. The people of a town may have their life savings in a bank. Since things can be valuable to individuals for many different reasons, it seems best in most cases to adopt a practice of protecting civilian property rather than trying to make guesses about what is central to people's lives.

A consideration of how property contributes to the meaning of life provides a further reason for insisting that civilian property should be immune from attack or appropriation. Life is valuable, but for most people it isn't the only thing of supreme value. Indeed, life without other valued things is for many people barely tolerable—or perhaps not tolerable at all. Because mere life can be a life without meaning or even a life not worth living, many philosophers have argued that it is not life itself that is valuable but life that has value to the person who lives it.[13] One of the implications of this plausible view is that it is not enough merely to protect life. We must also endeavour to preserve and protect those conditions that enable people to value their lives.

What makes it possible for people to value their lives is to some extent an individual matter. However, the value of life for most people will

---

[13] See Jonathan Glover, *Causing Death and Saving Lives* (Harmondsworth: Penguin, 1981), ch. 3.

depend on them not suffering from pain or insecurity, being able to have meaningful relationships with others, being part of a community, and being able to pursue goals that they find worthwhile. Having security, being able to maintain meaningful relationships, or to pursue worthwhile goals means having access to resources and some control over one's environment: that is, being able to enjoy or have access to property, private or public, including such things as a home, personal possessions, a business, a place of worship, public facilities, and the infrastructure on which social networks depend. People can lose valued property—even their homes and their personal possessions—and still believe that life is worth living, especially if they have reason to hope that they will be able to rebuild their lives. But the fact that access to, or possession of, property is an important prerequisite for a life worth living indicates that reasons for thinking that civilians should be immune from attack are also reasons for thinking that civilian property should be relatively immune.

An account of how property is conducive to conditions that make life worth living should not confine itself to the values that ownership has for individuals. Property in all societies is intrinsically connected to social values and relationships. The family home is at the heart of family life. A community is bound together through the places where people live and work, and its public buildings provide the infrastructure for their social relationships. Schools and places of worship or public assembly are the focus of the lives of many individuals, and provide resources that help to make their lives worth living. The role that property, public and private, plays in cementing and promoting social relationships is a further reason for regarding it as immune from destruction. It is also reason for avoiding other activities that tend to undermine communal life. A policy of removing civilians from their territory and herding them into protective hamlets or camps is highly disruptive to their lives, plans, and social relationships, even when it does not prove fatal. Humiliating civilians, forcing them to engage in activities alien to their cultural life, making it difficult or impossible for them to carry on their businesses or daily activities, are all actions that demonstrate a lack of respect for individuals and for activities that make lives meaningful.

A case for immunity that focuses on the value of property to individuals and one that appeals to what it means to respect life are similar in many respects. Both centre on the needs and interests of individuals, and both reach similar conclusions. There are strong reasons for prohibiting destruction of civilian property, but the prohibition is not absolute. Some kinds of property are more valuable to individuals than others. Some losses can be compensated for. Individuals can recover from even severe losses if they can be returned to conditions in which their lives can flourish. Nevertheless, the reasons for respecting individuals and the ways in which they have found meaning for their lives provide a presumption that civilian property should be protected unless there is a very good reason for not doing so. This proviso allows that if belligerents have to choose between saving civilian lives and saving their property, it is better to save lives. Though immunity means that belligerents should be prepared to take some risks in order to avoid destroying civilian property, the proviso allows that they are not required to take as many risks for the sake of protecting property as for the sake of protecting civilians.[14]

Agents of Destruction

De Vattel says:

We ravage a country and render it uninhabitable, in order to make it serve us as a barrier, and to cover our frontier against an enemy whose incursions we are unable to check by any other means. A cruel expedient, it is true, but why should we not be allowed to adopt it at the expense of the enemy, since with the same view, we readily submit to lay waste our own provinces?[15]

De Vattel is making two points that seem to tell against the reasoning in the last section. The first is that individuals are often willing, or ought to be willing, to allow their property to be destroyed or appropriated for the sake of the common good—especially in war. Russian peasants burned their own land in the face of Napoleon's invasion, and people in other times and places have been willing to sacrifice their property to the common cause of defending their country against an enemy. The fact that they are

---

[14] It should be noted that article 52 of the Geneva Convention says that 'in case of doubt whether an object which is normally dedicated to civilian purposes, such as a place of worship, a house or other dwelling or a school, is being used to make an effective contribution to military action, it shall be presumed not to be so used'. Abiding by this requirement would entail some risk to combatants.
[15] Emmerich de Vattel, *The Law of Nations*, ed. J. Chitty (Philadelphia: T & J. W. Johnson & Co., 1883), bk. III, ch. 9, sect. 167.

prepared to make that sacrifice, and that their government is justified in asking it of them, suggests that property is not so precious that it cannot be destroyed or appropriated for a higher good, like self-defence. De Vattel's second, and more important, point is that if we are prepared to destroy our own property in a war, then we should also be permitted to destroy the property of the enemy—at least if we think that our cause is just.

The destruction that de Vattel wants to allow might sometimes be justified by 'military necessity'. But in the absence of this justification, his reasoning is invalid. We cannot justify destructive attacks on the property of enemy civilians just because we would be prepared to sacrifice our own property for the sake of defending ourselves in a war. It is worthwhile to consider why the reasoning is invalid.

First of all, the people of a nation are likely to endorse the objectives and actions of their government and armed forces—especially if this objective is defence of their country. They are likely to accept that their properties have to be sacrificed for the sake of an important good. But when the enemy destroys property, it is being done for an objective that those suffering the harm are not likely to endorse. Second, the people of a country are likely to think of their government and military as representing them—at least when their government is responsive to their interests and in control of the military. This will be so even when they disagree with many of the decisions of the government—including the decision to go to war. Harm done to citizens' property by a government which represents them and acts legitimately (even if contrary to their point of view) is more acceptable than harm done by a government and military that doesn't represent them.

Respecting civilians includes understanding their point of view and respecting their political allegiances—at least, if they are not morally pernicious. But respect means that governments and armies must acknowledge a difference between visiting harm on the property of their own people for the sake of conducting a war and visiting harm on the property of enemy civilians.

It might be argued that this difference, and the prohibition against destruction that it is used to defend, exists only when governments do in fact represent their people, or at least are not oppressing them. If the invaders are liberators delivering the civilian population from an oppressive government, then why shouldn't civilians accept some sacrifices, including sacrifices of their property for the sake of an objective which serves their interest? Indeed, it might be clear in some cases that civilians do accept these sacrifices. But invaders should not too readily assume that they will be regarded as 'liberators'. Walzer points out that nations do not undertake the expenses and sacrifices of a war for purely altruistic reasons,[16] and so those who are being liberated have reason to be ambivalent about the objectives of the invaders. They will not necessarily regard all of their actions as legitimate or representing their interests, and this means that the invaders should not assume that the civilians of the conquered country will accept the same sacrifices as members of their own society.

Added to this is another consideration. People may despise their government, yet believe that there are aspects of their political and social relationships that are valuable and worth defending. If so, they may have reason to fear that the invaders will not respect valued relationships, or at least to fear the loss of an ability to control their future political destiny. Given that these fears are reasonable, a difference remains between the destructive actions of their own armed forces, at least when they are acting in defence of things people regard as worth defending, and destructive activities of invaders, however well motivated.

The respect that belligerents ought to have for the social and political relationships of civilians should also govern the behaviour of the occupiers of a country toward the civilian population. Occupiers are justified in destroying or appropriating weapons and interfering with those activities and institutions that might enable the defeated enemy to be a danger to others in the future. They are justified in liberating victims of oppression. But they are generally not justified in forcing civilians to give up practices and relationships which are not implicated in the aggressive or oppressive activities of their government. The 1949 Geneva Convention prohibits an occupying power from interfering with civilian private and collective property (article 53). This means that it is limited in the reforms it can make to a society even when it believes that changes to property and other relationships are in the interest of its people. The prohibition is justified by the respect that occupying powers ought to have for the social relationships of civilians and for their right to decide their own political

---

[16] Michael Walzer, *Just and Unjust Wars: A Moral Argument with Historical Illustrations* (Harmondsworth: Penguin, 1977), 101 ff.

destiny. If the occupying power does sponsor reforms, there must be good reason to think that they are acceptable to a majority of the citizens, accepted by their legitimate government, or are necessary to prevent future aggression.[17]

Protection of Cultural Property

De Vattel also says:

For whatever cause a country is ravaged, we ought to spare those edifices which do honour to human society, and do not contribute to increase the enemy's strength,—such as temples, tombs, public buildings, and all works of remarkable beauty. What advantage is obtained by destroying them? It is declaring one's self an enemy to mankind, thus wantonly to deprive them of these monuments of art and models of taste.[18]

That achievements of civilization and works of art should not be destroyed in war is a widely accepted principle, and the Hague Convention of 1954 insists that cultural property should have 'immunity from seizure, placing in prize, or capture' (article 14). This immunity from destruction or seizure is supposed to exist because of what these objects are in themselves or what they represent.

The justifications that have been given for the protection of cultural property in war and occupation are of two kinds. The Hague Convention echoes the view of de Vattel and declares that cultural property should be immune because 'damage to cultural property belonging to any people whatsoever means damage to the cultural heritage of all mankind'. It emphasizes the human, and thus international, significance of cultural property. The second Additional Protocol to the Geneva Convention, 1977, prohibits 'hostility against historic monuments, works of art or places

---

[17] When the USA invaded Japan after its unconditional surrender, it decided to destroy the feudal system in the countryside through extensive land reforms which involved taking property away from large landowners (with little compensation) and distributing it among their tenants. The American action can probably be morally defended, because the Japanese had already taken steps toward land reform in their parliament and because the Japanese Supreme Court decided in favour of the reforms. It is notable that the opposition of the landlords collapsed when this ruling was made. See Nisuke Ando, *Surrender, Occupation, and Private Property in International Law: An Evaluation of US Practice in Japan* (Oxford: Clarendon Press, 1991), 20 ff.

[18] De Vattel, *Law of Nations*, bk III, ch. 9, sect. 168.

of worship which constitute the cultural or spiritual heritage of peoples',
thus emphasizing the significance of cultural objects for the people of
particular communities or nations.

These justifications promote different ideas about the meaning and
significance of cultural property. A statue or a historical monument may
be of little or no significance to humanity—it may not be a great work
of art—and yet be of great symbolic value to the people of a nation. On
the other hand, a work of art can be of value to humanity and of no, or
negative, significance to the particular community in which it is located.
The Bamiyan Buddhas, destroyed by the Taliban, are an example. Let us
examine each of these justifications for protecting cultural property in war,
beginning with the second—the appeal to cultural property as heritage.

It might seem that a prohibition against harming or seizing the cultural
and spiritual heritage of a people follows from a general prohibition against
harming the public property of civilians, and that nothing more needs
to be said on this topic. But cultural property that counts as heritage
has a value that goes beyond its utility, and for this reason seems to call
for a special degree of protection. Some have suggested that its preservation is more important than the protection of civilian lives and private
property:

The destruction of a mosque or a church is different from the destruction of a
Bosnian's house. Your life is a series of accidents. But the mosque or the church,
it represents an order to the world. It's often been said to me … 'We get used to
being killed. We know that human life is no more tangible or permanent than the
life of a butterfly. But when we see these other buildings being destroyed, we see
the rest of the world starting to crumble around us, and we become lost.'[19]

A church or a mosque, this passage suggests, belongs to a whole people, past
and future, as well as to present members of a community, and for the sake
of continuity, permanence, and the survival of a heritage, its preservation
should take precedence over the saving of civilian and military lives or
civilian private property.

This position exaggerates the value of heritage. A tradition is, after all,
maintained and passed on by people, and it is their survival as individuals
and as a community which is of overriding importance. The people can

---

[19] National Arts Journalism Program, *War and Cultural Property*, p. 68 (viewed at <www.najp.org/
conferences/cultural/058-071%20War%20and%20Cultural%20Property.pdf>).

continue to practise their religion without their churches or mosques, but the churches and mosques would be meaningless without the people. What made the destruction of religious sites of such great significance to people in Bosnia was the fact that both sides deliberately destroyed these things—as an expression of contempt and a symbol of their desire to destroy or drive out a people and their tradition. Such acts against civilians are immoral for obvious reasons. Because of their central place in the lives of individuals and the practices of their communities, respect for civilians requires that places of worship, heritage buildings, and monuments should get at least as much protection from attack as civilian homes, and that looting of these things should be strictly prohibited.

The other justification for protection of cultural property focuses not on the value of an object as the heritage of people of a particular community or nation, but on its aesthetic, scientific, or educational value—those properties which make it of value to all of humankind. That things that have these values—particularly things that have them to a high degree—should be protected in war and occupation is not difficult to justify. Paintings or artefacts of great aesthetic value, for example, should be preserved and protected so that they can continue to be appreciated by present and future generations. Nevertheless, two issues arise in relation to the treatment of these objects in war and occupation. The first is determining how much protection they should get. The second is whether items that are of value to all of humanity are necessarily immune to seizure and capture.

The Hague Convention for the Protection of Cultural Property allows that military necessity can be a justification for endangering or destroying cultural property. 'Military necessity' is a slippery term subject to different interpretations. The difficult cases are those where cultural property can be protected only by endangering the lives of civilians or combatants. Some people take the view that saving works of major artistic value is worth considerable loss of life:

I should assuredly be prepared to be shot against a wall if I were certain that by such a sacrifice I could preserve the Giotto frescoes; nor should I hesitate for an instant (were such a decision ever open to me) to save St. Mark's even if I were aware that by so doing I should bring death to my sons…. My attitude would be governed by a principle which is surely incontrovertible. The irreplaceable is more important than the replaceable, and the loss of even the most valued human life is ultimately less disastrous than the loss of something which in no circumstances can ever be created again.[20]

The problem with this reasoning is that each human being is also precious and irreplaceable. What we are required to compare is not the value of something irreplaceable and of intrinsic worth with something that can easily be replaced, but the value of beings or things that are all irreplaceable and of intrinsic worth. On the other hand, the principle invoked by General Eisenhower gives too little weight to the value of works of art:

If we have to choose between destroying a famous building and sacrificing our men, then our men's lives count infinitely more and the buildings must go.[21]

If people's lives are infinitely more precious than buildings, however artistically significant, then it seems that no risk whatsoever can be justified for their sake. It was this thinking which led to the destruction of Monte Cassino, which most people now see as not justified by military necessity.[22]

Cultures as well as individuals are likely to have different opinions about how much should be risked in war to save works of art (and which works of art are worth the risks). But there is reason to agree that commanders should be prepared to risk lives in order to protect works which exemplify the achievements of a civilization. The requirements of just war theory are motivated by the moral importance of limiting war, of making it possible for important values to survive armed conflict. Above all, it should be possible for the opportunities intrinsic to civilized life to survive and be enjoyed by future generations—and these include being able to appreciate its greatest products.

The second problem raised by the universal significance of great works of art and other products of human creativity has to do with reparations and restitution. The Hague and the Geneva Conventions prohibit seizure and appropriation of cultural property. When this property belongs to the cultural heritage of a community—if, for example, it is used in their religious ceremonies or symbolizes their identity as a people—then the

---

[20] Sir Harold Nicolson, quoted in John Henry Merryman, 'Two Ways of Thinking of Cultural Property', in Merryman, *Thinking about the Elgin Marbles: Critical Essays on Cultural Property, Art and Law* (Cambridge, Mass.: Kluwer Law International, 2000), 76.

[21] Merryman, 'Two Ways of Thinking', 77.

[22] The German High Command had issued orders that troops were not to enter this seventeenth-century monastery. However, the advancing Americans thought that Germans might be there and reduced it to rubble.

justification for this prohibition is clear. A respect for civilians entails respect for the things that play such an important role in their communal life. But not all the pictures, statues, and other things that they hold in their museums play this role, and if these things have value for the whole of humanity, then this suggests that other considerations besides legal ownership could play a role in determining where they are located. Indeed, the idea that some artefacts, because of their universal significance, are the 'property of humanity' seems to weaken the hold over them of the possessing nation. Warren, for example, believes that some artefacts are not anyone's property, and that no one can be properly said to own them.[23] Can we hold this view, yet insist that appropriation is always wrong?

Napoleon brought wagon loads of artistic treasures to Paris from the lands that he conquered, operating on the assumption that the French nation offered the best repository for works of great human value. The Soviet Union in the years after World War II carted off an estimated 2.5 million 'trophies of war' which included works of art from all over Europe, but especially from Germany. These artefacts, which the Russian parliament has expressed its determination to keep, are widely regarded by Russians as 'compensatory reparations' owed to them for the destruction of so many Russian monuments, buildings, and artefacts.[24] And why shouldn't a nation which, because of poverty or the disasters of war, is relatively poor in universally significant works of art take whatever chance it has to seize its 'fair share' of this precious resource?

One objection that can be made against such appropriations, however they are justified, is their lawlessness. The Soviets simply took what they wanted without consulting anyone or giving an account of what they took. This kind of behaviour not only encourages abuses; it also causes resentment, enmity, and a desire to retaliate in kind when the opportunity arises. One of the motivations behind prohibitions on seizure was to prevent such retaliation—so destructive of relationships and of the works of art themselves. Moreover, it is an act that is disrespectful of the social and political relationships of the civilians from whom the property was taken. They are given no say in the matter.

---

[23] K. J. Warren, 'A Philosophical Perspective on the Ethics and Resolution of Cultural Property Issues', in P. M. Messenger (ed.), *The Ethics of Collecting Cultural Property* (Albuquerque: University of New Mexico Press, 1989).

[24] National Arts Journalism Program, 63 ff.

A further objection is that the possessors of works of art, whether they truly own them or not, must be accorded some rights. Even if these possessors are merely the stewards of things of universal value, as Warren supposes, they are the ones who have made a special effort to care for these works, have learned to appreciate them, and have developed a relationship to them. Some of the reasons we have for not destroying or appropriating the property of civilians are also reasons for not appropriating the works of art in the possession of their community.

It might be argued, however, that those who have fought a war of defence or who have liberated others from oppression can rightly demand reparations for the damage or expenses they have sustained. These payments will often come from the pockets of the civilian population of the nation they have fought or liberated, or from their public property. But if a nation can rightly demand reparations and rightly require that civilians give up some of their property for this purpose, then why shouldn't it be able to demand some of their cultural property in payment—at least those artefacts that are not part of their cultural or national heritage?

One answer to this question is that respect for civilians requires that they have some say in how they are going to meet requirements of reparation, and should not be forced to give up something they value in order to meet an immediate demand for payment. But there is a larger issue at stake—the justifiability of demanding reparations of any kind. Though nations that fight what they regard as a just war have often expected to extract payments from their defeated enemy, there are some serious objections to this practice. One of them is that civilians of a defeated or liberated nation are often in a very bad position to pay anything whatsoever. They are often poor and needy, and the resources they still possess are needed to rebuild their lives and businesses. Any attempt to make them pay would be seriously detrimental to their interests and destructive of their economic and social life. Another is that forcing people of defeated or liberated nations to pay reparations is often at odds with basic ideas about justice. Thomas Pogge has argued that citizens should not be expected to pay the debts that their dictatorial leaders incurred.[25] By the same reasoning, it seems unjust to make civilians pay reparations for the aggression of leaders over whom they had little or no control. This does not mean that demands

---

[25] Thomas Pogge, 'Achieving Democracy', *Ethics and International Affairs*, 15 (2001), 3–23.

for reparation can never be justified, but the difficulties, moral and practical, suggest that other means should be found for financing those wars that can be justified.[26]

Conclusion

I have examined three reasons for thinking that civilian property, or property of some kinds, should be immune from attack or appropriation in war or in occupation. None of these reasons supports absolute immunity for property, or indeed supports the idea that protecting property is as important as protecting life. However, they do indicate that protecting civilian life is not enough. Belligerents and conquerors ought to respect civilians, and this includes respecting what is of value to their lives as individuals and as members of communities. Respect for civilian property, private and public, follows from this requirement, and so do other requirements and restrictions on the behaviour of combatants.

---

[26] It should be noted that some recent interventions have been financed from a number of sources. For example, the First Gulf War was paid for largely by Germany, Japan, Kuwait, and Saudi Arabia (though Iraq paid some reparations to Kuwait), and the Kosovo intervention was financed by members of NATO. If there are important international reasons for an intervention, then there are also good reasons for an international means of paying for it.

Select Bibliography

Alexander, Lawrence A., 'Self-Defence and the Killing of Noncombatants: A Reply to Fullinwider', *Philosophy and Public Affairs*, 5 (1975/6).

Anscombe, G. E. M., 'Mr. Truman's Degree', in *Collected Philosophical Papers*, iii: *Ethics, Religion and Politics* (Oxford: Basil Blackwell, 1981).

—— 'War and Murder', in Walter Stein (ed.), *Nuclear Weapons: A Catholic Response* (London: The Merlin Press, 1961). Reprinted in Anscombe, *Collected Philosophical Papers*, iii: *Ethics, Religion and Politics* (Oxford: Basil Blackwell, 1981).

Bevan, Robert, *The Destruction of Memory: Architecture at War* (London: Reaktion Books, 2006).

Brandt, Richard, 'Utilitarianism and the Rules of War', *Philosophy and Public Affairs*, 1 (1971/2).

Brocklehurst, Helen, *Who's Afraid of Children? Children, Conflict and International Relations* (Aldershot: Ashgate, 2006).

Carpenter, R. Charlie, *'Innocent Women and Children': Gender, Norms and the Protection of Civilians* (Aldershot: Ashgate, 2006).

Carr, Caleb, *The Lessons of Terror: A History of Warfare Against Civilians* (London: Little, Brown, 2002).

Coady, C. A. J. (Tony), 'Terrorism and Innocence', *Journal of Ethics*, 8 (2004).

—— *Morality and Political Violence* (New York: Cambridge University Press, forthcoming).

Coates, A. J., *The Ethics of War* (Manchester: Manchester University Press, 1997).

Coppieters, Bruno, and Fotion, Nick (eds.), *Moral Constraints on War: Principles and Cases* (Lanham, Md.: Lexington Books, 2002).

Dobos, Ned, 'Democratic Authorization and Civilian Immunity', *Philosophical Forum*, 38 (2007).

Draper, Kai, 'Self-Defense, Collective Obligation, and Noncombatant Liability', *Social Theory and Practice*, 24 (1998).

Ford, John C., 'The Morality of Obliteration Bombing', *Theological Studies*, 5 (1944). Reprinted in Richard A. Wasserstrom (ed.), *War and Morality* (Belmont, Calif.: Wadsworth Publishing Co., 1970).

Fullinwider, Robert K., 'War and Innocence', *Philosophy and Public Affairs*, 5 (1975/6).

Garrett, Stephen A., *Ethics and Airpower in World War II: The British Bombing of German Cities* (New York: St Martin's Press, 1993).

Green, Michael, 'War, Innocence and Theories of Sovereignty', *Social Theory and Practice*, 18 (1992).

Hartigan, Richard Shelly, *The Forgotten Victim: A History of the Civilian* (Chicago: Precedent Publishing, 1982).

Holmes, Robert L., *On War and Morality* (Princeton: Princeton University Press, 1989).

Johnson, James Turner, 'Maintaining the Protection of Non-Combatants', *Journal of Peace Research*, 37 (2000).

Koontz, Theodore J., 'Noncombatant Immunity in Michael Walzer's *Just and Unjust Wars*', *Ethics and International Affairs*, 11 (1997).

Lichtenberg, Judith, 'War, Innocence and the Doctrine of Double Effect', *Philosophical Studies*, 74 (1994).

Mavrodes, G. I., 'Conventions and the Morality of War', *Philosophy and Public Affairs*, 4 (1974/5).

McKeogh, Colm, *Innocent Civilians: The Morality of Killing in War* (Basingstoke: Palgrave Macmillan, 2003).

McMahan, Jeff, 'The Ethics of Killing in War', *Ethics*, 114 (2003/4).

_____ 'Innocence, Self-Defense and Killing in War', *Journal of Political Philosophy*, 2 (1994).

Murphy, Jeffrie G., 'The Killing of the Innocent', *Monist*, 57 (1973). Reprinted in Murphy, *Retribution, Justice, and Therapy: Essays in the Philosophy of Law* (Dordrecht: D. Reidel Publishing Co., 1979).

Nagel, Thomas, 'War and Massacre', *Philosophy and Public Affairs*, 1 (1971/2). Reprinted in Nagel, *Mortal Questions* (Cambridge: Cambridge University Press, 1979).

Nathanson, Stephen, 'Terrorism, Supreme Emergency, and Noncombatant Immunity: A Critique of Michael Walzer's Ethics of War', *Iyyun: The Jerusalem Philosophical Quarterly*, 55 (2006).

Norman, Richard, *Ethics, Killing and War* (Cambridge: Cambridge University Press, 1995).

Orend, Brian, 'Just and Lawful Conduct in War: Reflections on Michael Walzer', *Law and Philosophy*, 20 (2001).

Palmer-Fernandez, Gabriel, 'Civilian Populations in War, Targeting of', in R. Chadwick (ed.), *Encyclopedia of Applied Ethics* (San Diego: Academic Press, 1998), i.

_____ 'Innocence in War', *International Journal of Applied Philosophy*, 14 (2000).

Paskins, Barrie, and Dockrill, Michael, *The Ethics of War* (London: Duckworth, 1979).

Phillips, Robert L., 'Combatancy, Noncombatancy, and Noncombatant Immunity in Just War Tradition', in James Turner Johnson and John Kelsay (eds.), *Cross,*

Crescent, and Sword: The Justification and Limitation of War in Western and Islamic Tradition (New York: Greenwood Press, 1990).

Primoratz, Igor (ed.), *Terror from the Sky: The Bombing of German Cities and Towns in World War II* (Oxford: Berghahn Books, forthcoming).

——(ed.), *Terrorism: The Philosophical Issues* (Basingstoke: Palgrave Macmillan, 2004).

Wallace, Gerry, 'Area Bombing, Terrorism and the Death of Innocents', *Journal of Applied Philosophy*, 6 (1989).

Walzer, Michael, 'Emergency Ethics', in *Arguing about War* (New Haven and London: Yale University Press, 2004).

——*Just and Unjust Wars: A Moral Argument with Historical Illustrations*, 3rd edn. (New York: Basic Books, 2000).

Index

Albright, Madeleine 140
Alexander, Lawrence A. 53
Anscombe, G. E. M. 21, 42–3, 57, 146
Aquinas, Thomas 68–70, 74 n. 27, 77–8
Augustine, St. 62–7, 70, 73, 74, 75, 77, 79,
    82–3, 204
Austin, J. L. 143

balance of terror 3
Bentham, Jeremy 141
Bica, Camillo 80 n. 38
blockades 3, 96–7
Bosnian War 15, 16, 217, 219, 221, 224 n.
    23, 233–4, 235, 252
Butt, D. M. 172
bystanders, *see* responsible bystander
    argument

Carpenter, R. Charli 18
Chamberlain, Neville 167–8, 169
Cherwell, Lord 172–3
Churchill, Winston 13, 169, 170, 171
Cicero 239
civilian, definition of 10, 88, 89, 198–9
    civilian/non-combatant
        distinction 138–9
civilian contractors 139
civilian property, destruction of 16–18,
    239–50, 256
    cultural property 17, 18, 250–5
Clausewitz, Carl von 81
Coady, C. A. J. 10, 12–13, 38–9
Coates, A. J. 49–51
collateral damage 12, 136–7, 156–7; *see
    also* double effect, doctrine of
    accidental 142–4
    incidental 145–6
collective responsibility 33, 10–11,
    127–30, 140, 212
    and culpable omissions 131–5
combatant, definition of 10, 30, 43, 89, 108
consensual justification of killing 6, 66
consequentialism/utilitarianism 7, 21,
    25–7, 40, 46, 57, 59, 60, 139, 150

convention theory 8, 44–5, 56, 57, 59–61;
    see also consequentialism/utilitarianism
crimes against humanity 16, 111, 112, 219,
    229, 230, 231, 233, 234, 236, 237

defence model 6, 7, 8, 15, 27–31, 35,
    51–4, 55, 56, 58, 60–1, 65–6, 73 n.
    25, 77–8, 206, 210
democracy 31–4, 47–51
Dixon, Rosalind 235
double effect, doctrine of 9, 12, 77–82,
    146–9, 187
Douhet, General Giulio 163
Draper, Kai 32–3, 35
Dresden 3, 140, 178–9, 183
dual purpose targets 96, 97–9, 107, 155–6,
    199–200; *see also* civilian property,
    destruction of
Dunlap, Colonel 242

Enzensberger, Hans Magnus 23–4
Erhard, Johann Benjamin 236

Fabre, Cecile 244
Fullinwider, Robert 51–3, 57

Gardam, Judith G. 219 n. 6, 226 n. 24
Garrett, Stephen 13
Geneva Conventions and Additional
    Protocols 4, 10, 16, 85–112, 225–8,
    247 n. 14, 249, 250–1, 253
Gilbert, Paul 9, 14–15
Green, Michael 46, 47–8, 60 n. 32
Grossman, Lieutenant Colonel Dave 149
Grotius, Hugo 8–9, 62, 73–4, 76, 77,
    78–9, 239
Gulf War 32, 33–4, 151, 183, 185, 197–8;
    see also Iraq War (2003)

Hague Conventions 2, 5, 106, 165, 250,
    252, 253
Hague Draft Rules 165–7

Hamburg 3, 175–6
Harris, Arthur 'Bomber' 13, 171, 173, 174,
    175, 186
Hart, Basil Liddell 180
Hartigan, Richard Shelley 5, 6, 64 n. 5
Hegel, Georg Wilhelm Friedrich 244
Hertzberg, Hendrick 140
Hiroshima 3, 99, 140
Hitler, Adolf 115, 167, 169
Hobbes, Thomas 204
Hobsbawm, Eric 1–2
Holmes, Robert 47
Hull, Richard 80 n. 38
Hussein, Saddam 132, 140, 151, 192, 194
human rights, killing in defence
    of 114–19, 125–7
human shields 193–6

identity, politics of 15, 202–3, 204, 205,
    209, 212, 214, 215
identity requirement 108
Ignatieff, Michael 224 n. 23
indiscriminate attacks, definition
    of 99–100
intention/foresight distinction 141–2, 80
    n. 38; see also double effect, doctrine of
International Court of Justice (ICJ) 87
International Criminal Court (ICC) 102,
    111, 112, 214, 230–3, 234
International Criminal Tribunal for the
    Former Yugoslavia (ICTY) 86, 110,
    229–31, 233
International Criminal Tribunal for
    Rwanda (ICTR) 110, 229–31, 233
international human rights law 87, 95, 109
international humanitarian law 9, 16, 84,
    85, 86, 87, 90, 95, 100–2, 109,
    110–12, 219, 225
Iraq War (2003) 183, 185, 190–2, 194

Jarvis, Michelle J. 219 n. 6, 226 n. 24
Johnson, James Turner 206
Jus ad Bellum 56, 62 n. 1, 74 n. 26, 85,
    120–2, 123, 151, 225
Jus in Bello 21, 56, 62 n. 1, 64 n. 6, 74 n.
    26, 85, 123, 152, 225
Jus in Bello/Jus ad Bellum, relation
    between 30–1 n. 16, 61, 122–3; see
    also moral equality of soldiers
justifying emergency theory 8, 55, 57, 60

just war theory 12, 14, 16, 21, 25, 30 n. 16,
    36 n. 21, 40, 54, 62, 64, 66, 137, 139,
    150, 239, 242, 243, 253

Kaldor, Mary 3–4, 15
Kolb, Richard 62 n. 1
Kosovo War 4, 143, 183, 185, 194, 198–9,
    199, 109, 136 n. 1
Kretzmer, David 9

legal enforcement and remedy for breaches
    of civilian immunity 109–12, 231,
    227, 228
legitimate civilian targets 124–5, 130–1
Lewis, David 147
Locke, John 17, 240–1
Lomasky, Loren 244

McKeogh, Colm 6, 8–9, 11, 12, 241–2,
    243
McMahan, Jeff 59, 138–9
McVeigh, Timothy 136
Mavrodes, George 43–5
Mazowiecki, Tadeusz 229
mercenaries 232
Miller, Seumas 10–11
moral equality of soldiers 30 n. 16, 56–7,
    58, 60, 61, 74–5, 122–3
moral guilt principle 8, 56–60
Münkler, H. 222
Murphy, Jeffrie 43, 30

Nagasaki 3, 99
Nagel, Thomas 27, 30
Napoleon 247
Nielsen, Kai 26
new wars 15, 201–5, 207–16, 222–4
Nicolson, Harold 252–3
non-international armed conflict 107–8
Norman, Richard 44–6
nuclear weapons 99, 147, 187–8
Nuremberg Trials 4, 16, 110, 219

occupied territory 105–7
omissions, responsibility for, see collective
    responsibility and responsible bystander
    argument
Orwell, George 22–3

pacifism 21, 45, 149
participation in hostilities, definition
  of 90–4
Portal, Charles 170, 178, 179
precaution requirement 9, 10, 102–5, 143,
  152–5, 191
precision guided weaponry 3, 13–14,
  103–4, 182–6, 190, 193, 196–200
proportionality 5, 9, 10, 78, 84, 100–2,
  149–52
punitive model 6, 8–9, 15, 30, 51, 55,
  62–73, 76, 82, 211–12

rape, see sexual abuse in war
responsible bystander argument 7, 32–5,
  117–18
Roberts, Frank 190
Rodin, David 145
Rome statute 102, 105, 108, 111–12,
  230–1
Roosevelt, Theodore 169
Rousseau, Jean-Jacques 48, 203
Rwanda, massacres in 16, 124, 219, 233–4

sexual abuse in war 15–16, 217–25, 234–8
  and new wars 222–5
  and the laws of war 225–31
Shehada, Sheikh Salah Mustafa 154
Shue, Henry 29, 116
Stahl, Leslie 140
Stalin, Joseph 178
Steinhoff, Uwe 8
strategic bombing:
  and the laws of war 165–8
  in World War I: 162

in World War II: 3, 13, 64 n. 5, 140,
  161, 163, 164, 168–81, 182, 184
supreme emergency exception 36–40

terrorism 40–1, 132, 208, 212
  definition of 3, 18, 40, 137–8, 144–5
Thompson, Janna 17
Tokyo Trials 16, 110, 219
Tomuschat, Christian 227 n. 25
total war 2, 171
Trenchard, Hugh 163–4
Trotsky, Leon 3

unlawful combatants 10, 93–4, 95
Urban II, Pope 67 n. 9, 70 n. 16

Vattel, Emmerich de 74–5, 77, 79, 247–8,
  250
Vietnam War 188–9
Vitoria, Francisco de 48, 70–2, 153

Walzer, Michael 7, 28, 36–8, 49, 60 n. 32,
  152, 154, 187, 188, 190, 195, 196, 197,
  249
Warren, K. J. 254
wars of identity, see new wars
White, Hugh 14
Wilby, David 136 n. 1, 137 n. 1
World War I: 2–3, 150, 190, see also
  strategic bombing
World War II: 16, 37, 218–19, 222, 254;
  see also strategic bombing

Zanetti, Veronique 15–16, 18